USER INTERFACE DESIGN

Bridging the Gap from User Requirements to Design

Edited by
Larry E. Wood

CRC Press

Boca Raton   Boston   New York   Washington, D.C.   London

Acquiring Editor: *Ron Powers*
Project Editor: *Susan Fox*
Cover Design: *Denise Craig*
Prepress: *Kevin Luong*

Library of Congress Cataloging-in-Publication Data

Catalog record is available from the Library of Congress.

© 1998 by CRC Press LLC

No claim to original U.S. Government works
International Standard Book Number 0-8493-3125-0
Printed in the United States of America 2 3 4 5 6 7 8 9 0
Printed on acid-free paper

Preface

This book grew out of a workshop held at CHI'96 in Vancouver in April 1996 on "Transforming User-Centered Analysis into Concrete Design". The workshop was motivated by the lack of published accounts of how experienced designers use the results of user work/task analyses and other tools and resources to produce Graphical User Interface (GUI) designs (i.e., to *bridge the gap* between analysis and interface design). Interface designers with a wide variety of experience were invited to share their methods for addressing the problem. This book is a result of our collective efforts.

Several themes became apparent in our workshop discussions, such as representations and models of work, scenarios (examples of user tasks), and high- and low-fidelity prototyping; designing for heterogeneous vs. homogeneous user populations; designing "breakthrough" systems vs. supporting existing work or redesigning legacy systems; and the virtues of objected- vs. task-oriented interfaces. Authors of individual chapters elaborate the role of these issues as appropriate to their own methods and work context.

The book should be useful to anyone involved in or interested in the issues surrounding user-centered design of software applications. However, it was our intention to provide information that will be particularly useful to practitioners who have a role in designing GUI's. The emphasis on examples from real GUI design projects will hopefully accomplish that goal.

PARTICIPANTS

There were fourteen people who participated in the workshop, among whom there was a wide variety of design experience. Including the organizers, there were three from academia, ten from large software development companies, and one who operates her own consulting firm. The participants included the following individuals:

- Larry Wood, Brigham Young University, USA (organizer)
- Ron Zeno, Intuitive Design, USA (organizer)
- Tom Dayton, Bellcore, USA
- Joseph Kramer, Bellcore, USA
- Tom Graefe, Digital Equipment Corporation, USA
- Frank Ludolph, SunSoft, Inc., USA
- Andrew Monk, University of York, U.K.
- Peter Nilsson, Linné Data, Sweden
- Martin Rantzer, Ericsson Radio Systems AB, Sweden
- Allan Risk, IBM SWS Toronto Laboratory, Canada
- Sabine Rohlfs, IF Interface Consulting Ltd., Canada
- Jean Scholtz, Intel Corp., USA
- Kevin Simpson, University of Guelph, Canada
- Colin Smith, Northern Telecom, Canada

Acknowledgments

I express my appreciation to the workshop participants for their willingness not only to share their knowledge and experience in interface design at the workshop, but especially for their efforts in writing the chapters that make up the substance of this book. I regret that after his enthusiastic participation in the workshop, Allan Risk was unable to complete a chapter to be included in the book. Likewise, following his efforts at organizing the workshop, Ron Zeno was unable to contribute to the book, which is unfortunate.

I also want to thank our CRC publisher, Ron Powers, and his assistant, Cindy Carelli, for their patience and flexibility in working with us to produce this volume.

Finally, I express my gratitude to Shannon Ford, who "found" us and was willing to provide helpful feedback on the chapters, expecially the introduction (Chapter 1).

The Editor

Larry Wood is a professor of cognitive psychology at Brigham Young University, who has taught human-computer interaction and interface design courses and consulted on design projects for 10 years. His research interests include all aspects of user-centered design.

Contributors

Tom Dayton
Bellcore
Piscataway, New Jersey

Thomas M. Graefe
Digital Equipment Corporation
Littleton, Massachusetts

Joeseph Kramer
Bellcore
Piscataway, New Jersey

Frank Ludolph
Sun Microsystems, Inc.
Mountain View, California

Al McFarland
Bellcore
Piscataway, New Jersey

Andrew Monk
Department of Psychology
University of York
York, United Kingdom

Peter Nilsson
Linné Data
Frolunda, Sweden

Ingrid Ottersten
Linné Data
Frolunda, Sweden

Martin Rantzer
Systems Engineering Lab
Ericsson Radio Systems
Linköping, Sweden

Sabine Rohlfs
IF Interface Consulting Ltd.
Ottawa, Canada

Tony Salvador
Intel Corporation
Hillsboro, Oregon

Jean Scholtz
National Institute of Standards and
    Technology
Gaithersburg, Maryland

Kevin T. Simpson
Financial Models Company
Mississauga, Canada

Colin D. Smith
Corporate Design Group
Nortel Technology (Northern Telecom)
Ottawa, Ontario, Canada

Larry E. Wood
Brigham Young University
Department of Psychology
Provo, Utah

Table of Contents

CHAPTER 1

Introduction: Bridging the Design Gap

Larry E. Wood
Brigham Young University, Provo, Utah
email: WoodL@byu.edu

TABLE OF CONTENTS

1. GOOD INTERFACE DESIGN

Design is both a product and a process. The product is an artifact designed *for* a specific purpose, *given* a set of components, resources, and constraints within which a designer has to work. The process consists of techniques and procedures for constructing the desired product. While there are principles and laws that guide effective design, there is usually a certain amount of craft and creativity involved in producing effective designs.

Whether or not the design is effective obviously depends on the criteria used to define effectiveness. In his book *The Design of Everyday Things*, Norman (1990) makes a strong case for the need to emphasize usability (in addition to functionality and aesthetics) through the design of artifacts that we frequently encounter in our everyday lives (e.g., doors, VCRs, and automobiles). He does so by providing many examples of *good* and *bad* designs (from a usability perspective) and in listing attributes of artifacts that make them usable (e.g., providing visible affordances, providing feedback regarding actions performed, and preventing users from making errors).

The same principles and guidelines outlined by Norman can also be applied to the design of a software application, particularly the user interface, which is the focus of this book. To be *usable*, a user interface must provide access to the functions and features of an application in a way that reflects users' ways of thinking about the tasks that a potential application will support. This requires that the application not only provide support for necessary aspects of the users' work, but must also provide the means for them to interact with the application in ways that are intuitive and natural. Great improvements in the effectiveness of a user interface have been made during the last 15 years, through (1) the improved components and resources available in Graphical User Interfaces (GUIs), pioneered by such systems as the Xerox Star, precursor to the Apple Macintosh desktop and in Windows (Smith et al., 1982) and (2) in the transition from "system-centered" to "user-centered" design methods (Norman and Draper, 1986).

The Star and related GUI systems introduced new hardware resources and components, while the user-centered design orientation focused design methods on the potential users of an application. In essence, the new hardware and software resources provided the building blocks of more usable computer applications, while the user-centered orientation provided the impetus to develop methods to insure that the building blocks were used in ways that fit the users' way of thinking about and performing their work. In this way an interface could be made more natural and intuitive than had previously been the case.

2. THE GAP: OR THEN A LITTLE *MAGIC* HAPPENS

By definition, user-centered design techniques focus on potential users (including their characteristics, their tasks, and their environment) whose work is to be supported by an application (i.e., functional requirements were developed from a user's perspective and are referred as *user requirements*). Typical activities of a user-centered design development process are listed in Figure 1.1. It should be noted that, while an order is implied in Figure 1.1, a critical aspect of user-centered design is that it is iterative, as is emphasized in the chapters of this volume.

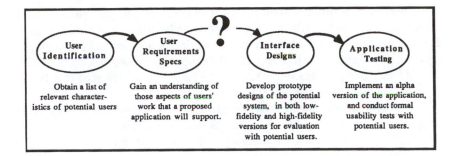

User Identification	User Requirements Specs	Interface Designs	Application Testing
Obtain a list of relevant character- istics of potential users	Gain an understanding of those aspects of users' work that a proposed application will support.	Develop prototype designs of the potential system, in both low- fidelity and high-fidelity versions for evaluation with potential users.	Implement an alpha version of the application, and conduct formal usability tests with potential users.

Figure 1.1. Typical activities in a user-centered design process.

Considerable effort has been expended to document methods related to each of the activities in Figure 1.1. In support of the activities for identifying users and determining their support requirements, there are sources discussing methods for gathering user information through field methods (e.g., Wixon and Ramey, 1996) and formal task analysis methods (e.g., Johnson, 1992). Furthermore, there are sources that emphasize the importance of representing work-related tasks via scenarios (e.g., Carroll, 1995) and use cases (e.g., Constantine, 1995). For produc- ing potential designs, there are a variety of sources that provide guidelines regarding the important characteristics of a usable interface (e.g., Fowler and Stanwick, 1995) and for producing design prototypes using both low- (e.g., Monk et al., 1993) and high-fidelity methods (e.g., Hix and Shulman, 1991). Also, much has been written about the methods for evaluating a user interface, once it has been produced, either by expert review (e.g., Nielsen, 1993) or by formal testing with potential users (e.g., Dumas and Redish, 1993).

As indicated above, while there are some excellent sources of information on user interface design, none contains specific descriptions of how a designer *transforms* the information gathered about users and their work into an effective user interface design. This is indicated in Figure 1.1 by the question mark between *User Requirements* and *Interface Designs*. Some might argue that is to be ex- pected because that process is a highly creative one and that creative processes are inexplicable by their nature. While this may be true in a limited sense, designs don't really appear as if by magic.[1] They are largely the result of thoughtful, conscious processes, and the chapters in this volume represent an attempt to make more explicit just how designers *bridge the gap*.

3. BRIDGING THE GAP: MAJOR ISSUES/CONSIDERATIONS

The *bridging* process can be conceptualized as a series of transformations that begins with the gathering of user requirements and ends with the creation of a design. While all of the methods discussed in this volume can be viewed that way,

---

[1] For more on this topic, the interested reader is referred to the Creative Cognitive approach (Ward, Finke, and Smith, 1995) which assumes that the same methods used to understand *normal* cognitive processes apply equally to the understanding and description of creative activities.

each contributor construes it somewhat differently, as would be expected. Each method has its relative merits and appropriate conditions of application. In most chapters the author(s) describes that transformation in the context of a methodology used with a specific design project. While the projects, the processes, and the methods vary considerably, the common theme is the *building* of that bridge between *User Requirements* and *User Interface Design*.

Some contributors view the design process as overlapping, but distinct stages within a reasonably well-defined theoretical framework. One example is Graefe (Chapter 3), who construes the design process as transformations on a set of representations, emphasizing the nature of the representations. Ludolph (Chapter 4), espouses a similar framework, although he chooses to speak in terms of transforming models, beginning with important user background information and ending with a concrete representation of how a user will interact with an application.

In contrast to a well-defined theoretical framework, some of the contributors tend to be guided more from a pragmatic perspective, describing their bridging process as a design *story* (Nilsson and Ottersten, Chapter 6) or describing the process from the perspective of design-related activities and their relative contribution to the effectiveness of the process (Simpson, Chapter 10). Some of the techniques have been developed for smaller projects designed by small, nonspecialized teams (Monk, Chapter 5), while others are suited for converting large, complex, mainframe systems to a GUI interface (Rohlfs, Chapter 8). Rantzer (Chapter 7) describes a framework where the notion of user interface is expanded to include user documentation. Two of the chapters discuss techniques that are particularly well suited to the development of products not yet on the market (Scholtz and Salvador, Chapter 10) or what Smith (Chapter 11) refers to as *new generation* products that introduce new technology. Finally, Dayton, McFarland, and Kramer (Chapter 2) describe a methodology for developing object-oriented GUIs, asserting their general superiority over task-oriented GUIs, whereas Rohlfs (Chapter 8) argues the opposite for her work in redesigning so-called *legacy* systems.

4. INDIVIDUAL CHAPTER DESCRIPTIONS

4.1. DAYTON, MCFARLAND, AND KRAMER (CHAPTER 2)

Dayton, McFarland, and Kramer describe a methodology (which they refer to as the *Bridge*) for quickly designing object-oriented (OO), multi-platform GUIs. The methodology produces an OO interface, which means that the GUI reflects the users' focus on the discrete units of data — data objects — with which they do their tasks, and the interface concretely represents each task object as a GUI object. Dayton et al. point out that their OO GUIs differ from procedural GUIs, which are oriented around particular procedures for doing tasks, and from application-oriented GUIs. Furthermore, they claim that the OO GUI style generally provides the most natural and easy-to-learn user interface. This position is in contrast with that put forth by Rohlfs (Chapter 8), who maintains that redesigned legacy systems need to be more task oriented.

Having been developed at Bellcore, the Bridge method draws heavily on previous, related techniques developed there (e.g., CARD and PICTIVE, Muller et al., 1995). All design activities are performed in a participatory manner with a five-member design team (consisting of an expert user, a novice user, a usability engineer, a developer, and a system engineer) surrounding a small table. The team is assisted and encouraged in their work by two facilitators who are intimately familiar with the method. The authors describe their methods in the context of an application to support a hotel reservation system.

The major activities of the Bridge method are (1) expressing user requirements as task flows, (2) mapping task flows to task objects, and (3) mapping task objects to GUI objects. They are carried out in a series of very intense workshops over a period of a few days, under the guidance of the facilitators. The results of design activities are first written on cards and placed on the table, where they are easily accessible to all participants and can be altered or even discarded. As consensus is reached on results, they are attached to the surrounding walls of the room, where they are conveniently available for reference.

Once the definitions of task objects and the outline of task flows have been established, these are usability tested by having one team member talk through each step in the task flows and the other members verifying that all objects with accompanying attributes and actions are available for performing the required tasks. This is performed at an early stage and is independent of any GUI representations of the objects. After the task objects have been mapped to GUI objects using paper prototypes, usability testing is again performed by the team members. Final detailed design specifications for a particular platform are performed by a usability engineer in accordance with appropriate style guides.

4.2. GRAEFE (CHAPTER 3)

Graefe proposes that the design gap lies between various representations used in the design process (i.e., between a represented world and a representing world). As with many other cognitive tasks, bridging the gap is a process of transforming various representations from one to another, in this case, beginning with user work descriptions and ending with an interface design. He discusses a theoretical framework in which he specifies a series of representations and the transformations that lead from one to the next. This process is shaped by mediating abstractions such as metaphors and by the rules governing the chosen user interface paradigm.

The context of Graefe's discussion is a system management application to be used for monitoring hardware and software processing resources, typically functioning as servers within a computing environment. Scenarios provide content and structure for the subsequent steps, beginning with the development of use-cases, which define the high-level system interactions, the setting of usability goals, and the development of low- and high-fidelity prototypes. Specific user scenarios are gathered from interviews with users and from direct observations of their work. Interviews are also conducted with others involved in the context of use (e.g., managers).

From scenarios, Graefe generates use-cases, which are defined as "a sequence of transactions in a system whose task is to yield a result of measurable value to an individual actor of the system". Initially, a use-case is defined at a high level of task interaction, then extensions are developed, which account for more detailed subtasks. The use-cases capture the users' work, and Graefe describes how the designer's task of creating a user interface is facilitated by the use of effective meditating representations.

Both the user scenarios and use-cases contain descriptions of user objects and are the source of metaphors defining the contents of the interface. This interface is captured first in a paper prototype storyboard, which is reviewed with users. These data are used to create a computer simulation prototype that can be tested for more detailed feedback. Graefe concludes that iterative, user-centered design can be thought of as a corrective measure for biases that occur in more traditional software development processes. He suggests some rules-of-thumb for successful design practice.

4.3. LUDOLPH (CHAPTER 4)

Ludolph contends that people use models to explain complex systems. He therefore bases his approach to interface design on the construction of models and their transformation from one into another until there is finally a finished design. He begins with background information, transforms that into an essential model, transforms the essential model into a user's model, and finally, transforms the user's model into the user interface presentation and interaction elements. It is this series of transformations that allows the designer to bridge the gap between user requirements and the finished design.

The context for Ludoph's discussion is the development of an application builder, where a developer constructs an application, using reusable chunks of software as building blocks. The user locates and selects the software chunks to be used. The first stage in design is the gathering of background information, consisting of goals, a description of the work environment, the people involved (including their roles and their characteristics), real-life scenarios (including task frequencies, artifacts produced, and obstacles), and environmental constraints.

From the background information, essential task models (use-cases) are constructed by taking real-life work scenarios, focusing on goals, and then abstracting away details of specific technologies and descriptions of how the tasks are currently performed. The essential model includes necessary tasks with objects and their relationships and essential actions.

Essential models are then transformed into user models, primarily by putting the tasks, objects, and relationships of the essential model into the context of a familiar metaphor. In the case of the application builder project, candidate metaphors were a catalog, a components data handbook, and a parts bin/cabinet. The characteristics of the candidate metaphors are compared to those of the essential model to choose the best candidate for the application. Once a metaphor is chosen, the use-cases are restated in terms of the metaphor to construct the user model. Another important part of the user model is a hierarchical task tree which describes functionally what the user does to accomplish each task, but not how the user actually does it.

The interface design results by transformations on the essential model. First, rough layouts are constructed by transforming task flows into simples sketches of window layouts with indicators of flow between them. Interaction design is produced by transforming the task tree and objects into plausible object views and controls. Finally, rough layouts are transformed into visual prototypes (high-fidelity prototypes), which mimic the intended appearance, interaction, and feedback in a way that allows the designer to validate the design with potential users. The process of developing the high-fidelity prototypes also brings many interaction issues to light and also forces the designer to consider details easily overlooked in rough layouts (i.e., it is part of the design development process itself).

4.4. MONK (CHAPTER 5)

Monk makes a strong point that the *bridge* is better built if one uses the correct representation for communication and for reasoning about user activities. To be maximally useful in those two roles (i.e., communication and reasoning), documents in which representations are captured must be tailored to the context. He refers to his techniques as *discount* design methods, making it clear that they are well suited to everyday, relatively small scale projects, rather than very large ones. Thus, they are particularly well suited to small development teams, where resources are scarce and few team members are highly skilled in the various areas needed for effective design. Monk also assumes a relatively small and well-defined user base, either because of in-house tool development or for development of a product in a relatively narrow, vertical market. Because small projects have small teams, the members cannot be specialists, so techniques must lend themselves to being easily and quickly learned by members of the team.

The context for Monk's discussion is an application used in a warehouse handling food products for a large group of stores in the U.K. His method begins with a representation of the "rich picture", which is a high level description of the work to be supported and that includes the work environment described broadly enough to demonstrate that thought has been given to the impact the new application will have on everyone who might be affected by it. The rich picture takes the form of a rough, annotated sketch, broadly describing the work being performed and identifying all of the stakeholders that need to be consulted about the final design.

From the rich picture, a work objective decomposition (WOD) is performed to produce a representation in terms of required states of the world. This requires the designer to think clearly about the purpose of each process, rather than their interdependencies or the means by which they are achieved. Later on, this helps promote reasoning about alternative ways in which the work might be supported. The WOD is a hierarchical representation of objectives with each decomposed into subobjectives as far as it seems useful. Because the WOD is an idealized view of the work, it must be supplemented by an "exceptions" list, indicating things that can go wrong and/or points where the work might be interrupted for various reasons.

Because the WOD and exception list are relatively abstract, user scenarios are then constructed to add detail and make the understanding of the work more concrete. Functionally, they are fictional, but typical stories describing the user's work. They also function as effective means for evaluating the design alternatives.

The four representations described above are preparatory to actually producing an interface design and are intended to enable the designer to incrementally and iteratively refine the understanding of the necessary aspects of the user's work environment. Once that goal has been achieved, then the beginnings of a design are formulated in terms of a dialogue model, which frequently consists of a set of rough screen sketches and some indication of the flow among them. The dialogue model is at the same level of abstraction as the WOD, the exception lists, and scenarios, and thus can be verified against them. The verification might suggest a useful metaphor for data representations or other presentation/ manipulation aspects of the final interface. Necessary constraints on the order of the work can be imposed in the dialogue model, but should be restricted to only those that are necessary.

4.5. NILSSON AND OTTERSTEN (CHAPTER 6)

Nilsson and Ottersten provide an experiential, narrative approach to their chapter in an attempt to focus on the process of bridging the design gap, rather than the end result. Consequently, they avoid discussing details of a specific project, in the interest of portraying the design process as a whole, rather than risking the confusion of important issues with less significant details. They begin their chapter with a design story about a project that describes a collaborative effort between two designers, describing the activities they perform and how they accomplish their goals. They also describe their interactions with other members of a design team (e.g., a context and requirements analyst) as they attempt to bridge the design gap.

The approach taken by Nillson and Ottersten emphasizes the importance of designers' reflecting on their efforts as a way of promoting creative processes that result in new insights about the design goals. They describe activities such as free sketching, *Bubbling*, and ways to consider appropriate metaphors. In particular, the Bubbling technique is designed to get a quick start on the design process by putting one key issue from the design space in a bubble in the middle of a piece of paper. The designer (or designers) associate freely to that issue, drawing connecting bubbles. The next step is to find ideas on how to create one or more designs for each of the associated words. The Bubbling technique is part of a more general method called Linné-VISA™ used at Nilsson and Ottersten's company, Linné Data AB. While much of the their discussion focuses on creative activities, they point out the need for a designer to have a clear and defensible rationale for each design decision.

For Nilsson and Ottersten the final phase of the bridging process begins with a conceptual design, describing at a high level how the various parts of the user's work fit together in a way that matches the user's mental model. These conceptualizations are represented in rough sketches for further exploration in design. In the second phase of design, a "functional" design is created by making rough sketches of potential screen designs, also showing some preliminary information about potential GUI controls. The controls are then used in user evaluations with design guidelines based on principles of human perception and cognition, which is part of Linné Data's AnvändarGestaltning™ method.

4.6. RANTZER (CHAPTER 7)

Rantzer's design methodology is called the *Delta* method, which expands the concept of user interface to include not only functions provided by the system and the graphical presentation, but also the enabling information (i.e., user documentation). It thus raises usability requirements to the same status as the technical and functional requirements.

Rantzer discusses the Delta method in the context of the development of a next-generation telecom simulation system used for installing and testing of switched and cellular communication equipment. On the requirements side of the *gap*, the Delta method begins with a system definition where the goal is to set the scope of the project and to gather some preliminary customer requirements. The next phase consists of gathering user profiles and generating descriptions of user work tasks and the work environment. This also includes creating user scenarios describing at a high level the work that will be performed (including new tasks) with a new system in place.

In the Delta method, the *bridging* process begins with a conceptual design produced by the design team in a design room through activities such as structured workshops, contextual walkthroughs, and construction of activity graphs (user scenarios) and user environment diagrams. This is done in an interactive, iterative manner, progressing from one to the other. Because user environment diagrams reflect the work at a high level, they become the basis for creating low-fidelity prototypes through rough sketches of the layout of potential screens and the flow among them. During this process, appropriate metaphors are also chosen, which play an important role in the final design. As the low-fidelity prototypes are developed and evaluated with users, high-fidelity prototypes are then developed, embodying specific visual design details and navigational issues.

4.7. ROHLFS (CHAPTER 8)

Rohlfs describes methods which she has developed for redesigning complex *legacy* systems. She defines the typical legacy system as a transaction-oriented, mainframe-based system used for administrative and/or customer service support. Examples are systems for financial/insurance portfolio management and for management of supply, warehousing, and distribution of retail products. Her techniques are described in the context of a hypothetical system to support a large company that offers a wide range of financial and insurance services, with branch offices and mobile sales representatives.

Rohlfs distinguishes between approaches appropriate to fire-prevention vs. firefighting situations. Work done on firefighting assignments is aimed at quickly addressing the most glaring usability problems within the confines of project schedule, resources, and budget. On the other hand, work done on fire-prevention assignments allows extra time and effort to ensure higher quality information for decision making and more exploration of alternatives, which in turn leads to a higher level of quality in the final GUI design.

Because the context of the work is redesign, it is particularly important to specify the new user tasks by carefully considering the current tasks along with a malfunction analysis of those tasks. Rohlfs places a heavy emphasis on the development of an appropriate metaphor and claims it is the most challenging, far-reaching, but enjoyable part of a project. Another important issue is the decision regarding whether a system should provide a task-oriented dialogue or if it should be more object-oriented (as proposed by Dayton, Kramer, and McFarland, Chapter 2). Rohlfs acknowledges that generally novice users prefer a task-oriented dialogue, whereas more experienced users prefer an objected-oriented one. However, she maintains that the type of work supported in a redesigned legacy system is by nature more task than object-oriented.

When it comes to the translating the user information (including the choice of a metaphor) to the actual GUI design, Rohlfs proposes a horizontal-first, vertical-second approach. *Horizontal-first* refers to such decisions as major windows, their relationship to each other, and placement of tasks in a foreground/background relationship. Such decisions are based on information regarding frequency of task performance as well as the information about user classes, objects, and functions. This stage is intended to ensure that all tasks and user classes are considered from the perspective of high-level navigation so that users are able to find and initiate key tasks. *Vertical-second* design means that after high-level navigational concerns are addressed, then the design to support each individual task is worked out using storyboards and scenarios, with the entire design being refined by iteration.

4.8. SCHOLTZ AND SALVADOR (CHAPTER 9)

Scholtz and Salvador have developed a framework called *Systematic Creativity*, which can be used throughout the entire development process. This allows not only design issues, but also development questions and usability issues to always be traced back to product requirements. This technique also demonstrates how conflicting requirements from users and marketing and technological constraints can be quickly identified. The general context in which this framework was developed was a corporate mission to produce products (based on new technology) that would enhance the home and professional lives of users. Thus, the challenge for Scholtz and Salvador was to produce requirements and designs for products not currently on the market. An additional challenge facing them was that their customers were usually not actual end users. In the case of corporate products, customers were the Information Technology groups in the corporation, not the final corporate workers, who would actually use the product. Home products were marketed to computer manufacturers who would bundle some form of the software on their new hardware. All of these constraints required a design methodology that would allow effective communication among design team members and that would facilitate minimal time to market in order to take advantage of a small window of opportunity.

The Systematic Creativity framework is discussed in the context of a revision of an application that allowed users to collect and read news stories on-line. Although the first version of the application had been available for some time, the functionality being added was quite different from what was available previously, and there was great concern about how this functionality should be represented. With the Systematic Creativity framework, design activities begin with the development of product goals and a definition from a marketing point of view. Designers then work closely with potential users to determine the work related goals this product could support. Designers also identify both the obstacles users face in their current work tasks and the facilitators that are present to assist them to accomplish their goals. The information gathered from users is then merged with the marketing information to form a set of prioritized goals that the product will support.

The specific interface design phase is begun using the supported goals as well as the actions and objects that will enable those goals. The enabling objects and actions are then used to generate and evaluate potential metaphors that will convey the appropriate information to users through an interface. Low-fidelity prototypes are then generated and evaluated by comparing the new user tasks with the current user tasks. All tasks, actions, and objects can be traced back to the user goal or goals that they support. This helps designers, implementors, and usability engineers to evaluate the effect of high- and low-level changes throughout the development cycle.

4.9. SIMPSON (CHAPTER 10)

Simpson emphasizes two particular techniques that he has developed to help bridge the gap, the UI War Room and the Design Prism. The context in which the War Room was developed was a computer-aided software engineering tool and that for the Design Prism was an application for computer control of processes in a nuclear power plant. The UI War Room is a dedicated room used for interface design. User requests (capabilities they would like) and user objects (those objects mentioned in descriptions of their work) are extracted from user task analyses. These are written on cards and pasted on to separate walls, where they can be easily modified, and re-organized to reflect the emerging understanding of designers. A third wall in the UI War Room contains a white board that can be used for reflection and brainstorming.

The fourth wall of the UI War Room is used to place rough sketches (low-fidelity prototypes), which can easily be compared to the user requests and objects to make certain that design ideas are capturing the important aspects of the users' work. These are produced after the user objects have been organized in diagrams showing their relationships. Having a wall on which to place the sketches helps to encourage a variety of alternative design ideas from which to choose, as the design is refined.

The Design Prism draws on the notion of subdividing the user objects and functions identified in the UI War Room into four mutually exclusive and exhaustive categories: user information, objects, goals, and actions. The relationships among members of each category are then specified. Low-fidelity prototypes (in the form of sketches) are then constructed from each perspective, and finally, those are consolidated into one coherent design.

4.10. SMITH (CHAPTER 11)

Like Scholtz and Salvador (Chapter 9), Smith's chapter deals with the challenges present when introducing new technology, or what he calls *new-generation products*. He points out that this makes the design gap even larger and more difficult to bridge. As a result, he emphasizes the need for an exploratory design stage that has to proceed the work/task analysis stage involved in designing for current technology. The level of user involvement is particularly high at this stage. The context for Smith's discussion is the design of a new wireless voice communication device (called Orbitor) that supports an integrated voice and note message center, electronic business cards, and various interactive network-based services. Design encompassed both hardware and software components. Smith describes a design process consisting of three overlapping stages: exploratory design, analysis and refinement, and formal design.

In exploratory design, new concepts are created through having potential users consider *user interaction scenarios* (narrative descriptions of what people do and experience as they attempt to make use of a new product). These new concepts are then visualized through rough sketches and simple physical models, paper-based storyboards, computer-based simulations with voice-over, and even scripted play with live actors. Scenarios provide an effective method for brainstorming about and for clarifying new product concepts. Once a potential set of viable concepts is established by the design team, they are further refined in focus groups with potential users. The final result of the exploratory stage is a set of high-level user values, which encompass the intended customers' future needs, wants, and goals.

The goal of the analysis and refinement stage is to verify the user values and to define the new product attributes. In defining new-generation products, there is a larger than usual discrepancy between the existing task model (use of current products) and an enhanced task model (how the tasks will change, given the new product). Bringing them together is accomplished using more explicit and detailed scenarios to help users understand the implications and impact of the new product on their work. These scenarios are often presented as videos of actors using the new products, which helps convey more realism to potential users and helps to elicit more useful feedback.

In the formal design stage, scenarios are used to choose, design, and verify the conceptual model and the metaphors that will be used in the final product. The scenarios are presented as low-fidelity (paper) prototypes to design and verify the high-level dialogue model of the interface. High-fidelity prototypes (computer simulations) are then used to further refine the interface details. In the Orbitor project, a composite metaphor was chosen from the various types of tasks that were being combined into the final product. At the highest level, an environment metaphor was used (call environment, message center environment, and filing cabinet environment). Within each environment, appropriate visual metaphors were used (e.g., telephone and file folder icons) for specific tasks.

5. CONCLUSION

User interface design is a complex process, resulting in many different issues that need to be considered and many questions that need to be answered. Some issues are more pervasive than others and recur across different contexts. To push the *bridging* analogy, it is important to use effective building methods, but it is equally as important to have the proper materials. Some of the issues most central to design (as emphasized by the contributors to this volume) are scenarios and use-cases, metaphor use, high-level dialogue (or interaction) design, high- and low-fidelity prototype development, and the issue of object- vs. task-oriented dialogue style.

Those familiar with user interface design will note that none of these issues are new or unique. Our attempt here is simply to make more explicit how they contribute to the building of that elusive *bridge*. Various authors emphasize these issues to a greater or lesser extent, as outlined in the descriptions of individual chapters above. What is obvious from the various approaches described in this volume is that there are many effective ways to build the bridge, each suited to particular contexts and constraints. Our hope is that readers will be able to use them to suit their own needs and circumstances as they also attempt to bridge that gap between User Requirements and GUI design.

6. REFERENCES

Carroll, J. M., *Scenario-Based Design: Envisioning Work and Technology in System Development*, John Wiley & Sons, New York, 1995.

Constantine, L. L., Essential modeling: use cases for user interfaces, *Interactions*, ii.2, 34, 1995.

Dumas, J. S. and Redish, J. C., *A Practical Guide to Usability Testing*, Ablex, Norwood, N.J., 1993.

Fowler, S. L. and Stanwick, V. R., *The GUI Style Guide*, AP Professional, Boston, 1995.

Hix, D. and Schulman, R. S., Human-computer interface development design tools: A methodology of their evaluation, *Communications of the ACM*, 34(3), 74-87, 1991.

Johnson, P., *Human Computer Interaction: Psychology, Task Analysis, and Software Engineering*, McGraw-Hill, London, 1992.

Monk, A. F., Wright, P. C., Davenport, L. and Haber, J., *Improving your Human-Computer Interface: A Practical Technique*, BCS Practitioner Series, Prentice-Hall, 1993.

Muller, M. J., Tudor, L. G., Wildman, D. M., White, E. A., Root, R. W., Dayton, T., Carr, B., Diekmann, B., and Dykstra-Erickson, E., Bifocal tools for acenarios and representations in participatory activities with users, in *Scenario-Based Design for Human Computer Interaction*, Carroll, J. M., Ed., John Wiley & Sons, New York, 1995, 135-163.

Nielsen, J., *Usability Engineering*, Academic Press, Boston, 1993.

Norman, D. A. and Draper, S. W., Eds., *User Centered System Design : New Perspectives on Human-Computer Interaction*, Erlbaum Associates, Hillsdale, N.J., 1986.

Norman, D., *The Design of Everyday Things*, Doubleday, New York, 1990.

Smith, D. C., Irby, C. H., Kimball, R. B., Verplank, W. H., and Harselm, E. F., Designing the star user interface, *Byte*, 7(4), 242, 1982.

Ward, T.B., Finke, R.A., and Smith, S.M., *Creativity and the Mind: Discovering the Genius Within*, Plenum Press, New York, 1995.

Wixon, D. and Ramey, J., Eds., *Field Methods Casebook for Software Design*, John Wiley & Sons, New York, 1996.

CHAPTER 2

Bridging User Needs to Object Oriented GUI Prototype via Task Object Design

Tom Dayton, Al McFarland, and Joseph Kramer
Bellcore, Piscataway, New Jersey
email: tdayton@acm.org   mcf52@aol.com   jkramer@bellatlantic.net

TABLE OF CONTENTS

ABSTRACT

This chapter sketches out The Bridge, a comprehensive and integrated methodology for quickly designing object-oriented (OO), multiplatform, graphical user interfaces (GUIs) that definitely meet user needs. Part 1 of The Bridge turns user needs into concrete user requirements represented as task flows. Part 2 uses the Task Object Design (TOD) method to map the task flows into task objects. Part 3 completes the bridge by mapping the task objects into GUI objects such as windows. Those three parts of the methodology are done back-to-back in a single, intense session, with the same team of about five participants (notably including real users) working at a small round table through several consecutive days. The methodology is unusual in its tight integration not only of its explicit steps, but also of several pervasive techniques and orientations such as Participatory Analysis, Design, and Assessment (PANDA) methods that involve users and other stakeholders as active collaborators. This chapter describes both the underlying portions and the explicit steps of this bridge over the gap between user needs and GUI design.

1. INTRODUCTION

Traditionally, designing the fundamentals of OO GUIs to meet user needs has been done seemingly by magic. There have been methods for the surrounding steps — gathering user requirements before, and polishing the fundamental design after. However, there have been few if any systematic ways to step over the gap in between. Some concrete examples: Once the users' task flows are designed, how does the designer decide which of those flows' data elements are to be represented as entire windows and which merely as object attributes within the client areas of those windows? How should users navigate between windows? Style guidelines help decide the exact appearance of a menu in a window, but how does the designer decide which user actions need to be represented at all, which windows they should be in, and whether to represent them as menu choices or buttons? This chapter describes how to bridge that gap between user requirements and OO GUI design by using "task objects" in a participatory methodology we call "The Bridge". Arguments for the value of methods — any methods — in human-computer interaction work are in Karat and Dayton (1995) and Dayton (1991). The Bridge methodology is an example of a very practical way to apply the philosophy of advancing human-computer interaction by actively cultivating eclecticism (Dayton, 1991).

At the beginning of 1994, Dayton and McFarland synthesized this methodology for fundamental GUI designing and used the methodology in several high-pressure software development projects in several companies over the next year. Most of the components of this approach were not new. What was new was the combination of those components into a comprehensive and integrated methodology for end-to-end GUI designing. Kramer then joined the team, which (with many other people, including design session participants) continued to apply the methodology to dozens of projects in several companies, and to refine and extend the methodology. The methodology has been used in many commercial GUI development projects in big and small companies from areas such as telecommunications, finance, software development, and air travel; projects whose lives from conception to delivery ranged from 3 months to 3 years; and projects whose total development staff sizes ranged from four to hundreds.

This chapter describes the entire three-part methodology that is the bridge over the gap between user needs and GUI design prototype, being most thorough in describing the center span — Part 2, Task Object Design.[1] We set the stage by describing the Bridge methodology's broad context within a sequence of other methodologies that cover GUI design projects from start to finish, and give an overview of the explicit steps of The Bridge itself. Then we describe some of the techniques and orientations that pervade, underlie, and are the medium of its three explicit steps. Finally, we describe those explicit steps in more detail. Before all of that, let's get a feel for the atmosphere and dynamics of Bridge sessions.

[1] The full methodology has not yet been fully described in any generally available publications. The most complete description other than this chapter is handed out as notes when the methodology is taught in all its breadth and detail, for a consulting fee. Portions of the methodology have been taught at conferences such as UPA (Dayton and Kramer, 1995, July; Kramer, Dayton, and Heidelberg, 1996, July), OZCHI (McFarland and Dayton, 1995, November), CHI (Dayton, Kramer, McFarland, and Heidelberg, 1996, April), APCHI (Kramer and Dayton, 1996, June), and HFES (Dayton, Kramer, and Bertus, 1996, September).

1.1. A TYPICAL SESSION

The Bridge methodology uses a participatory session as its primary medium. Every session is somewhat unique, there being many dimensions along which a session exists. For example, sessions typically last 3 days but for large complicated projects can last 7 days. To give you a flavor before we get into the details of those variations, here is a short story of a typical session:

Monday begins with the two facilitators directing the five participants (expert user, novice user, usability engineer, developer, system engineer) to the five seats at a small round table. The facilitators briefly explain the session's goals and approach, and lean into the table to start the group writing the Big Picture index cards. Within a few minutes the participants themselves are writing task steps on cards and arranging the cards into flows on the blank flip chart paper in the table's communal center. After push-starting the group, the facilitators fade into the background, floating around the edges of the table and becoming most noticeable when introducing each step of the methodology. Within the first half day the five participants have become a well-functioning team and feel that they are running the session with only occasional help from the facilitators. The atmosphere is fun, sometimes goofy, with periodic showers of paper as discarded index cards and sticky notes are torn up and thrown over shoulders. At the end of Monday the walls are covered with the task flows that were created on the table. Each flow is composed of a set of index cards connected with sticky arrows, all attached with removable tape to a piece of flip chart paper (see Figure 2.1 left side). Commentaries are stuck on top of the task flows in a riot of fluorescent stickies of assorted sizes and shapes.

By lunch time Tuesday the table holds an additional dozen cards, each having stuck to its lower edge a sequence of blue, pink, and yellow sticky notes (top right of Figure 2.1). The team designed those dozen "task objects" to represent the units of information that are needed by users to do the task flows posted on the walls. The floor is littered with an additional dozen cards that were discarded as the team refined its notion of what information qualifies as a task object. The team has verified that the set of task objects is usable for doing the tasks, by walking through the task flows while checking that there exists a task object listing both the data and the action needed for each task step.

Up to now the facilitators have banished the GUI from the conversation, to keep the participants focused on the abstract task and its units of information. However, after lunch on Tuesday, the facilitators give to the participants photocopies of GUI windows whose client areas and title bars are blank. Participants make a window for each task object by hand drawing some of the attributes from the blue sticky of that task object into the client area of a window (bottom right of Figure 2.1). By the end of this second day only eight of the original task objects remain on the table, the participants' notion of objecthood having been refined by their act of translating task objects' attributes into window views.

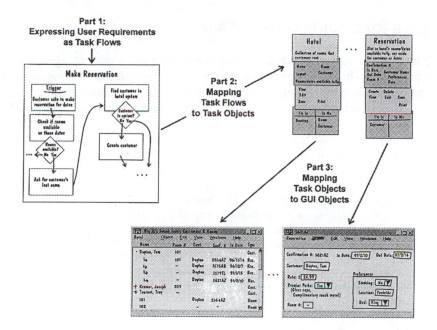

Figure 2.1 The three types of artifacts resulting from the three consecutive parts of The Bridge methodology. Part 1 yields a set of hand-lettered index cards and removable sticky arrows representing task flows. Part 2 extracts task objects from those flows and represents them as hand-lettered index cards with removable sticky notes. Part 3 expresses each task object as a GUI object, usually as a window; the window contents are hand drawn on photocopied empty windows.

Wednesday starts with participants drawing additional paper windows to represent additional views for some objects' attributes. After the coffee break comes the first GUI usability test. The facilitators use masking tape to delineate a computer screen as a big empty rectangle on the table. A user points and clicks with a finger within the rectangle, the other participants serving as the computer by adding and removing paper windows as dictated by the user's actions. As the task flows on the wall are executed in this way, the team discovers flaws in the paper prototype, revises the prototype and the task objects, and resumes the test. At the end of this third day the team does another usability test, this time with windows to which the team has added menus and buttons as GUI expressions of the actions that were listed on the task objects' pink stickies. There are only four objects left. The usability engineer walks away Wednesday evening with a usability-tested paper prototype of the fundamental GUI design (bottom right of Figure 2.1).

1.2. BROAD CONTEXT OF THE BRIDGE

The Bridge for fundamental GUI designing is itself one methodology in a complete start-to-finish approach to taking a GUI project from proposal creation through checking the implementation against the user requirements document. The major methodologies in that approach are listed below, with the Bridge methodology italicized.

- Proposal Creating
- Project Planning
- Detailed Customer Requirements Creating
- *Fundamental GUI Designing — "The Bridge"*
  - *Part 1: Expressing User Requirements as Task Flows*
  - *Part 2: Mapping Task Flows to Task Objects*
  - *Part 3: Mapping Task Objects to GUI Objects*
- Detailed GUI Designing
- Formal User Requirements Document Writing
- Conformance Checking of the Implemented GUI Against the User Requirements Document

The Bridge does not require use of any of those other methodologies because The Bridge is only one component of *any* start-to-finish software development process. For instance, writing a detailed, formal user-requirements document happens after The Bridge, if at all. Such a document that dictates the developers' coding is the best way to get efficient coding, traceability, maintainability, and extensibility. However, The Bridge will successfully output an excellent GUI design and paper prototype even if the project as a whole fails to quickly produce a corresponding formal requirements document or software product.

The Bridge can be used with great effect even if the system requirements are already written. Of course, The Bridge *should* be done before the system requirements are decided, since Bridge sessions always address the software product's deep functionality in addition to its GUI look and feel. For example, the underlying database and the contracts between the GUI and that underlying system should be designed to quickly return all the data that will appear in the same GUI window. You don't want half of the data in the window to appear instantly and the rest 5 minutes later! However, if the system requirements and underlying system code have already been set, The Bridge is still very useful. In this example, the system engineer and developer participating in the Bridge session would warn the team as soon as those fast- and slow-returning data were hand drawn into the same paper window. The team would then immediately redesign and reprototype so that the different data were displayed separately, such as in different views, different notebook pages, or different Include settings. All of those activities would happen within minutes, in the same Bridge session, without any resources being wasted in writing up or coding the poor design.

The above is an illustration that The Bridge is not the type of user-centered design process that just records whatever users say they want. Instead, The Bridge's resulting design realistically can be developed, with usability compromised as needed to get the GUI delivered on time. The Bridge has an advantage over many competing approaches, in its provision of excellent support for making those tradeoffs rationally and with minimum expenditure of resources on infeasible or poorly usable designs. Not just users are present in the session; various management camps are represented in the persons of the usability engineer, developer, system engineer, and perhaps others. Those participants are selected partly for their knowledge of management perspectives and for their power to represent management in making at least rough commitments.

Another important support for management is that not all decisions need be made finally during The Bridge session. The session outputs priorities on portions of the task flows, on portions of the GUI, and on the issues that are documented during the session. There is even a Blue Sky version of the task flows that is acknowledged by everyone to be infeasible, but that is publicly documented as an ideal goal of the project. All this information guides the development team during the months or years after the session, as the teams adjusts the design to suit the unfolding practical realities of the software development project.

This chapter does not explain any of the methodologies in the above list other than The Bridge. Before we delve into details of The Bridge, here is a brief overview of its three major, explicit steps.

1.3. OVERVIEW OF THE BRIDGE'S EXPLICIT STEPS

All of The Bridge's integrated three parts are the bridge from user needs to GUI design. This three-step methodology is done in a single, intense, participatory session that takes a minimum of three consecutive days. Four days is really the minimum desirable length of the session, and 5 days is more realistic if the participants are not to feel rushed and driven by the facilitators. Large projects may require multiple sessions, each session having a slightly different set of participants working on a slightly different portion of the project. Figure 2.1 shows a few examples of the outputs of the methodology's three parts.

Part 1 of The Bridge produces one or several well-documented task flows from the user perspective. The task flows concretely represent what the user wishes to accomplish with the proposed software product. However, the task flows do not refer to underlying system architecture or existing system representations of the data that the user wishes to access or manipulate. For example, the task flows would indicate that the user wants to know the customer's total billable amount of charges rather than the user wanting to view "The Billing Summary Screen". The task flow representation is index cards taped to flip chart paper, lines of flow between the cards being drawn on long, skinny, removable sticky notes ("stickies"). Each step in the task is represented as a noun and a verb written on a card, such as "Print Customer's Bill".

Part 2 (Task Object Design) bridges the task flows to the GUI design via creating somewhat abstract "task objects" from the nouns embedded in the task flows that came out of Part 1. Each task object's name is copied from a task flow step onto an index card and thrown onto the table around which the group works. For example, if one step in a task flow is "Print Customer's Bill", then "Bill" is written on an index card that is thrown onto the table.

The mapping and verification process continues within Part 2 by noting each task object's attributes on a sticky note attached to that object's index card. Many attributes are copied from their mentions in the task flows, but others come from the team's knowledge. This step eliminates many objects by discovering that their data can be adequately represented merely as attributes of other objects. If a task step is "Print Customer's Bill", then the "Customer" index card's sticky note might get the attribute category name "Billing Info" written on it, allowing the "Bill" index card to be thrown out. Then the actions that users take on that object are listed on yet another sticky; if a task step is "Print Customer's Bill", then the "Customer" index card's sticky has the action "Print" written on it.

The most difficult step in Part 2 is creating a strict hierarchy of all the task objects. The hierarchy is the mental model that the users feel best represents the relationships among the task objects on the table. For example, in designing an interface for managing a hotel, a user may want the Hotel object to contain a Customer object. This relationship can be totally different from the data structure being used by the developers and does not necessarily imply object-oriented inheritance. The attributes that are not child objects are "properties". A concrete example is that a "Closet" object will have the clothing it contains as its child objects, and "Type of Material The Closet Is Made Of" as a property. In the hotel example, a Customer object has multiple Reservations as child objects, and an address as a property. Each object's index card gets a sticky that is marked with that object's parent and children.

Part 3 translates the task objects, with their attributes, actions, and hierarchical containment relations, into GUI objects. A GUI object is represented as a window when open and as an icon, list row, or other GUI element when closed. The window client area contents are GUI representations of the attributes listed on the task object attributes sticky. The form in which an attribute is represented in a client area depends partly on whether that attribute is listed as a child object or just a property. Each GUI object's windows are roughly prototyped in paper, with enough detail to give an idea of the type of representation (e.g., graphical, textual, list). Any object can be represented by multiple types of windows — multiple "views" — that can be open simultaneously.

What remains after the three-part Bridge is the filling in of design details. Those details are important, of course. However, they are much less important than the fundamental organization, appearance, and behavior that The Bridge does design. The remaining details are most efficiently designed by the usability engineer outside of a participatory session, though with consultation from users and others.

The output of the three-part Bridge methodology is a working paper prototype of an object-oriented GUI's foundation, whose design has been *driven* by the user requirements via the Task Object Design center span.

2. PERVASIVE TECHNIQUES AND ORIENTATIONS

Just as important as the three explicit steps of The Bridge are several techniques and orientations that are used in all the steps. These pervasive techniques and orientations do not just ease the steps, they are the medium in which the design team executes the steps. Here are brief descriptions of the most important ones.

2.1.PARTICIPATORY ANALYSIS, DESIGN, AND ASSESSMENT (PANDA)

PANDA methods involve users and other stakeholders as active collaborators in analyzing, designing, and assessing. PANDA is a general term for a whole class of methods invented and used by people throughout the world. Several overviews, and detailed descriptions of some methods, are in Muller and Kuhn (1993). A catalog of a great many PANDA methods, among which ours are just a few, is Muller, Hallewell Haslwanter, and Dayton (in press). Our task analysis, design, and assessment method that is Part 1 of The Bridge is an advanced descendant of the CARD method described in Muller et al. (1995). Part 2, Task Object Design, is briefly mentioned in the catalog by Muller, Hallewell Haslwanter, and Dayton (in press). Part 3, our low-tech GUI designing- and paper prototyping-method, is an advanced descendant of the PICTIVE method described in Muller et al. (1995).

Every activity in the three-part Bridge involves, from start to finish at the small round table, a team of representatives of the major stakeholders in the software product's usability: users, usability engineer, system engineer, developer, and perhaps others such as subject matter experts, trainers, documenters, and testers. You should substitute whatever titles you use for the people who have those responsibilities, but in this chapter here is what we mean by those titles:

- *Users* are real potential users of the software product. Users are not just people who think they know what users want (e.g., users' managers, purchasing agents) nor people who were users once upon a time. If there are several classes of users, for instance experts and novices, each class should have a representative participating in the session. Users do act as designers during the session. Like all the other participants, they are more expert in some aspects of designing than in others, but the methodology facilitates users acting to some degree as designers during all phases of the session.
- *Usability Engineers* are the people primarily responsible for the usability of the software and for all the activities that directly contribute to usability. Other people also are involved, but the usability engineers have formal responsibility and so initiate, coordinate, and complete the activities:

- Gathering preliminary data about the user, task, and work environment populations and about the business needs that the worker-computer combination is supposed to meet
- Analyzing, documenting, and sometimes redesigning the users' task flows
- Designing the GUI
- Prototyping the GUI
- Designing, executing, and analyzing usability tests on the prototype, then redesigning the GUI on the basis of those results
- Writing and maintaining the user requirements formal document that drives the GUI coding and testing
- Helping the testers evaluate the final software product's conformance to the formal requirements document
- Helping the learning support people design the user support documentation, on-line help, and training

If there is room at the table for only one usability engineer, that person should be the one with the most knowledge and skill in the GUI style and the Bridge methodology. The other usability engineers may observe from an adjacent room. The project's usability engineers probably should not be facilitators of that project's sessions, because they have a stake in the project (e.g., a complex design will take more time to write up in the user requirements document). Even if the usability engineers really can act neutrally, the other participants may suspect them of bias and so not respect them as facilitators.

- *System Engineers* are the people responsible for the underlying system requirements, such as the exact natures and sources of the data that the underlying computer systems must provide to the GUI code layer. The system engineers write a formal system requirements document that, together with the user requirements document, drives the developers' work. Naturally, the system engineers must work closely with the usability engineers to ensure that the user requirements are feasible for the underlying systems, and sometimes the system requirements document is combined with the user requirements document. Ideally, The Bridge is used right at the project's start, before any system engineering requirements have been written. That allows the user needs to drive the software product's deep functionality as well as its look and feel. However, even if the system requirements are already set, a system engineer must participate in the session to help the team cope with those constraints and to help invent workarounds. If there is room at the table for only one system engineer, that person should be the one most capable of estimating feasibilities and of committing system engineers to work.
- *Developers* are the people who write the code that provides the functionality that is specified in the GUI and system requirements documents. Sometimes there are separate developers for the GUI layer of code than for the underlying back-end system code; the GUI coders are the most relevant to the GUI design sessions, but the back-end developers also can make excellent contributions. The Bridge should be used at the project's start, before any back end code, or contracts between the GUI and the back end, have been written. Even if the GUI is being laid on top of a legacy system, the GUI developers participating in the session can help the team by explaining those underlying constraints as soon as they become relevant to the GUI designing and by helping create GUI design workarounds. If there is room at the table for only one developer, that should be the GUI developer most capable of estimating feasibilities and of committing the developers to work.

All those participants work together at a single, small, round table, actively collaborating in every activity. Of course, each participant contributes the most from one area of expertise. Users, for example, are most expert in the task and work environments, so are most active in designing the task flows and in doing the usability testing. The usability engineer is the most active during designing of the GUI per se. However, all the participants are quite capable of contributing to some degree and from some perspective during every step of the methodology.

The Bridge facilitates everyone contributing to all the activities. One way is by educating every participant in the other participants' areas of expertise. That education is done mostly informally, sprinkled throughout the analysis, design, and testing activities as the topics naturally arise. Another way is getting participants to support each other by using their particular expertises to fill in the information missing from the other participants' ideas. For example, a user might compensate for the usability engineer's lack of task knowledge by designing a window — by writing some field names on a photocopied empty window. The user might then complain that there is so much information in that window that the pieces needed at any one time are hard to find. The usability engineer might instantly respond, filling in the users' missing GUI design knowledge by suggesting segmenting the window's contents into notebook pages. This symbiosis is no different than the usability engineer relying on the developer and system engineer for new ideas about how the underlying technology can help.

Getting even one representative of each of the stakeholder groups sometimes would lead to more than the five or six session participants that we allow. In that case, only the stakeholders most critical to the GUI per se sit at the table — three users, one usability engineer, one system engineer, and one GUI developer. The other stakeholders are allowed to silently observe, preferably from another room. There are other techniques for handling too many stakeholders for a single session, such as having successive design sessions with overlapping membership, and running two tables at once with synchronization of the tables after each substep of the methodology. With techniques such as those, The Bridge has been used successfully in projects having more than 30 distinct user populations, and in projects having over 100 staff (developers, system engineers, usability engineers, etc.). Such advanced techniques are beyond the scope of this chapter.

The presence of representatives from all the stakeholder groups at the same table allows rapid iterations of designing and testing, via two mechanisms of increased efficiency:

- *Iterations are speeded.* Time is not spent creating a design, writing it up, and sending it to the developers and system engineers for review, only to have the developers and system engineers reject it as infeasible. Instead, a developer and system engineer are sitting right there at the table, commenting on feasibility as soon as the design ideas pop up. Similarly, usability engineers do not waste time detailing, documenting, creating a computerized prototype, and arranging and running formal usability tests, only to have users reject the fundamental design. Instead, users are sitting right there at the table, giving feedback the instant the design ideas arise.

- *Iterations are eliminated.* Rapid feedback on ideas generated by other people is not the main benefit or point of participatory methods. "Participation" means active collaboration of all the stakeholders in *generating* the ideas. The initial ideas are better than they would have been if the stakeholders were working isolated from each other, so the initial iterations of creating really bad designs and testing them are just skipped.

PANDA improves the *effectiveness* of design as well as its efficiency. The ideas generated by the team collaborating in real time often are far superior to the ideas that could have been generated by the same people working isolated from each other for any amount of time, even if they were communicating with each other asynchronously or through narrow bandwidth media (Muller et al., 1993).

The great efficiency and effectiveness of the PANDA approach cannot be attained merely by throwing this bunch of people together into a room. Standard-style meetings do not encourage true collaboration. These stakeholders can actively collaborate best in a fluid atmosphere that is barely on the organized side of chaos — a "whitewater" model of analysis, design, and assessment.

2.2. WHITEWATER APPROACH

In contrast to the "waterfall" and "spiral" models of software design and development, our "whitewater" approach encourages *very* rapid iteration of analyzing, designing, and testing. All those activities occur within the same participatory session. An entire cycle for a piece of the GUI design might take only 2 minutes — a 30-second analysis of a subtask, yielding a design modification that is added to the paper prototype in 60 seconds, which is usability tested for 30 seconds before the user discovers a problem, sparking another 2-minute cycle of analysis, redesign, and testing.

The team rarely spends much time thinking about or discussing design alternatives in abstract. Usually it is more efficient to get concrete immediately, by usability testing the alternatives after quickly representing them in the low-tech materials. Iterations can take as little as a few seconds, because of the speed of using the low-tech materials and the instant availability of users and other stakeholders right there at the table. This principle applies not just to designing of the GUI per se, but also to designing of the task flows and task objects. A related principle is that the team must keep moving. When the participants spend much time discussing any point, when silence descends on the room, or when there is too little writing and drawing, the team immediately moves to the next activity. If the team's best guess from that earlier step turns out to be wrong, the team can discard that solution and return to the activity in which it made the guess. This flexibility is made possible by the team's low investment in any idea that has not yet been tested — low investment of time, labor, materials, and ego.

We call our approach "whitewater" because the activity as a whole moves rapidly toward its goal in a messy way due to the high total energy. There is churning, surging, boiling, and even some convulsing and eddying, but if those things are kept just enough under control, the activity as a whole makes much more rapid progress than it would if enough control were imposed to keep the activity smooth.

Two ingredients are needed for whitewater: a medium that not just allows, but encourages, a headlong pursuit, and strong but loose guidance to keep that energy pointed toward the goal. The guidance is provided by two elements: the explicit steps of the methodology and the session facilitators. (Facilitators are different from participants; the facilitator role will be described later.) The medium is provided by those same facilitators, by the composition of the participant group, by the low-tech materials, and by the gathering of participants about a small round table.

2.3. ROOM SETUP

Only five or six people participate in any session. Any more than that interferes with the group acting as a team, due to the emergence of side conversations, the difficulty of everyone reaching the center of the table, and so on. Other, less-relevant stakeholders may observe from another room. The two facilitators do not count as participants, since they do not sit at the table and are not the center of the session. The participants are all seated at a single round table that is small enough to give the group a feeling of intimacy, but large enough to give everyone adequate personal space. The table is two arms' distance from the walls on which flip-chart paper can be attached, but the room is spacious enough for the facilitators to easily walk around. The chairs should be armless, to allow people to sit close to each other and to encourage people to sit close enough to the table to rest their arms on the table rather than lounging back away from the table and so becoming socially disengaged. Most important is that the table be small enough for all participants to easily reach the center while staying seated, since *all* the activities are done by *all* the participants manipulating low-tech materials in the communal center of the table.

2.4. LOW-TECH MATERIALS

The task flows are documented with index cards for the steps and with removable sticky notes ("stickies") for the flow arrows. (The foundation of that method is CARD, an early version of which is described in Muller et al., 1995.) Stickies are also used for labeling problems and solutions on the flows. The task objects are documented with index cards and stickies. The GUI design is documented with photocopies of empty windows and menus and with stickies for everything else. (The foundation of that method is PICTIVE, an early version of which is also described in Muller et al., 1995.)

Low-tech materials have many benefits (Virzi, 1989). They provide an "equal opportunity work surface", as Muller says, because users who have little experience with computers can express themselves with those materials just as readily as the computer-savvy participants can. If instead we used computerized tools for flow charting or GUI prototyping during the session, the less computer-savvy users would be inhibited and would have their ideas documented only as the interpretations of whomever was controlling the computerized tools. Low-tech materials are usable with little investment of time, effort, or money, thereby supporting the technique of gradually increasing investment (see the next section). Participants are encouraged to create only low-fidelity prototypes, to quicken iteration by reducing participants' investments in the intermediate ideas. Eventually the design should be expressed in a high-fidelity, computerized, running prototype. But that should not be done until after the low-tech prototype has been thoroughly tested, redesigned, reimplemented, and retested, during the participatory session and probably after as well. Investing the considerably greater resources needed for a high-tech prototype makes little sense until the risk of throwing away and replacing that expensive prototype has been made very small.

2.5. GRADUALLY INCREASING INVESTMENT

This technique is related to the techniques of whitewater, breadth-and-context-first, and low-tech materials. The team designs first at a high level, then tests that high level design. Time, effort, and ego are invested in the next lower level of detail only when the team has reasonably high confidence in the quality of the high-level design. There are many layers of detail, from task flows through task objects to GUI windows. The participants do not invest in the GUI fundamentals or even in the task objects until they have designed and tested the task flows that the GUI will be used to execute. Then they do not invest in designing the GUI until they have designed and tested the task objects that the GUI must represent. Then they do not invest in designing the details of the GUI windows until they have usability tested whether the identities of the windows are good for doing the task flows; why spend time designing the menus for a window when there is a risk that you are going to eliminate that window?

2.6. BREADTH AND CONTEXT FIRST

Both the explicit steps of the methodology and the facilitators encourage participants to understand the context of any issue before making decisions about it, and to work breadth first. These techniques are important for keeping the session on the organized side of chaos and for keeping the session moving rapidly toward its goal. Note that chaos is not quite the same as muddle and that the latter must be avoided at all costs — participants should never be seriously confused. The high speed of the session makes excursions out of scope costly, since the team can get very far into territory that is irrelevant or contrary to the goals of the project. The short time available for the session makes premature work on details dangerous, because that work could consume a substantial part of the session's time, and could be pointless if later, higher-level work reveals as irrelevant the entire area that was detailed. A more important danger of spending time on details before context, and depth before breadth, is that the motivation of the participants could suffer. That danger is especially great in one of these sessions, because of the session's tenuous organization and high time pressure; participants can easily become disoriented, frustrated, and dispirited. Skilled facilitators are essential for skirting that danger.

2.7. TASK ORIENTATION

The methodology produces a GUI that helps users do their work, instead of one that the users like only in the abstract. The fact that our methodology produces an object-oriented GUI does *not* mean that the methodology and resulting GUI support the task only tangentially. The focus of the team is exclusively on the tasks for at least the first full day of the session and on the task objects for at least another half day. During most of that initial day and a half, mentions or pictures of any GUI elements (e.g., windows, screens, lists, icons) are prohibited. Only during Part 3 are the GUI objects designed and they are designed to support the users' tasks. Indeed, the GUI objects are direct representations of the task objects, and the task objects are extracted directly from the task flows. Even when the session finally turns to the details of the GUI per se, the task flows are constantly on the walls for reference and refinement. Vigilance for task relevance is kept by usability testing very frequently, during not only designing of the GUI per se, but also during designing of the task flows and task objects.

2.8. CONSISTENT, OBJECT-ORIENTED GUI STYLE

The last two parts of the three-part methodology — the task objects designing and the GUI designing — are object-oriented (i.e., data-centered). "Object-oriented" means that the GUI reflects the users' focus on the discrete units of data — data objects — with which they do their tasks. The data objects are based on the users' desires rather than on the underlying computer system's organization. In our methodology, those user data objects are called "task objects", and they are discovered/designed by the users and the rest of the team extracting them from the users' task flows. The GUI concretely represents each task object as a GUI object — as a window when the object is open, and as an icon, row in a list, graphic element, or other compact representation when the object is closed.

OO GUIs provide a consistent and relatively small set of rules for users to follow in creating, viewing, manipulating, and destroying GUI objects within and across software products. OO GUIs provide a graphical environment that lets users

- visually see the relationships among GUI objects (e.g., the containment of a customer within a hotel is reflected as a "Tom Dayton" row in a list within the "Big Al's Swank Joint" window);

- change those relationships naturally and directly, by direct manipulation (e.g., move a customer from one room to another by dragging the "Tom Dayton" icon from the "Room 101" window into the "Room 106" window);
- change the way the GUI object's contents are displayed (e.g., change the "Big Al's Swank Joint" window's appearance from a list of customers and rooms to a floor plan of the hotel).

Consistency of GUI style, that is, of rules for the user viewing and manipulating the GUI, is important to users regardless of the GUI's other style attributes (Dayton, McFarland, and White, 1994; McFarland and Dayton, 1995). Consistency within the single GUI being designed in this Bridge session allows users to do many tasks once they have learned to do *any* task. Consistency of this GUI with industry-wide style standards allows users to utilize their knowledge of other software products in their use of this product and vice versa. Consistency of GUI style also is important to our *methodology*, because the participants in our sessions need learn only a small set of GUI style rules for designing and testing the entire GUI.

Global optimization of the GUI to suit the users' entire job rather than any subset of the job is an important property of OO GUI style and an important consequence of our design methodology. The tradeoff is occasional local suboptimization — the GUI's usability for some narrow task may not be as good as in some alternative designs. The reason for global optimization is that the users' entire job is more important than any individual task. That is not to say that all tasks are given equal weight. The OO style is flexible enough to accommodate differences in task frequency, difficulty, and importance, and our methodology actively seeks out and accommodates such differences. In contrast, many procedural interfaces and the methods to design them optimize locally at the expense of the entire job.

OO GUIs differ from procedural GUIs. Procedural GUIs are oriented around particular procedures for doing tasks, with the users' data elements shown only as support for the procedures. Typically, procedural interfaces have one window for each step in a procedure, with all the data elements relevant to that procedure being in that window. If a data element is needed in several procedures, a procedural interface represents the datum equivalently in each of those several windows. Consequently, related data elements such as a customer's name and address will not be in the same window, unless those elements must be dealt with in the same step of the particular procedure that the GUI designers have chosen. A consequence of such procedural organization is difficulty in doing the task any other way.[2] Doing the task in a different way often requires using the data

---

[2] Occasionally, law or safety *requires* that the task be done in only one way, making a procedural interface more appropriate than an OO interface. A procedural interface may also be appropriate if there is only one way to do the task *and* if speed of task execution is critical. Except in those circumstances, guiding novices should be done with training and on-line procedural help for an OO interface, rather than with a procedural interface. If automated procedural hand-holding is provided, it should be in the form of a wizard layered on top of an OO GUI, with users given the power to escape from the wizard's clutches at any time.

elements in a different order than how they are organized in the current procedural interface. Users must move among many windows to get at the scattered individual data elements they need, but users get few clues to guide their search; for example, they cannot just look for the single window that contains all the attributes of a "customer". In contrast to such a problematic procedural GUI, a well-designed OO GUI matches the users' mental model of the data elements' relations to each other; therefore, users can be guided by their mental model of the data elements, regardless of the procedure they are trying to execute.

OO GUIs also differ from application-oriented GUIs. Application-oriented GUIs may or may not be purely procedural, but they all focus on the application being used to handle the users' interactions with the data. For example, to open a word processing document object, a user of an application-oriented GUI must start up the word processing application, then open the document from within that application. The "application" is an extra layer between the user and the data that are the user's true objects of desire. In contrast, pure OO GUIs hide the application from the user; users see no representations of the applications, they see just the data objects. Only the computer should have to deal with whatever code must be run to let users see and manipulate those data objects. To reflect the secondary role of the code, OO GUI designers often call the code the "handler" of the data object. There are necessary deviations from that pure object model, such as users needing to be aware of the existence of handlers in order to be able to choose which handler they want to use for a data object at a given time. However, the basic difference between OO and application-centric GUIs remains profound.

The "OO" in "OO GUI" is relevant only to the user interface, not to the underlying computer programming code. An OO GUI need not be coded in OO style — you can program an OO GUI in COBOL if you want (though we have heard rumor of an object-oriented COBOL). Nor do all the concepts of OO programming or analysis apply to OO GUIs; for example, inheritance has little to do with OO GUI containment.

We agree with the great many people in the usability engineering community who contend that OO GUI style is the most natural and easy to learn user interface style for the majority of computer users, tasks, and task situations. Some of the places to read those contentions, along with principles and rationales of OO GUI style, are Collins (1995), the CUA™[3] style guide (IBM™[4], 1992), the Windows®[5] style guide (Microsoft®[6], 1995), and McFarland and Dayton (1995). The industry's degree and extent of conviction in the superiority of the OO GUI style is evidenced by the reliance on OO GUI style by most major GUI platform vendors (e.g., CUA and Windows styles). Partly for that reason, the OO style allows for multiplatform GUI design, as the next section explains.

---

[3] CUA is a trademark of IBM Corp.
[4] IBM is a trademark of IBM Corp.
[5] Windows is a registered trademark of Microsoft Corp.
[6] Microsoft is a registered trademark of Microsoft Corp.

2.9. MULTIPLATFORM, INDUSTRY-STANDARD GUI STYLE

Our methodology can be modified to support design of interfaces in *any* OO GUI platform style, but at this moment the methodology fully and explicitly supports these four:

*   Microsoft Windows (Microsoft, 1995)
*   IBM Common User Access™[7] — CUA (IBM, 1992)
*   OSF/Motif™[8] (Open Software Foundation™[9] 1993)
*   Common Desktop Environment — CDE (X/Open®[10] Company Ltd., 1995)

The multiplatform style common to those four GUI platform-specific styles is expressed most completely in the design guide by McFarland and Dayton (1995), which includes, supplements, and extends design guidelines from all four platforms' style guides. It is based not only on those four guides, but also on industry trends for GUI design, and on guidelines derived from successful GUI design at Bellcore and elsewhere. Designs following that multiplatform style are completely compatible with all four platform-specific styles.

Our methodology produces designs compatible with those multiple platforms mostly by

*   developing an object model for all the data that users need for their tasks
*   using the highest common denominator of the four GUI platform styles
*   leaving until last the details on which the platforms diverge (e.g., exactly where to position command buttons in a dialogue box)

The multiplatform compatibility of the fundamental design guarantees that the details can be expressed in any of the four platform-specific styles and that the resulting detailed design can be easily translated into any of the other four styles. The industry-standard style allows this GUI to be immediately usable, at least in basic ways, by users having even a little experience with other industry-standard GUIs.

2.10. DESIGN FIRST FOR LESS-EXPERIENCED USERS

Our methodology designs first for less experienced users — people who know only the industry-standard OO style's basic look and feel and the content domain of the GUI (e.g., hotels). The GUI's fundamental organization matches the users' mental model of the domain's data objects, their containment relations, and the actions that can be done to them. That organization forms the GUI universe in

---

[7]   Common User Access is a trademark of IBM Corp.
[8]   OSF, Motif, and OSF/Motif are trademarks of Open Software Foundation, Inc.
[9]   Open Software Foundation is a trademark of Open Software Foundation, Inc.
[10] X/Open is a registered trademark of X/Open Company LTD.

which users operate. The only other knowledge that users really need is knowledge of the basic laws of physics in that GUI universe, such as how to open, close, and move objects.

Take, for example, hotel desk clerks who are familiar with the industry standard, multiplatform, OO GUI style by virtue of either using another software product or brief training in the fundamentals common to all such GUIs. As long as the clerks know that hotels contain rooms and customers, and that customers contain reservations, they can do their work with a GUI that was designed via The Bridge. They will need to explore the GUI a bit, but they can do so safely and with confidence.

GUI features for expert users are important, but should be layered on top of, or carefully woven into, the fundamental GUI design. Part of the reason for this is that few people are *always* experts in *all* of the uses of any particular GUI. Most people use some aspects infrequently, so are novices in those aspects. At times of high cognitive load, only the most rudimentary and well-learned knowledge may be available (e.g., using the GUI while talking on the phone and gesturing to someone in your office). An example of an expert feature is showing objects in an indented hierarchical list so users can directly view and manipulate closed grandchild and great-grandchild objects without having to open their parents first (see the top left window in Figure 2.6).

At the other end of the spectrum are features for rank novices who lack knowledge of even the basics for using an industry-standard GUI. The best example is a wizard that steps users through a procedure for doing a task. A wizard should be layered on top of the OO design, so that users can escape the wizard at any time to directly manipulate the OO GUI themselves.

Features for experts and rank novices are two kinds of the polish that should be designed only at the end of Part 3 of The Bridge, so that the foundation design for less-experienced users is not distorted. Deciding when to shift the session's focus toward such design details is part of the skill of a good facilitator.

2.11. FACILITATORS

The facilitators are one of the sources of the loose but strong guidance that keeps the session barreling along toward its goal instead of flying apart or bounding off somewhere else. However, the facilitators are not leaders — at least not explicitly. They try to guide subtly enough for the participants to feel that there is no particular leader, that the group as a whole is leading. The most difficult part of the facilitator's job is to simultaneously provide that strong guidance *and* goad the team toward chaos. The facilitators must keep the session at the highly productive but delicate balance between unproductive chaos and unproductive rigidity.

As guides, the facilitators prompt the participants through the explicit steps in the methodology by demonstrating, by diving in to start each activity themselves, and sometimes by showing a few overhead transparencies. The facilitators act most forcefully when reining the errant group back into the scope of the session and when confronting the group with their limited time. (One of Tom's favorite methods is to lean over the table while staring at his watch and muttering "tick, tick, tick, ...") Even at their most forceful, the facilitators avoid explicitly leading the group. Instead they act as the group's conscience, forcing the group to acknowledge the hard reality of the need to go through all of the methodology's steps, and the hard reality of the group's previously and publicly documented goal-and-scope definitions and time allocations. In each incident of reining in, the facilitators first force the group to acknowledge their previous consensus about goal and scope and time, then to acknowledge that they are at this moment pursuing a different goal, or are out of scope, or are almost out of time. Then the facilitators force the group to either get back on track or to change its consensus definition of goal, scope, or available time (e.g., extend the session by a day). In any case, it is *the group* that must decide what to do. The group should view the facilitators as fancy alarm clocks that are indispensable, but which are unavoidably annoying on occasion.

For the group to trust and value the facilitators in that way, the group must see the facilitators as impartial. "Impartial" means not just toward the project itself, but also toward the project's politics and the session's participants. Such impartiality is most thoroughly attained by having the facilitator be ignorant of the project and its stakeholders. Ignorance is also helpful for preventing the facilitators from getting sucked into the session — listening, seeing, thinking, and then behaving like a participant. Without knowledge of the project's domain, the facilitators can do little more than what they are supposed to do — float right at the surface of the session, using as cues their observations of the social interactions, facial expressions, long silences, too-long discussions, repeated conversations, and other subtleties. But facilitating without knowledge of the users' domain is difficult because those general social and other cues are the only hints available.

As goads, the facilitators constantly recommend that the participants take their best guesses at decisions and move along, instead of discussing anything for very long. When the team slows after making reasonable progress in a step, the usual facilitator response is to prod the team to go to the next step. If the team seems to have invested too much ego in an idea that no one really likes, the facilitators encourage the team to crumple up that piece of paper and throw it on the floor. It can always be picked up and straightened out if the team decides it really likes the idea after all.

Another, more neutral, role of the facilitators is lubricant for the session. Facilitators help transcribe statements onto the low-tech materials. Facilitators get the participants to switch seats around the table periodically to prevent stagnation of the social relations, to equalize power relations around the table, to break up side conversations, and to give people a different view of the ideas on the table. When participants mutter something, the facilitators hand them pens as a subtle suggestion to write their comments on the public materials.

Many of the facilitators' goals and activities are subtle. Their role most apparent to the participants is facilitating the team's execution of the explicit steps that complement the pervasive techniques and orientations we have described so far.

3. EXPLICIT STEPS

Having described some of the pervasive, easily undervalued parts of The Bridge methodology, we turn to the explicit steps. The Task Object Design step is the center span of the bridge from user needs to GUI, but you can't have a useful bridge without entrance and exit spans as well.

- **Part 1: Expressing User Requirements as Task Flows**
  - *Goal:* Translate user needs for the task into requirements that reflect the task flows and that can be input to the next step.
  - *Activities:* Analyzing, documenting, redesigning, and usability testing task flows.
  - *Output:* Scripts of what users will do with the new GUI. The format is an index card for each step, sticky arrows between cards, and those materials taped as flows onto pieces of flip chart paper.
- **Part 2: Mapping Task Flows to Task Objects**
  - *Goal:* Map the user requirements output by Part 1 into task objects — discrete units of information that users manipulate to do the task — with specified behaviors and containment relations.
  - *Activities:* Task Object Design — discovering, designing, documenting, and usability testing task objects.
  - *Output:* Each task object shown as an index card, with the object attributes, actions, and containments described on attached stickies.
- **Part 3: Mapping Task Objects to GUI Objects**
  - *Goal:* Design a GUI guaranteed to be usable for executing the task.
  - *Activities:* Designing, documenting, paper prototyping, and usability testing the GUI fundamentals by translating task objects from Part 2 into GUI objects represented by GUI elements such as windows.
  - *Output:* Paper prototype, usability tested for goodness in doing the task flows that were output from Part 1. Includes the fundamentals of the GUI — window definitions and window commands — but not the fine details.

Throughout the following descriptions of the three parts we will illustrate with the coherent example of a GUI for hotel desk clerks to make reservations, check in customers, and check out customers. Do not be confused by the incompleteness of the example as it is described here; this chapter shows only the pieces needed to illustrate key points. Figure 2.1 shows examples of the outputs of the three parts of the methodology; in reality this GUI would have more task flows, more steps in the task flows, more task objects, and more windows. All the figures in this chapter diagram materials that are mostly hand lettered and drawn by the session participants.

3.1. PART 1: EXPRESSING USER REQUIREMENTS AS TASK FLOWS

The goal of Part 1 is to produce an explicit representation of a desirable but feasible way for doing the users' tasks, to be input to Part 2. The input to Part 1 is the participants' (especially the users') knowledge of how users do their work now and of users' needs and desires. The activities in this step are varied — analyzing, documenting, redesigning, and usability testing. The output is a set of task flows showing each task step as an index card. Removable sticky notes are used as arrows to show the flows among steps. See Figure 2.2 for partial examples of the output task flows for a hotel desk clerk's work with a hotel GUI. Each card has one noun and one verb, which Part 2 will use by taking each noun as an object and each verb as the action on that object. The task flows never reference computer screens, windows, or other superficial representations of the information that users manipulate to do their jobs. Instead the flows show only the information abstractions behind the representations. For example, if users say they "go to the Customers screen", the facilitators insist that they write on an index card something more generic such as "view all of the Hotel's Customers".

The pervasive techniques and orientations we described earlier are very important. The task flows are produced by the small team of participants, including users, sitting at the small round table. All the participants create the physical artifacts of the task flows as a natural part of doing the task designing because the index cards, removable notes, and felt-tipped pens are the medium in which the team works. The task flow designing process follows the below steps in strict order only in the sense that no step is started until its predecessor step is completed at least roughly; there are always iterations, clarifications, and modifications. Following are brief descriptions of the steps within Part 1.

3.1.1. Big Picture

The team (including real users, as in every step of every part of The Bridge) puts together a very high-level set of current work flows on a single piece of flip chart paper, using an index card for each step and stickies for arrows between steps. These flows might have only one or two cards to represent the entire job that these users are supposed to do with this GUI. The rest of the flows show the steps that are the triggers to these users' work and the steps that are done with the output of these users' work. The scope of this GUI design session is shown on the Big Picture by circling the portion of this high level set of flows that is to be done by these users with this about-to-be-designed GUI. The Big Picture is posted on the wall to act as a scope map for the entire multiday session. If the session drifts to

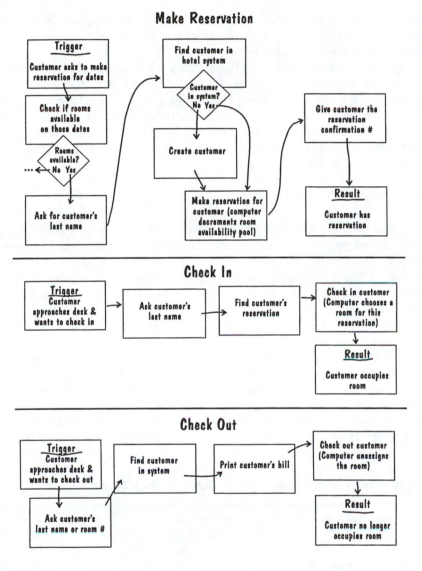

Figure 2.2 Realistic and Desirable task flows output by Part 1. This example is for a hotel desk clerk's work. Each rectangle is an index card, the other items are removable sticky notes, and all those materials are stuck with removable tape onto a piece of flip chart paper. The writing and drawing are done with felt-tipped pens by all the participants. A clerk's job using the GUI includes all three tasks — making reservations, checking in customers, and checking out customers.

an out-of-scope topic, the corresponding index card's position outside the scope circle is a public reminder and indisputable evidence that the topic must be abandoned or the scope redefined.

Figure 2.2 does not show a Big Picture, but the format shown there is the same — hand-lettered index cards with hand-drawn sticky arrows. A Big Picture for the hotel desk clerk GUI might include a single index card for each of the three tasks that are the target of this GUI — "Make Reservation", "Check In", and "Check Out" — with that set of three cards circled as being in scope. Index cards outside the scope circle might include "List the Rooms Needing Maintenance" and "List the Customers With Outstanding Bills".

3.1.2. Current Task Flows

The team now magnifies the circled portion of the Big Picture into a moderate level of detail on new pieces of flip chart paper. As before, the team places index cards on flip chart paper that rests on the small round table about which the team is huddled. The flows being documented are the current task flows, not redesigned ones. The focus is on describing the flows rather than critiquing them, but if problems are mentioned they are written on hot pink "issues" removable stickies and placed on the appropriate steps' index cards. As in the Big Picture, the flows must have triggers, results, and process steps in between. Not much time should be spent creating the Current task flows because the GUI will be based instead on the redesigned flows that are the ultimate product of Part 1.

A desk clerk's Current flows might look much like the desirable Realistic and Detailed flows illustrated in Figure 2.2. Certainly there should be strong resemblance of the triggers and results, since rarely can those be redesigned by the team designing the GUI. Often, though, the current flows are more complicated than the redesigned flows.

3.1.3. Issues and Bottlenecks in Current Task Flows

The completed, semi-detailed, Current flows now are critiqued by the team. Every team member gets hot pink removable sticky notes on which to write their critiques, just as throughout the entire methodology every team member has some of all the materials; there is no single scribe. Each hot pink sticky gets only one issue or bottleneck, and that sticky is placed on the index card representing the relevant task step. Any kind of issue or bottleneck qualifies, not just overt problems; there may be a task step that works just fine when considered in isolation, but that is obviously a bottleneck when the entire task flow is considered. Issues are written even if no one has a clue what the solutions might be. The focus of this step is on documenting issues rather than solutions, but if solutions happen to be mentioned they are written on square, blue, "possible solutions" stickies that are stuck to the relevant hot pink issue stickies.

An issue with the desk clerk's current task flows might be the need to go to different screens to see a customer's record for the different purposes of making a reservation, checking in, and checking out. A separate issue (written on a separate hot pink sticky) might exist within the check-out task; users might need to go to one screen to print out the customer's bill and to a different screen to unassign the room to that customer. An issue at check-in time might be the need for users to go to one screen to find the particular room to give to the customer and a different screen to make that assignment. Similarly, at check-out time the users might have to go to one screen to unassign the room to the customer and to another screen to increment the hotel's room availability tally.

3.1.4. Scoping the Current Task Flows

Users mark each hot pink sticky issue with its priority, for example, "High", "Medium", and "Low". It's okay for all issues to be the same priority. The team then draws a circle around the portion of the Current flow that they will work on during this session. They inform that scoping decision with the Current flows' publicly visible evidence of the breadth and depth of the users' tasks and with the arrangement and priorities of the hot pink issue stickies. In the best case, all the high-priority hot pink stickies are clustered on a small portion of the task flows, and the team has the power to throw most of the resources of the GUI project into improving those steps. In the worst case, the hot pink stickies are scattered evenly across the task flows, but at least that gives the team confidence that it isn't wasting resources on an unimportant portion of the users' work. The scoped Current flows now are posted on the wall for reference during the rest of the session.

Perhaps desk clerks think the issue of going to different screens is low priority when the different screens are for the different tasks of making a reservation, checking in, and checking out, because desk clerks have a fair amount of time to shift gears between those three tasks. However, they might give high priority to the related issue of different screens within the check-in task and within the check-out task because within those tasks the users are pressed for time.

3.1.5. Blue Sky Task Flows

The team now spends a maximum of 30 minutes documenting an ultimately desirable set of task flows that lacks the problems of the Current flows and that ignores feasibility. This set of flows usually is not quite as detailed as the Current flows, since time spent laying out infeasible details is liable to be wasted. The goal of this phase is to expand the imaginations of the team members. For that reason, the flows must not be mere replicas of the Current flows with each step replaced by one that lacks a problem. This Blue Sky set of flows should be a radical solution, one that fixes problems by redefining the Current flows so drastically that the problematic steps are just absent. This is not merely an accumulation of generally keen ideas, however; each flow must really be an integrated process from triggers to results. Users are the primary players in this phase, but other team members begin to contribute more because users often are unfamiliar with the possibilities of the technology behind the upcoming version of the GUI. This is a brainstorming activity so criticism is not allowed. This set of flows is expressed as index cards and sticky arrows, as were the previous flows and as is illustrated by Figure 2.2.

A Blue Sky version of the desk clerk's flows might use a single "Check In Customer" step that causes the computer to automatically choose the room based on the customer's preferences and then to assign the room. That single user step would replace the two separate steps of the user choosing a room and then assigning it to the customer. Likewise, the Blue Sky flow might have a single "Check Out Customer" step that has the computer automatically do the heretofore separate steps of unassigning a room and then incrementing the room availability pool.

3.1.6. Scoping the Blue Sky Task Flows

Users now mark each Blue Sky step with its desirability (e.g., high, medium, low). The other participants, the developer and system engineer in particular, mark each step with its feasibility (e.g., easy, medium, hard). Then the team draws a circle around the portion of the flow that is in scope for this multiday design session. In fortunate cases the highly desirable steps are also the most feasible, allowing the team to reallocate the project's resources to yield the most benefit to users. The Blue Sky flows then are posted on the wall for reference.

Desk clerks might be more rushed while checking customers out than while checking them in, so higher priority might be marked on the single "Check Out" step than on the single "Check In" step.

3.1.7. Realistic and Desirable Task Flows

The team now designs task flows that solve some of the problems of the Current flows, that have characteristics of the Blue Sky flows, but that are feasible given the software project's resources. These flows must be more detailed than any of the flows produced so far, and like the other flows these must have triggers, process, results, and one noun and verb per index card. This is the set of flows that will be input to Part 2.

An example of a set of Realistic and Desirable flows is in Figure 2.2. There are three tasks that a desk clerk must do with the GUI about to be designed: make reservations, check in customers, and check out customers. Those three tasks have different triggers and results, so they are laid out as separate flows. But, the single GUI being designed will cover all three tasks.

3.1.8. Scoping the Realistic and Desirable Task Flows

The team now gets another opportunity to change its mind about how much of the task set can be handled during this multiday session. If the scope needs to be smaller than what is shown in the Realistic and Desirable flows, the team draws a circle around the portion that can be dealt with. However, the team must include all the major data objects in the circled steps. Otherwise the GUI's object framework will be difficult to extend later to accommodate the other data objects and so to accommodate the other tasks' steps. If this circle differs from the scope circles on the previous flows (Big Picture, Current, and Blue Sky), the team must redraw the previous flows' circles to match.

The final output of Part 1 is the set of Realistic and Desirable task flows, though the other task flows should be retained as context and as documentation of how the final flows were produced. The final set of flows must be detailed, well grounded, and well understood by the entire team because it is the input to the methodology's Part 2 for extraction of the task objects.

3.2. PART 2: MAPPING TASK FLOWS TO TASK OBJECTS

This part is the center span of our bridge between user needs and GUI design. It maps the Realistic and Desirable task flows (i.e., user requirements) from Part 1 into somewhat abstract task objects — discrete units of information that users could manipulate to do the task. By "manipulate" we really mean only in the abstract, since these task objects are represented in Part 2 only as index cards. What users will actually manipulate in the GUI is determined by Part 3, which expresses each task object as a GUI object having a concrete representation such as a window. The task objects themselves are abstract enough that they *could* be expressed as *any* OO work environment's artifacts. They could even be used to design a physical office by mapping them into office supplies such as real pieces of paper, file folders, and steel file cabinets. The precise destiny of the task objects is mentioned only briefly during Part 2 to orient the participants during their designing of the containment relations. Otherwise the participants work entirely in the abstract to keep focused on the pure information needed for the tasks.

Part 2 is done by all the participants, including the users, with the same pervasive techniques and orientations described above. Its explicit steps include discovering, designing, documenting, and usability testing the task objects; as was true of Part 1, this part is highly iterative and even somewhat messy. However, it does follow a strict sequence in that each of its substeps never begins until the previous substep has been done at least in a first pass. Our name for this entire Part 2 method is Task Object Design (TOD).

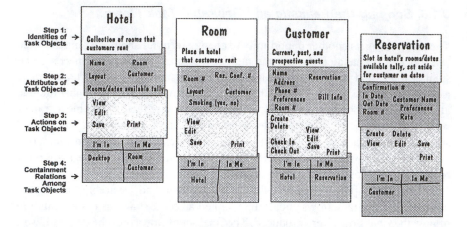

Figure 2.3 Task objects output by Part 2. Step 1 within Part 2 identifies the objects from the task flows, representing each object as an index card (Hotel, Room, Customer, and Reservation). Steps 2 through 4 add stickies to represent characteristics of the objects. It helps to place the task objects on the table in this vertically staggered way to reflect their containment relations — Hotel contains Room and Customer, Customer contains Reservation.

Figure 2.3 shows examples of task objects as they would appear at the end of Part 2. The figure also notes which steps within Part 2 produce the index cards and different stickies.

3.2.1. Identities of Task Objects

The goal of this first step within Part 2 is to discover and document the identities of the discrete units of information that users need for doing their tasks that are represented by the Realistic and Desirable task flows output by Part 1. This step is quite simple and fast and is similar to many object-oriented methods. Participants merely copy each noun from the task flows onto an index card and place the resulting cards on the table. They do not write verbs, just nouns. Participants must not write *GUI* object names such as "a scrolling list of customers", but only abstract *task* object names such as "a set of customers". Each card also gets a one-sentence definition written on it. The object must not be defined purely in the abstract, such as "Hotel — building used to accommodate travelers". Instead, the object must be defined as it relates to the GUI being designed, for example, "Hotel — collection of rooms that customers rent". To save time, everyone at the table does all this in parallel; then the group as a whole reviews the cards, revises them until getting consensus, and throws out the duplicates.

Participants should not spend much time debating whether all these task objects really qualify as full-fledged objects, but they should go ahead and throw out any cards that represent objects outside of the GUI being designed. For example, "call the bellhop" may be a step in a hotel check-in task flow, but if that is purely a manual procedure having nothing to do with the GUI (the desk clerk yells to the bellhop), then the "Bellhop" index card should be thrown out.

The output of this step would be just the topmost rectangles in Figure 2.3— the index cards labeled "Hotel", "Room", "Customer", and "Reservation". Each task object is really an object class, so the Customer task object represents the class of all customers. The actual user interface would have separate object instances such as the customers Tom Dayton and Joseph Kramer, but object instances are not represented explicitly in The Bridge methodology until Part 3.

3.2.2. Attributes of Task Objects

Next the participants more fully describe each object by writing its attributes on a blue sticky note that they attach to the bottom edge of that object's index card (see Figure 2.3). There are two basic kinds of attributes each object can have: child objects, which are themselves objects and so have their own task object index cards; and properties, which are not objects. Child objects are what the object is made up of, such as a hotel being made up of rooms and customers and a customer being made up of reservations. Properties are what the object *is*, such as a hotel having a name, a type (e.g., luxury), and a status (e.g., sold out). At this point in the methodology, no distinction is made between those two types of attributes; participants merely write all the attributes they can think of on the attributes sticky. Some of the attributes come from what is written on the task flows, but many come from the participants' knowledge of the domain.

Many of the index cards are discarded during this step, as the participants learn more about these nominal objects and refine their notion of objecthood. Participants should try to reduce the number of task objects during this step, because users find it easier to deal with a few object classes each having lots of attributes than with lots of object classes that are almost identical. Deciding which units of data qualify as bona fide objects is not based on hard and fast rules but on rules of thumb and the context of users doing their tasks. Objecthood is necessarily a fuzzy concept, and not until Part 3 of the session do participants get a good feel for it. Participants change their minds right through Part 3, usually by continuing to reduce the number of objects, and that is perfectly all right. Some rules *of thumb*:

- If users' domain knowledge has them think of the unit of data as an object (e.g., hotel, room, customer, reservation), then make it an object.
- If users ever want to see only a few of the attributes of the unit, but sometimes want to see all of them, then the unit should be an object so that it can be presented in the GUI as both closed (e.g., a row in a list) and open (a window).
- An index card having no attributes listed on its attributes sticky means that this "object" should instead be merely an attribute of other objects, listed on their attributes stickies but not having its own index card.

- If there might be several instances of the unit of data, and especially if the number of instances that might exist is unknown but could be large, then the unit of data might be an object.
- If users want to create, delete, move, and copy the unit of information, they are treating it like they would a physical object, so the unit might be an object.

In Figure 2.3, the second rectangle from the top in each of the four collections is an attributes sticky for that task object. One of the attributes listed on the Customer object's sticky is "Bill Info", which stands for an entire category of attributes. That attribute category was added to the Customer only after the participants realized that the attribute category served the task just as well as a separate "Bill" object did. In the Identities step they had created a separate Bill task object by copying "Bill" from the "Print Customer's Bill" task step card in Figure 2.2. But in this Attributes step they realized that the phrasing of the task step could be reinterpreted as "Print the Bill Info attributes of the Customer", making Customer instead of Bill the task object. Printing the bill would then be done simply by printing the Customer, setting the Print action's parameters to print only the bill information and in the bill format.

3.2.3. Actions on Task Objects

In this step, the participants record on pink sticky notes the actions that users need to take on the objects (the third rectangle from the top in each of the collections in Figure 2.3). These are actions done *to* an object, such as printing it, rather than actions done *by* the object. The only actions of relevance here are those actions done by *users* to the objects; actions done by the system are not the focus here, though they can be added as parenthetical annotations to the user actions. The starting point for discovering actions is the task flows, since each step card in the task flows has a verb as well as a noun. In addition to actions listed on the task flows, participants should consider standard actions such as view, create, delete, copy, edit, save, run, and print. Users may write whatever terms they like, such as "change" and "discard" instead of more computer-standard terms such as "edit" and "delete". For now, these action names need not match the style guide standards for menu choices and buttons, since the names on these stickies will be translated into GUI style standard terms during Part 3.

This Actions step of Part 2 is important, because it finishes gaining one of the benefits of the OO style of GUI — using each window to represent a single data object, with several actions easily taken on that data object. We and others contend that is easier for users than is a typical procedural interface's separate screens needed for doing different actions to the same data. "View" and "edit" actions are common examples: In many procedural interfaces users must tell the computer that they want to "view" before the computer will ask them what data are to be viewed, and they must issue a separate "edit" command before the computer will ask what data are to be edited. An OO GUI instead lets users find the data object without requiring them to specify what they want to do to it. Users can see the object's attributes, and if these users have permission to edit this object, they can just start changing what they are already looking at. For example, different steps called "Specify which customer to check in" and "Specify which customer to check out" might be replaced with a single "Find Customer" step that is common to the check-in and check-out tasks. Checking in a customer and checking out a customer might then become just "Check-In" and "Check-Out" actions on the same menu of that customer's window.

Figure 2.3 shows examples of actions on task objects. For instance, the task flow step "Create Customer" (shown in Figure 2.2) would have already stimulated participants to create a task object called "Customer," and now the action "Create" would be written on the actions sticky attached to the "Customer" task object index card shown in Figure 2.3.

3.2.4. Containment Relations Among Task Objects

The goal of this step is to ease users' navigation through the software by making the GUI represent the users' existing mental model. That is done by capturing the users' natural mental model of the real-world relationships among the task objects completely aside from any GUI, so that in Part 3 those relationships can be translated into visual containment among the GUI objects. The input to this step in Part 2 is the set of task object cards, each card having two stickies. The output is that set with a third (yellow) sticky on each task object, showing all parent and child (no grandchild) containment relationships of that object. See the bottom rectangle of each collection in Figure 2.3 for examples. The task flows are not especially relevant for this step because the goal is to capture the users' mental model of the objects' relations to each other aside from any particular task.

"Parent" and "child" mean only the visual containment relation between objects, not any kind of subclassing relation as is meant by those terms in object-oriented programming. These containment relations are not tied closely to the dynamics of the task flows, but are static relations. They are the intuitive hierarchies among the objects when users think about the objects they use to do their tasks. When participants design this containment hierarchy, they are designing the foundation of the users' mental model of the GUI universe. For example, a car mechanic's universe of cars has the car containing the engine and the engine containing the pistons, regardless of the particular activities the mechanic does with those objects:

Car
Engine
Piston

In this Containment step the distinction between child objects and properties is made sharply, in contrast to the Attributes step which listed both types on the attributes sticky. Child objects are attributes that are themselves treated as objects within the context of their parent. Properties are attributes that are *not* themselves treated as objects within the context of their parent. In this step the participants examine all the attributes listed on the attributes sticky for each task object and copy those attributes that are child objects onto the "In Me" (right hand) column of the containment sticky (see Figure 2.3). The child objects now are listed on both the attributes and containment stickies, whereas the properties are listed only on the attributes sticky. Then the "I'm In" (left-hand) column is filled with the names of the task objects on whose containment stickies *this* object is listed as a child.

Figure 2.3 shows the example of Hotel, Room, and Customer. Hotel is the ancestor of all objects within this desk clerk's GUI, but Hotel itself lives within the Desktop — the mother of all objects in this GUI platform, which fills the entire computer screen, in which all the other windows and icons appear (e.g., the Microsoft Windows desktop). Therefore, Hotel's third sticky has "Desktop" written in its "I'm In" column. Only two of the attributes of Hotel have their own task object cards (Room and Customer), and desk clerks do think of those two objects as children of Hotel, so "Room" and "Customer" are written in Hotel's "In Me" column. Consequently, the Room and Customer stickies have "Hotel" written in their "I'm In" columns.

This step of designing containment should be focused on the abstract containment relations among objects as represented by the containment stickies rather than being focused on any GUI representations of objects or containment. Not until Part 3 of the methodology will containment be given GUI form. However, part way through this step the participants usually need a glimpse into the GUI consequences of the containment relations they are now deciding. Figure 2.4 is the kind of picture that should be shown briefly to participants at this point: A hotel instance, Big Al's Swank Joint, is represented as the open window in the top left of the figure. Individual customer and room instances are children of that hotel and are represented when closed as rows in a list. The children's containment in the hotel means nothing more than visual containment of the children's closed representations within their parent hotel's open window. Users might be able to see enough information about the customers and rooms just by reading the attribute values displayed in columns across the rows. If users do need to see more information about Room 101, they double-click on that row to open it into its own, additional, window, as shown in Figure 2.4. The closed representation of Room 101 continues to exist within its parent's window, but Room 101 now has its own open representation as well. Only one or two examples of this kind should be shown to participants at this point in the methodology, since more than that would get them thinking too much about GUI details.

Participants must check that the hierarchy is not tangled — that each task object has just one parent. In the polishing phase of the design process, multiple parents may be allowed, but at this point in the methodology it is best to keep the hierarchy simple. It is also important to check that objects do not contain their own parents as their children.

Although the parent of an object must not be shown as a *child object* of that object, it is perfectly legitimate to show the *name* of the parent as a *property* of the object. For example, the Room object's attributes sticky may have "Hotel" written on it as a property, but certainly "Hotel" will not be written in Room's "In

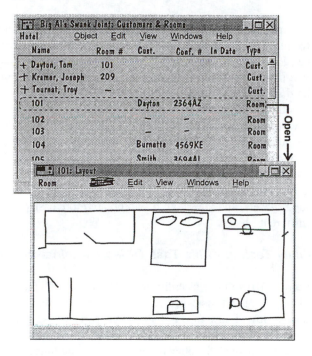

Figure 2.4 The eventual GUI consequences of task object containment. A few pictures such as this are briefly shown to participants during Part 2 to help them understand why they are deciding the containment relations among the abstract task objects; participants do not actually design GUI windows such as these until Part 3. This figure shows instances of the Hotel and Room objects as they appear after being mapped into GUI objects during Part 3. The Hotel task object had "Room" written in its "In Me" column (see Figure 2.3), so here the corresponding Hotel window contains closed Room instances as rows. Double-clicking on the closed Room 101 row opens that room into its own window, and double-clicking other rows would open yet more windows. The room windows are outside of the hotel window since containment means only that *closed* objects are shown within their open parents.

Me" column. Rather, "Hotel" will be written in Room's "I'm In" column. In general, context determines whether an object is shown on another object's card as a child object or just the name shown as a property. It's okay for an object to be a child of one object while having its name shown as a mere property of another object. One difference between child object and property in the GUI to be designed during Part 3 is that a child object can be opened by double-clicking on its closed representation. In contrast, object names shown as mere properties are just strings of text; to open the named object, users must find its representation as a true child in some other window.

There are ways to shortcut the single-parent restriction, but our methodology protects participants from such complexities until the end of Part 3. Here in Part 2, every object usually should have a single parent, with all other names of that object being mere properties. This produces a simple, strict hierarchy that is a solid basis for the steps of the remainder of the design process. During the GUI designing (i.e., Part 3), some of those object-names-as-properties may be turned into links, or a multiple-parent model may be adopted. Those activities usually should not be done here in Part 2.

Many task objects are converted to mere attributes of other objects during this step; in other words, their index cards are thrown out after their attributes stickies are moved to other objects. The team's bias should be to have very few task objects (i.e., object classes) even if that requires each object to have lots of attributes. A plethora of attributes in an object can later be managed in the GUI representation of the object by bundling the attributes into frames, notebook pages, Included subsets, and views, all of which are more easily accessible than are entirely different objects.

3.2.5. Usability Testing of the Task Objects Against the Task Flows

You don't need a GUI to do a usability test! The team (which, as always, still includes real users) now tests whether the set of task objects is usable for executing the task flows it designed in Part 1. One person talks through each step in the task flows, with the other participants checking the task object cards and stickies for the presence of all the objects, attributes, and actions needed to execute that task step. The team usually will discover that the task objects or even task flows are incomplete or incorrect. If so, the team should change them; this entire workshop methodology is an iterative process.

As of yet, any GUI is irrelevant. The team must do this usability test only at the rather abstract level of task flows and task objects. This *is* a usability test, but of the conceptual foundation of the GUI instead of the surface of the GUI. Discovering usability problems at this early stage saves the resources you might otherwise have spent on designing the surface of the GUI incorrectly. The earlier in the design process that usability testing happens, the more leverage is gotten on resources.

The output of Part 2 is a set of task objects sufficient and usable for doing the task, each task object documented as an index card with stickies as shown in Figure 2.3. This set of task objects is the input for Part 3, which maps those rather abstract task objects into GUI objects.

3.3. PART 3: MAPPING TASK OBJECTS TO GUI OBJECTS

The goal of this part is to translate the output of the Task Object Design step (Part 2) into GUI elements such as windows and menu choices. Our terminology is that the abstract "task objects" are mapped into "GUI objects". Task objects manifest only as index cards, whereas GUI objects are the corresponding abstract data objects that manifest as combinations of GUI elements such as windows. The resulting GUI is object oriented, conforming in fundamental look and feel with the four GUI platform styles we mentioned at the start of this chapter: IBM CUA (IBM, 1992), Microsoft Windows (Microsoft, 1995), OSF/Motif 1.2 (Open Software Foundation, 1993), and X/Open CDE (X/Open Company Ltd., 1995). A valuable tool for getting that multiplatform look and feel is the multiplatform design guide by McFarland and Dayton (1995).

Using any of those style guides (or any current or future ones) necessarily is too time consuming and difficult during the initial designing activities, especially in the midst of a participatory session. All style guides, by their essence, are useful mostly as references for designing the details of a GUI after the participatory session. Here is how our methodology largely eliminates the need to use style guides during the participatory session.

- It breaks up the design process into steps that each map strongly into well-bounded components of the style (e.g., most task objects are expressed as GUI windows).
- It uses paper prototyping materials that reflect the desired style (e.g., photocopies of empty windows printed from a screen of the desired style).
- For the few style guidelines that do require explanation during the session, the methodology communicates each by brief lecturing with just a few overheads, at just the time in the process when that particular guideline is necessary.
- It postpones designing of the details until after the participatory session. It does this by skipping some of the details (e.g., some of the standard buttons on secondary windows) and by letting participants draw some components on the paper prototype in any way they like (e.g., put the buttons either on the side or the bottom).
- It includes style experts either as participants (usually the usability engineer) or as facilitators.

Of course, many platform-specific characteristics must be specified during the session, in order to draw even the basic pictures used as the paper prototype. Therefore, one of the target GUI platform styles is chosen by the team for the purpose of paper prototyping. If the GUI must also be produced in other styles, then after the session the usability engineer copies the fundamental design while changing the platform-specific details in minor ways to make them conform exactly to the other styles.

Part 3 of the methodology designs only the fundamentals of the GUI per se. That means the resulting window definitions include window types, window views, and window commands (menu bar choices and control buttons), but not accelerator key combinations and icons. Those and other details are filled in by the usability engineer after the participatory session because the other participants usually can contribute less to those activities, and a participatory session is not a particularly efficient medium for doing that kind of detailed designing. Nor does Part 3 of the methodology design user support such as documentation and on-line help. Those things are important, but they need to be designed via methods that fully focus on them.

There are several steps in Part 3; they involve designing, documenting, paper prototyping, and usability testing the GUI fundamentals. As in the previous two parts, no step is begun until the previous step is mostly complete, but there is considerable small- and large-scale iteration among steps. Almost always, the participants gain insights during this GUI designing part that prompt them to change the task objects and even the task flows. Each step in Part 3 maps a different aspect of the task objects to GUI objects, as exemplified by Figure 2.5. The following sections briefly describe the steps that do those mappings.[11]

3.3.1. Identities of GUI Objects

The core mapping of task objects to GUI objects is done by deciding which GUI representations each task object should have. All task objects must be represented as closed objects in the GUI. There are many possible closed representations, such as list row, icon, and menu choice (for device objects). The decision on the particular closed representation is not made in this first step of Part 3. This step instead requires participants only to decide whether each GUI object's closed representation can be opened into a window, and if so, whether that should be a primary window or a secondary window. The bias should be toward primary windows, largely because primaries can remain open despite the closing of the windows from which they were opened. (This GUI style uses only Single-Document Interface style, SDI, not Multi-Document Interface style, MDI.)

Participants document their decision to show an object as a window by paper clipping a photocopied empty primary or secondary window to the task object card. They write in the window's title bar the name of an object instance; in the example in Figure 2.5, the title is "Tom Dayton" because Tom Dayton is one instance of a Customer. If the window has a menu bar, they name the leftmost menu with the name of the object class; in Figure 2.5 the leftmost menu is called "Customer" because the window as a whole represents a particular customer. Figure 2.5 actually shows more than the result of this first step, since this step uses only one photocopied window per task object and leaves the window's client area empty. The next step defines additional windows.

3.3.2. Views of GUI Objects

Then the team decides the basic appearance of each window's content, in other words, the "views" of the GUI object. The mapping is from each task object's attributes sticky into the corresponding windows' client areas (Figure 2.5). The team roughly sketches the view appearances in the heretofore empty client areas of the window photocopies and appends each title bar's object instance name with a view name. Each view of an object is drawn on its own photocopied empty window, with all the views for the same object having the same leftmost menu name and the same title bar object instance name.

---

[11] Readers wanting more GUI style descriptions as context for better understanding these method descriptions should see McFarland and Dayton (1995), IBM (1992), or Microsoft (1995).

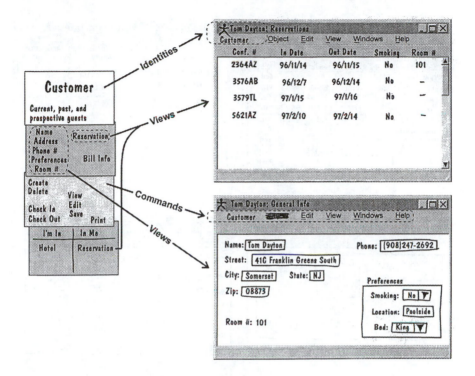

Figure 2.5 Mapping a task object to a GUI object in Part 3. In the Identities step of Part 3, participants map the object class name into the name of the leftmost menu of a window and into an instance name in the title bar. In the Views step, participants map the child objects and properties from the attributes sticky into the client areas of one or more window views — creating an additional paper window for each view — and append the view names to the window titles. (This figure does not show the Bill Info view.) In the Commands step, participants map the actions into choices from pull-down menus or into window-level buttons. Participants hand draw on photocopies of empty windows.

Views can be used to show *different* attributes, such as child objects in one view and properties in another (e.g., a customer's reservations vs. a customer's general information — see Figure 2.5); the containment sticky on the task object helps by identifying which of the attributes are child objects. For instance, the Room object might have one view showing a diagram of the room (see Figure 2.6) and another view showing the room's furniture, equipment, and maintenance history. Views can also be used to show the *same* attributes, but in different ways. An example is having one view showing customers as textual rows in a list and another view showing customers as pictures of the customers' faces.

Multiple windows showing the same object instance may be open simultaneously (e.g., the two windows in Figure 2.5). Multiple object instances may be open at once (e.g., a set of Tom Dayton customer windows and a set of Joseph Kramer customer windows), so the team may paper prototype multiple instances

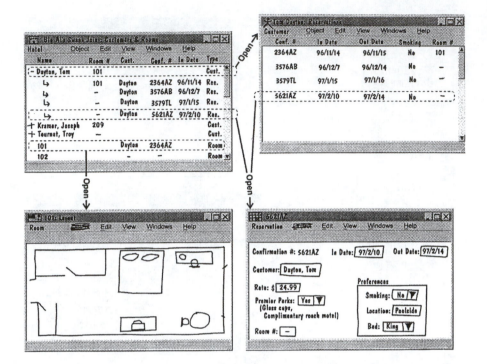

Figure 2.6 Prototype output by Part 3. These are just some of the windows needed for the
hotel example GUI. Each window is hand-drawn in a separate photocopied empty
window. The user tests the prototype by tapping and dragging a pen or finger on
these windows, while the rest of the participants respond by placing and removing
windows, menus, and other GUI elements. For example, the user double-tapping
on the Room 101 row in the Big Al's Swank Joint window causes Room 101 to
open into its own window that is an additional piece of paper on the table. The Big
Al's Swank Joint window uses an indented hierarchical list to let users see its
reservation grandchildren without opening their parent — Tom Dayton — into its
own window. However, if users want to focus just on Tom Dayton's reservations
without the distraction of any other customers, rooms, or reservations in the
window, they can still open Tom Dayton into its own window.

to increase the richness of the usability testing. These windows usually are
independent of each other, with users relying on the standard GUI windowing
environment mechanisms of window moving, sizing, layering, minimizing, maxi-
mizing, and closing to manage the large quantity of information.

Users easily know how and where to open closed objects into windows
because closed objects are shown inside the objects that users naturally think of
as their containers (Figure 2.6). The Bridge methodology produces a GUI that
reflects the users' natural mental model of those containment relations, in contrast
to many traditional approaches that force users to change their mental model to
match the GUI.

3.3.3. Commands for GUI Objects

Then the menu bars and entire-window-level command buttons are designed by mapping them from the actions sticky of each task object (Figure 2.5). The menus are represented by preprinted, style guide standard, menu pull-downs. The leftmost menu has a blank for its preprinted name so that the team can write in the names of object classes to match the paper windows' hand-lettered leftmost menu names. For example, if the actions sticky for the Customer task object says "Print", then the team leaves the standard choice "Print" in the preprinted leftmost menu that they have labeled "Customer". Preprinted menu choices that have no corresponding sticky entries are crossed off. Actions on the sticky that have no corresponding preprinted standard choice are written on the appropriate preprinted menus. To keep all the materials together, the menus for each object are removable-taped to an index card that is paper clipped to the object's windows and task object card.

Also in this step, participants design and paper prototype the major portions of the transaction dialogue windows that support the commands most relevant to view definition. The most important of these is the dialogue supporting the Include action, which makes visible only the subset of information that a user wants to see in a given window at the moment (i.e., it is an inverse filtering action). The Include action allows the team to avoid designing a separate view for every subset of information they might ever want to see. Some other dialogue windows that should be designed at this point are those supporting the New, Sort, and Find actions.

The team has now produced a paper prototype that contains the data needed by the users to do their tasks, the menu bars and window-level buttons to manipulate the data, and the navigational paths among the windows. The paper prototype is now ready to be thoroughly usability tested by these very same participants in this very same session.

3.3.4. Usability Testing of GUI Objects Against the Task Flows

Throughout Part 3, the team has done quick usability tests of the incomplete paper prototype. But now that even the commands have been prototyped, the usability testing can be more realistic and thorough. A rectangle representing the computer screen is marked off with masking tape on the table top. One participant points to and reads each step in the task flows. One user uses a pen as the mouse pointer for clicking through the paper prototype to execute the task step being read. The rest of the participants act as the computer, responding to the user's actions by adding and removing the appropriate windows and pull-down menus from the screen. Any time a problem is found, the team stops the test, changes the design and the paper prototype, then restarts the test. Usually, the task objects and even the task flows also are changed during this phase, in a rapidly iterative process.

If time allows during the session, the team now adds some polish and detail to the paper prototype. For instance, they may add shortcuts for expert users and complete more of the dialogue windows.

After all the documented task flows have been successfully executed with the paper prototype, the team tries other tasks to test the flexibility of the design. Thanks to the object-oriented style, often the design can handle tasks that were not foreseen during the initial design and the design can easily be modified to accommodate many other tasks.

4. CONCLUSION

What remains to be done after the three-part Bridge session is the filling in of design details such as some of the dialogue boxes, icons, precise window layouts, colors, and fonts. Those remaining details are most efficiently designed by the usability engineer outside of a participatory session, though the usability engineer must continue consulting with users and other team members. Those remaining details are, of course, important, but they are much less important than the fundamental organization, appearance, and behavior that The Bridge does design.

This chapter is not a complete description of The Bridge methodology. More extensive descriptions are in the notes handed out during educational sessions of the methodology, but a complete account will require its own book. In the meantime, this chapter should at least give readers a general orientation, especially to the critical Task Object Design center span of our bridge over the gap between user needs and GUI prototype.

5. ACKNOWLEDGMENTS

Many people have contributed in varying ways and degrees to development of The Bridge. Michael Muller was largely responsible for initially convincing us of the value of participatory methods in general. Michael also was a prime originator of the early versions of the CARD method (with Leslie Tudor, Tom Dayton, and Bob Root) and the PICTIVE method that we took as the starting points for developing Parts 1 and 3, respectively. Michael is also a prolific contributor to the usability lexicon, the "PANDA" acronym being his most recent. Bob Root added to CARD some explicit steps that we expanded and elaborated into Part 1. Jim Berney was a key to providing the various resources we needed for developing The Bridge. Much of what we have provided is just the overall structure and glue that made an integrated, end-to-end process out of component ideas that we adapted from many public sources, including common object-oriented methodologies. Our cofacilitators and the participants in Bridge sessions have provided not just valuable feedback but also original ideas. We heartily thank all the above people for their participation in the collaborative development of this collaborative methodology. We also thank Larry Wood, Andrew Monk, and Sabine Rohlfs for comments on this manuscript.

6. REFERENCES

Collins, D., *Designing Object-Oriented User Interfaces,* Benjamin-Cummings, Menlo Park, CA, 1995.

Dayton, T., Cultivated eclecticism as the normative approach to design, in *Taking Software Design Seriously: Practical Techniques for Human-Computer Interaction Design,* Karat, J., Ed., Academic, Boston, 1991, 21-44.

Dayton, T. and Kramer, J., *Testing Task Flows: A Participatory, Object-Oriented Approach*, tutorial presented at UPA 95, the annual meeting of the Usability Professionals Association, Portland, ME, July, 1995.

Dayton, T., Kramer, J., and Bertus, E. L., *Participatory Design of Data Centered, Multiplatform, Graphical User Interfaces*, tutorial presented at HFES 96, the annual meeting of the Human Factors and Ergonomics Society, Philadelphia, September, 1996.

Dayton, T., Kramer, J., McFarland, A., and Heidelberg, M., *Participatory GUI Design from Task Models*, tutorial presented at CHI 96, the annual meeting of ACM SIGCHI, Vancouver, April, 1996. Summary in *CHI 96 Conference Companion,* 375–376.

Dayton, T., McFarland, A., and White, E., Software development — keeping users at the center, *Bellcore Exchange, 10*(5), 12–17, 1994.

IBM, *Object-Oriented Interface Design: IBM Common User Access Guidelines*, Que Corp., Carmel, IN, 1992.

Karat, J. and Dayton, T., Practical education for improving software usability. *Proceedings of CHI 95,* 162–169, 1995.

Kramer, J. and Dayton, T., *After the Task Flow: Participatory Design of Data Centered, Multiplatform, Graphical User Interfaces*, tutorial presented at APCHI 96, the annual meeting of the Asia Pacific Computer Human Interaction Group, Singapore, June, 1996.

Kramer, J., Dayton, T., and Heidelberg, M., *From Task Flow to GUI: A Participatory, Data-Centered Approach*, tutorial presented at UPA 96, the annual meeting of the Usability Professionals Association, Copper Mountain, CO, July, 1996.

McFarland, A. and Dayton, T., *A Participatory Methodology for Driving Object-Oriented GUI Design from User Needs*, tutorial presented at OZCHI 95, the annual meeting of the Computer Human Interaction SIG of the Ergonomics Society of Australia, Wollongong, Australia, November, 1995. Summary in *OZCHI 95 Conference Proceedings,* 10–11.

McFarland, A., and Dayton, T. (with others), *Design Guide for Multiplatform Graphical User Interfaces* (LP-R13, Issue 3), Piscataway, NJ, 1995. Bellcore (call 800-521-2673 from US and Canada, +1-908-699-5800 from elsewhere).

Microsoft, *The Windows Guidelines for Software Design,* Microsoft Press, Redmond, WA, 1995.

Muller, M. J., Hallewell Haslwanter, J., and Dayton, T., Participatory practices in the software lifecycle, in *Handbook of Human-Computer Interaction,* 2nd ed., Helander, M., Prabhu, P., and Landauer, T., Eds., Amsterdam, North-Holland, in press.

Muller, M. J. and Kuhn, S., Eds., Participatory design [Special issue], *Communications of the ACM,* 36(6), 1993.

Muller, M. J., Miller, D. S., Smith, J. G., Wildman, D. M.,White, E. A., Dayton, T., Root, R. W., and Salasoo, A., Assessing a groupware implementation of a manual participatory design process. *InterCHI 93 Adjunct Proceedings,* 105-106, 1993.

Muller, M. J., Tudor, L. G., Wildman, D. M., White, E. A., Root, R. W., Dayton, T., Carr, B., Diekmann, B., and Dykstra-Erickson, E., Bifocal tools for scenarios and representations in participatory activities with users, in *Scenario-Based Design for Human-Computer Interaction,* Carroll, J. M., Ed., John Wiley & Sons, New York, 1995, 135-163.

Open Software Foundation, *OSF/Motif Style Guide: Rev. 1.2.,* Prentice Hall, Englewood Cliffs, NJ, 1993.

Virzi, R., What can you learn from a low-fidelity prototype?, *Proceedings of HFES 89,* 224-228, 1989.

X/Open Company Ltd., Application style checklist, in X/Open Company Ltd., *CAE Specification: X/Open Common Desktop Environment (XCDE) Services and Applications,* Reading, Berkshire, U. K., 1995, 355-441.

CHAPTER 3

Transforming Representations in User-Centered Design

Thomas M. Graefe
Digital Equipment Corporation, Littleton, Massachusetts
email: graefe@tnpubs.enet.dec.com

TABLE OF CONTENTS

ABSTRACT

This chapter describes the activity of bridging the gap between user-centered analysis and a concrete design as a cognitive process of transforming representations of information. Like other cognitive tasks, such as remembering or problem solving, success in design hinges on the ability to code and recode information effectively. A case study illustrates this process within the proposed framework, and shows how the use of appropriate mediating representations facilitates bridging the gap. Finally, it is argued that user-centered design can be thought of as a corrective for biases in traditional system design and further that metaheuristics can and should be developed to guide design.

1. INTRODUCTION

Planning, installing, controlling, and repairing the infrastructure on which society's pervasive Information Technology (IT) is based has engendered a new software application domain. Loosely defined this new industry comprises the network and systems management applications used to support near real-time monitoring and control of this widely distributed infrastructure. Any given IT network is made up of many heterogeneous resources, each of which can be a complex system itself. Moreover, the whole inevitably has emergent properties unanticipated by the makers of the individual parts. This variability, and the magnitude and technical content of the problem domain, creates a significant mismatch between the complexity of the managed technology and the capabilities of the people who manage it. User-centered design techniques must be used to simplify, integrate, and infuse network and system management applications with purpose and intelligence.

User-centered design prescribes involving the end users of a technology in the definition of how the technology is applied within a problem domain. The diverse techniques for bringing users into the development process all provide for including user-based data to determine the make up of systems. However, these techniques are less clear on how the user-centered data are transformed into a specific design. This chapter examines the question of how user-centered analysis becomes a concrete design with two particular issues in mind: what is the nature of the transformations a designer makes to move from the user-centered analysis to concrete design and how does the process of transformation relate to the psychology of the designer? The next section describes a framework for discussing these issues, after which an example is given. Finally, in light of this analysis the last section looks at psychology of the designer.

2. WHAT IS THE GAP?

User-centered design can be thought of as a cognitive task that requires the designer (or group of designers) to encode and transform information in the course of application definition. For example, in general, transformation occurs when the designer combines end user work descriptions with a user interface syntax (e.g., the rules governing a graphical user interface) to produce a new means to accomplish some task. A more specific example within this general category is when the designer makes word choices to try to adhere to a maxim such as "Use terms familiar to the user". In either case the designer is taking information in one context, transforming it, and expressing it in another. This ability to code and recode information is basic to human cognition and has been the focus of much psychological research. Psychological accounts of the efficacy of coding often rely on the concept of "representation" whereby coding results in representations more amenable to completing some particular cognitive task (e.g., Miller, 1956). Familiar elementary school rhymes used to help recollect the number of days in each month, or acronyms such as "ROY G BIV" for the colors of the spectrum, are simple instances of coding. The psychological literature abounds with other examples, including studies of chunking as a means to increase the amount of information that can be retained, studies of mental rotation (Shepard and Metzler, 1971), theoretical accounts of the structure of memory (e.g., Anderson, 1976), and accounts of how choice of representation can be critical to success in problem solving (e.g., Simon, 1981). In all cases a key part of the account given of human performance has to do with the mediating role played by internal representation or coding. Similarly, it is argued here that representation is key to defining the gap bridged in design because this gap lies between representations used in the design process.

One representational metatheory characterizes any discussion of representation as necessarily a discussion of a "representational system."[1] A representational system must specify:

1. What the represented world is
2. What the representing world is
3. What aspects of the represented world are being modeled
4. What aspects of the representing world are doing the modeling
5. What are the correspondences between the two worlds

User-centered design entails the creation of a particular "representational system" through a process that begins with user data and ends with a hardware and software system for some end user task. To fulfill the necessary conditions for a design the designer will have implicitly or explicitly addressed each of these five

---

[1] This discussion is based on a chapter by S. E. Palmer, "Fundamental Aspects of Cognitive Representation", p. 262. Norman (1993) also discusses the notions of represented and representing worlds, but from the vantage of the end user rather than the designer.

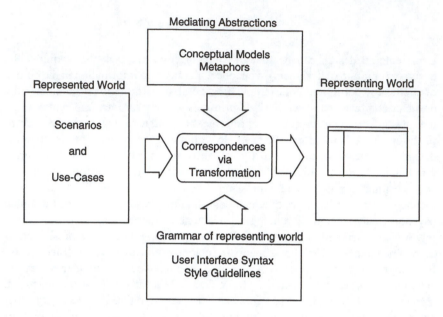

Figure 3.1 The representational system in design.

elements. In this view, the gap between user data and concrete design is a gap between a "represented world" and a "representing world". The represented world is the end user data, and the representing world is the application user interface.[2] Bridging the gap requires the definition of items 3 through 5, although sometimes the designer's job may begin with the basic choices of what the represented world is and what the representing world should be.

The selection of aspects of the represented world to be modeled and appropriate aspects of the representing world doing the modeling are bound up in the process for developing the correspondences between the two. This is the crux of the designer's decision making, leading to a concrete design. Figure 3.1 illustrates the Gap between the represented and representing world and graphically shows the idea that correspondences developed through information transformation span the gap.

Artifacts containing the results of user analysis make up the represented world. In this paper the represented world comprised the results of contextual inquiries (Wixon and Ramey, 1996), rendered in scenarios and extracted use-cases that distilled many hours of meetings with end users. As will be described later, successive iterations during design elaborated the initial view of the repre-

---

[2]   The epistemological question of how the represented world is known, its correspondence with the "real world", and the objectivity of this knowledge is an interesting one and affects how the representational system is defined. However, for this context it will be sidestepped with the caveat that how user-centered analysis is captured has a significant impact on the design process, as will be discussed later.

sented world. On the other side of the gap, the representing world was a software application based on Windows NT/Windows 95™ operating systems and user interface look and feel. Two additional factors shape the development of correspondences in the representational system during design. First, the upper box in the middle of the figure shows mediating abstractions as important transformations for bridging the gap. They help manifest the represented world in the representing world by suggesting appropriate interpretive structure. Examples here include metaphors for the represented world and other conceptual models at once removed from the data of user experience, but sufficiently linked to it to serve as the basis for users' understanding. These mediating abstractions can "have entailments through which they highlight and make coherent certain aspects of our experience" to use Lakoff and Johnson's phrase about the role of metaphor in understanding (Lakoff and Johnson, 1980, p. 156). This understanding is shared between the designer and the end user. The designer creates the representing world around such models and metaphors, and the user comprehends the laws of that world via the same devices.

Whatever the data defining the represented world, or the derived mediating abstractions, the representing world will have its own constraints. In Figure 3.1 the lower middle box shows these constraints as the grammar of the representing world. While the designer can expand the realm of possible components from which they choose, even these new components typically fall within some general paradigm, such as defined in the visual graphical user interface. Expanding the possible grammars of user interaction (e.g., looking beyond direct manipulation or adding gesture to the repertoire of means of manipulation) is an important topic in human computer interaction design, since any chosen paradigm has its own particular affordances with regard to the aspects of the represented world that can be included or the facility of the end user to access those aspects.

3. REPRESENTATIONS IN DESIGN: DECISIONS AND TRANSFORMATION

The rationale for user-centered design is that research shows continuous and iterative inclusion of end user information is the best way to create useful and usable products (Landauer, 1995). The previous section argued that user-centered design requires mediating information be generated and applied in the creation of the representing world within the representational system. The purpose of this section is to outline one process for realizing a concrete design and show how facilitating the systematic transformation among the different representations is the *raison d'être* for useful process steps.

The discussion that follows covers design work for a system management application for monitoring hardware and software processing resources typically functioning as servers within a corporate computing environment. The application was distributed and could be used to monitor resources in a single site, worldwide

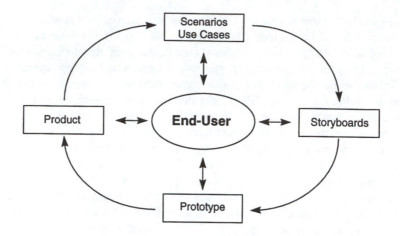

Figure 3.2 Iterative design — spanning the gap in increments.

or in between. It also was intended to support proactive and reactive automation of operations. The time scope of the work was about 1 year, although the majority of the user interface design covered about 3 months (post contextual inquiries). The development team consisted of about 15 software engineers, supported by a usability engineer working about half time on this project.

The next section describes the overall process. The example pertains to one aspect of the product and was one of numerous design problems.

3.1. PROCESS OVERVIEW

This project used an iterative design process through which alternative user interface designs and system behaviors were tested and refined in the course of product development. This means that the "gap" was not bridged once, but rather was bridged incrementally as the design was refined. User-centered analysis was the starting point for design, but feedback from users on that analysis, on intermediate approximations of the concrete design rendered as storyboards, prototypes, and ultimately on the product itself informed the final concrete design. Thus, repeated interactions with end users shaped decisions about both the form of the representing world and the correspondences between it and the represented world. Figure 3.2 shows the steps of iterative process used for testing approximations of the concrete design.

At the center of the figure is the end user. At the top of the figure the square-labeled scenarios and use cases represent the initial user data. The scenario information also described the work environment, education, and experience of

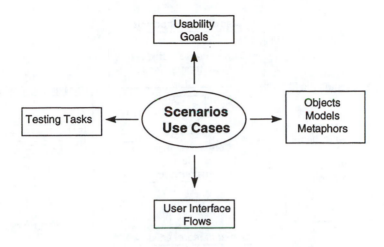

Figure 3.3 Use cases and scenarios provide data for many design steps.

end users and their existing tools. The other three squares are types of artifacts used to capture the concrete design at different stages in its evolution. User feedback was gathered on storyboards (sequences of paper screen designs arranged as flows, serving as a paper prototype), software prototypes, and the actual product.

The methods used to gather user feedback changed as the rendering of the design changed, but they consistently linked to the originating scenario and use-case data. Figure 3.3 shows for this project where the scenarios provided content and structure for other steps in the interface design and testing process.

The use cases had corresponding usability goals, usually defined in measurable terms such as time to complete an operation or number of errors. The use cases also provided a high level definition of the important system interactions, especially since user-case structure defined related operations. Finally, the use cases were executed as test tasks, using storyboards, a prototype, and in testing field test versions of the product.

Thus, by combining an iterative design approach with the appropriate description of the represented world, it is possible to shape the design and the design process with end user information. The concrete design is derived from content of the analysis and modified in accord with ongoing feedback. The process (e.g., setting usability goals and test tasks and then testing via the storyboard walkthroughs and prototype testing) is linked to the same analysis. The user-centered analysis can be augmented as well during the design cycle (e.g., new use cases may emerge as users note how their work is being changed by the application itself).

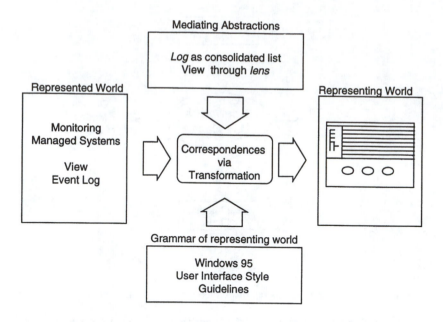

Figure 3.4 Example case study elements in a representational system.

3.2. VIEWING THE MANAGED RESOURCES: THE OPERATOR'S WINDOW ONTO THE WORLD

In design a good deal of the work is detailed examination of the results of user-centered analysis, extraction of key information, and laborious development of correspondences between the data and the elements of the representing world. The ability to recognize recurrent patterns in end user data and to manipulate the possibilities of the representing world (e.g., knowing the grammar and style or idioms) is developed with practice. The following subsections use the definition of the main application window as a case study to elaborate on the process overview provided above. Figure 3.4 gives an overview of this case study within the diagram for a representational system. The four squares show the elements of the system described earlier, but now labeled with the instances of information from this case study. Each element is explained below.

3.2.1. Scenarios and Use Cases

The raw data for this design were gathered from contextual inquiries (CIs) conducted with users from six different corporations. These data included infor-mation on their existing work practice and tools, as well as on possible changes to the current practice that this new application might support. The hours of discussions and observations were summarized into reports for each customer, which were circulated back to the customer for comment and revision. These summaries were structured according to high-level scenarios. These scenarios were an amalgam of narrative information, as well as some observation and interpretation from the CI team. A scenario did not typically correspond to a single task, but usually captured a flow of tasks — in a sense how the users defined their job responsibilities and means to fulfill them. The data captured within a scenario included task information, critiques of current tools, policies, and opinions. The customers all found these reports accessible and useful. The separate reports were consolidated into a single, cross-customer summary.

There are several different types of end users of system management applications who were observed at work in operations centers using existing tools and manual procedures. In the case study scenario below, the end user is the operator, who uses the application to watch the status of resources, gathers first level information when there is a problem, and then usually notifies an expert for problems they cannot solve. The operators report to a manager, who also has specific requirements for the application, but is not typically using it day in and day out to monitor (they often set up and administer the application, as well as set policies for the operators). The scenario is simply called "Monitoring", and was derived from general and specific information from operators and their managers. The comments below were descriptions given by end users and are accurate reflections of observed work as well.

- **Managers**
  - "Our operators need to be able to monitor thousands of systems from a central location and detect a problem in any one."
  - "Our operators have specific areas of responsibility based on what operating system technology they know — UNIX, NT, and VMS. We also have people responsible for applications that can cut across operating systems. Often they will need to see problems in other areas."
  - "We usually have some specific key systems that are particularly important to the company, and we want to make sure these are highly visible."
- **Operators**
  - "I need to be able to quickly focus on a critical event."
  - "I like to keep all my systems in view and watch for an icon to change color."
  - "I can't be swamped by thousands of events."
  - "I can't afford to miss a single important event."
  - "Often I need to find all the events for a system and their status."

Such quotations are taken from an overall discussion and are meant to show how simple narrative serves as a starting point for design. Even this small sample of data outlines several critical (and sometimes conflicting) requirements the user interface needs to fulfill. One obvious example is the ability to monitor many objects at once while at the same time avoid being swamped or creating a condition where individual systems cannot readily be brought into focus. Also,

Scenario: Monitoring

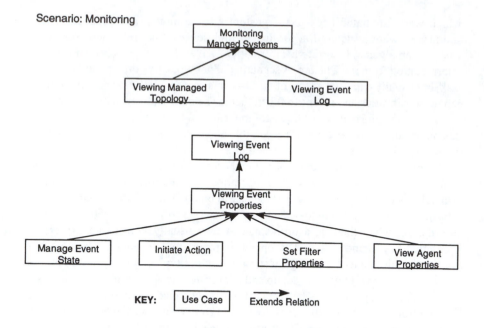

Figure 3.5 Example use case analysis and structure.

users made it clear that accurate detection of problems was critical, and discussion surrounding this point suggested that, if not actual compensation, at least customer satisfaction was strongly influenced by success in this regard.

As useful as the scenario data were, they lacked sufficient structure for all aspects of design. Strength of the data in conveying the end user perspective was also a weakness because it did not provide a systematic decomposition that could be related into the overall software design process. Therefore, from the scenarios a set of use cases was defined. A Use-case is "a sequence of transactions in a system whose task is to yield a result of measurable value to an individual actor of the system" (Jacobson, I. et al., *The Object Advantage*, 1994, p. 105). While use cases are sometimes described as defined in the absence of users, for this project the use case definition was driven from the end user data and then reformulated, if need be, to tie into relevant details of the underlying system architecture.

The Monitoring scenario had a corresponding Monitoring use case, in which the value is bound to the fundamental challenge for the operator, namely being able to observe efficiently and effectively status changes. Two more specific use cases, as extensions of the basic use case defined specific interactions between the actor — an operator — and the management system. These extension use cases specify a substantial subcourse of actor-system interactions and capture two ways monitoring can be done. Figure 3.5 illustrates the use cases and their relationship. The textual definition of the main monitoring use cases is below.

Monitoring Managed Systems — Events provide information about the systems, and are used as the basic indicators of system state change for operators. Access to the state change information comes from two modes: looking for a change in the system icon or some related icon (e.g., parent icon) or through viewing the event log.

Viewing Managed Topology — Viewing managed topology is started when the operator launches the application. They use a graphic display of the managed systems to watch for changes in health of the systems. The topology includes all managed systems and any superimposed hierarchy (e.g., grouping by type). The health of the system is visually indicated.

Viewing Event Log — Viewing the event log is started as soon as the operator wants to look at the text descriptions of the real-time event stream being received from the managed systems. The event log is the default destination of all received events and unless otherwise altered shows all events from all managed systems.

Figure 3.5 shows additional subcourses of transactions for the Viewing Event Log use-case. View event properties and the four extension uses cases capture the different likely actions the operator might take in reaction to a specific event they have chosen to view. The structure of the use cases defines a relationship between transactions with the system and captures an abstract view of the flow of these transactions.

The use cases themselves provide summaries across observations and specific individual differences, and can then support and structure design as a useful "chunk" of information. The scenario data (e.g., the quotations) are important just because they are not abstracted — they capture the actual flavor of users' understanding of their work and give evidence of users' "schemas" for understanding their tasks.

3.2.2. Objects, Conceptual Models, Metaphors

Scenarios and use cases are the substance of the represented world. The information they contain must be transformed to develop correspondences with the representing world. Objects, conceptual models, and metaphors play a major role in this activity and are derived from the scenarios and use-cases to facilitate design of specific interface elements and flow. The objects defined here, although capable of having a formal connotation within a full Object-oriented system, can be thought of less formally as the entities upon which the user acts. The user actions can be thought of as services being requested of the object, but no formal requirement is made in this regard. A conceptual model is a simplified rendering of how proposed objects will behave and interact. The behavior in question is not just that of the graphical user interface *per se*, but of the software functions supporting that interface. One analogy here is between a blueprint and a finished house. The blueprint describes how the components of the house will be put together so that the finished structure is sound and can be used for the designed purpose. When you walk into the house you do not see many of the elements

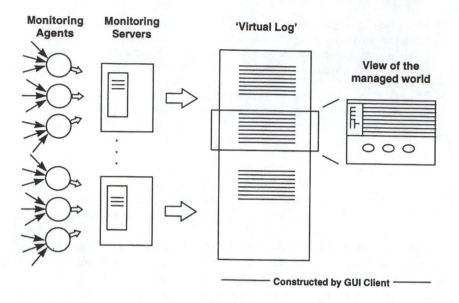

Figure 3.6 Conceptual model for distributed architecture and consolidated user view.

contained in the blueprint, especially if it was built correctly. However, it is possible to relate the finished appearance and the internal structure of the house to the blueprint. Therefore, a conceptual model is in a sense a user view of the architecture of the system, if such a view was to be revealed to the user.[3] A conceptual model helps the user interface designer and the development team make consistent decisions across user visible objects of a system and to relate these objects to the internal system view. This definition is somewhat different from others in the literature because it emphasizes the integration of the user view with system behavior, instead of focusing only on the user's conceptual model. A metaphor effectively likens a model or an aspect of the represented world to some other commonly understood object, behavior, or characteristic of the world. The metaphor then provides both literal and behavioral structure to the user interface. Conceptual models and metaphors should work synergistically as system design centers.

Conceptual modeling is useful for ensuring that internal system designs are projected selectively to the end user, or conversely, hidden as required. Figure 3.6 illustrates some aspects of an important conceptual model underlying the Monitoring scenario.

This figure shows six agents[4] on the left, each of which can detect important changes within their domain (typically a single computer). These agents are

---

[3]   Such models were used in documentation, information support, and training on this project, where
they were the basis for explaining the application.
[4]   In this context "Agent" refers to an architectural component within a common management model
in which an agent communicates with and can act on instructions from a Manager application to
effect changes within the managed resource (object).

Table 3.1 Example Abstractions Drawn from User Data

End User data	Objects	Model	Metaphor
"Monitor Key Systems"	Systems	Log as consolidated list	View through lens
"Focus on Critical Events"	Events		Zoom/wide angle views
"Keep all Systems in View"			

software modules within monitored corporate servers. They send notifications of these changes to other servers running the system management application, which collect these events and store them, each in its individual log file. The large rectangle into which the servers place events is the event log viewed by the operator as part of the use case "Viewing the event log". It is a consolidated repository of data (i.e., all the log files) based on a subscription constructed by the GUI client and sent to distributed event servers. Thus, the underlying software is responsible for supporting this virtual view. The end user sees this single "log" in the list view and only cares about the distributed sources if there is some problem making the "virtual" log incomplete. In the contextual inquiries, users made a clear distinction between the distributed elements they managed and their own requirement to have the application support a centralized, logical view of that distributed domain. Part of the user interface design problem was arriving at the correct user view of the information, its use, and the end user's expectations. Part of the overall system design problem for support of the Monitoring use case was ensuring underlying software services were available to maintain and manage the virtual view.[5] The conceptual model is important because it makes the potential impact of nominally "internal" design decisions explicit and thereby enables the designers to address how such decisions might affect end users.

Table 3.1 summarizes some of the flow between the data gathered from users into scenarios and use cases, the generation of metaphors and models, and the subsequent selection of specific user interface components.

For example, in discussing monitoring users often described their work by saying "I need the big picture most of the time, but then I need to be able to focus in really quickly on a problem." Combined with the other information about operator responsibilities (e.g., manager statements about central monitoring of many systems) this user statement defines some basic structural issues for the user interface display and navigation mechanisms. There is some form of representation of the managed resources. These resources themselves have certain relationships to one another and to the scope of the operator's interest. There are specific notifications of problems, a need to determine what the problem is, and so on. These characteristics constitute the user elements of the conceptual model for how

---

[5] This indirection also affects the definition of the underlying system architecture and thereby the structural elements or services made available to modules. A classic instance where system internals are painfully revealed to the end user in many network management systems occurs within the context of SNMP-based Management systems. Here typically the user must directly and in a piecemeal fashion manipulate low-level data structures because a data model has been equated with the user's view.

users want to use this application for monitoring. Further, the user's description itself suggests a reasonable metaphor for the operation — that of a lens onto the managed world with both wide angle and zoom capabilities. Therefore, the general requirements for the interface (expressed in Monitoring Managed Systems → Viewing Managed topology, Viewing Event Log), the model of the system supporting these requirements, and a metaphor for the operation of that interface can be linked to the detail of the user-centered data.

More generically, the use cases themselves were mined to create a candidate pool of user visible objects and operations. These are the nouns and verbs of the use-case narrative. The user descriptions that underlay the use-cases were examined for specific language and nuance, and together this information was used to create candidate dialogs for display of the objects and menu commands capturing the actions. Specific terms can derive from either standards (e.g., for dialog control) or domain semantics.

In summary, objects are the nominal targets within a direct manipulation interface, but how they are portrayed — their context and meaning within the concrete design — is shaped by the mediating devices of the conceptual model and metaphor with which they are aligned.

3.2.3. Detailed Screen Design

The objects, models, and metaphors generated from the use-cases were first transformed within Windows 95™ Graphical User Interface standards into a paper prototype storyboard. As discussed above, detailed analysis provides a view into the user's world in terms of the relevant objects and operations. Models and metaphors are abstractions helping to link the user data to the software system design and implementation. Detailed screen design is the step where specific user interface components must be chosen to express these metaphors and models as they will be used to manipulate the target objects. Figure 3.7 is a copy of a paper prototype screen used in the storyboard for the Monitoring use case. It shows the main application window and is made up of three subwindows within an overall Multiple Document Interface (MDI) application window. The three panes of the child window are the tree view (upper left), the list view (upper right), and the map or icon view (bottom panel). Table 3.2 lists these elements and some brief notes about the rationale for their design.

Viewing topology and viewing event lists were two main ways of monitoring, as reflected in the use case analysis. The icon color status provided quick alerting and the event list provided more information about a specific event (the rows in the list view were also color coded for severity). To support both overall monitoring of a large number of systems and quick focus (wide angle and zooming) whenever any object in the tree or map view was selected the event view would be automatically filtered to show only events for the selected object and its children. In this design the metaphorical focus is implemented with explicit feedback from direct manipulation of the tree, as well as with filtering to reduce

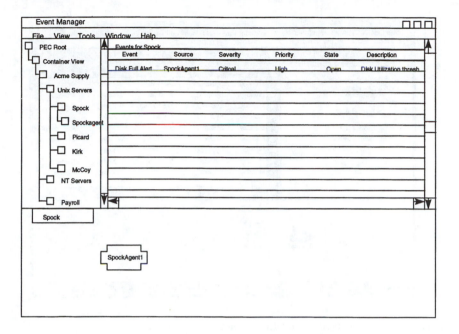

Figure 3.7 Paper prototype of main window for operator view used within storyboard walkthrough.

Table 3.2 Example Component Analysis from Main Window Design

GUI Component	Design Rationale
MDI application window	MDI structure accommodated multiple child windows; windows standard; note both child windows and application itself could be cloned or opened in copies respectively
Tree control	Hierarchical view allowing flexible containment definition for grouping managed resources (by technology, by application etc.); familiar and standard component; easy drag and drop
Icon\map view	Alternative representation of systems allowing use of geographic map backgrounds for added information in icon placement; preferred by subset of users for monitoring
List view	Simple means to show large number of event text descriptions; supported sorting and customization of contained fields; standard control
Linked child window navigation	Selection of a given object in tree or map view automatically filtered events in list to those generated by the specific selected item (or it children if a 'directory' level object); this was indicated in the status bar
Main menu items	Reuse of all standard menu items for generic functions; some customization for view

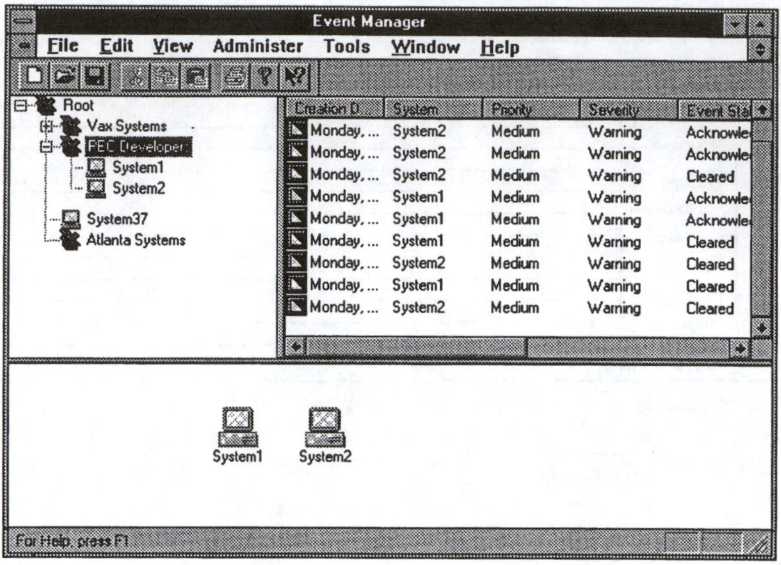

Figure 3.8 Screen capture of prototype screen for main window.

the data. Other features helped focus and alerting. For example actions could be defined to produce a pop-up message box when certain events were detected. Figure 3.8 shows a screen capture of an early version of the actual running application.

3.2.4. Storyboards and User Interface Flow

Storyboards were used in two ways on this project. First, they were used within the design team as a working tool for sketching out user interface flows and navigation. In this case, the storyboards were often hand-drawn User Interface sketches on sticky notes arranged in possible flows placed on large sheets of paper. The context for each individual display was its use-case and scenario of execution. Because the use-case analysis defined relationships among use cases (as shown with the extension relationship for the example in Figure 3.5) the user interface flow from screen to screen was aligned with the scenarios of use and in turn the end user goals. As these were reviewed by the design team changes were made, and questions and issues were noted right on the storyboard for later resolution.

Once the design team felt the storyboards were reasonable approximations of the system they could build they were captured as black and white drawings with a computer drawing package. These more polished assemblies of screens were used to conduct storyboard walkthroughs with end users. Four of the original companies, and a total of ten users, participated in the walkthroughs, which took between 3 and 6 hours to cover about 30 total use cases. The walkthroughs combined an opportunity for the end users to play through the paper prototype and for real-time design. Storyboard review is particularly useful for covering a large amount of material and providing for both detailed screen design review and overall work flow discussion. The joint walkthrough-design sessions often empowered users to elaborate on their work practices and then to describe their own visualizations of interface designs. Comments often provided straightforward alternatives designs. For example, users pointed out a relationship among a group of objects they felt was central to how they worked and suggested this relationship should be captured (e.g., hierarchical organization in a tree view). Thus, two critical types of data were gathered. First, initial usability data were gathered — where were users confused? Where did they make errors in trying to walk through the design? Second, the users could talk about how they would use the capabilities embodied in the design and describe how it integrated with their work practice.

3.2.5. Usability Goals

It is a great help in design and testing to establish early on some goals for the usability of the system. Usability goals provide measurable targets for the design and give a development team a tangible expression of the desired system behavior. Scenarios, as stories, can provide the context for defining tasks and goals. Two example goals (drawn from a set of about 30 goals) are defined below, using the same data from which other elements of the design have been motivated.

1. **Goal**: Detect Key system status change immediately, regardless of current task.
    - **Metric**: Note key system change within 5 seconds of appearance in display.
    - **CI Data**: "Besides monitoring overall network and system health, there is often a need to focus monitoring on specific systems that are particularly important to the company."
    - "We want simultaneous roll-up and key system view."
    - "Make critical events highly visible."
    - "We would like a pop-up window on an event."
2. **Goal**: Detect and display high priority event for any one system out of 100 systems rapidly (30 seconds or less).
    - **Metric**: Measure time from occurrence of high-priority event to user displaying event detail for that event.
    - **CI Data**: "We need an easy way to get specific information quickly."
    - "It would be useful to be able to see what actions the event has triggered and perhaps start some others."
    - "Make critical events highly visible."

These goals were tested with the prototype application, as described below.

3.2.6. Prototype and Field Testing

Besides the storyboard walkthroughs, two other steps were used to gain user feedback. A Visual Basic prototype was created about the same time a first draft of the storyboards was available. This prototype was tested with five operators in 1-hour sessions. Test results provided many comments about how the linked navigation needed to work, how status should be indicated, and how transition from monitoring and detecting problems to problem resolution should be supported. Regarding the usability goals, users were able to note events as desired and quickly access the event detail information. However, they needed additional color coding for status indication and it took practice to discover some of the navigational mechanisms used.

Field test of preproduction versions of the software revealed relatively few new comments when conducted with users who had participated in the storyboard walk through. On the positive side this indicated that early and repeated inclusion of user feedback can help resolve problems. On the negative side, because these users were more experienced with the application design, their feedback was not representative of that from naive users. For a variety of reasons subsequent usability testing with naive users was not done.

4. LINKS AMONG SYSTEM REPRESENTATIONS

A basic tenet of this project is that human-computer interaction design must embrace *system usability*, and system usability emerges from programmatically linking the end-user characterizations that drive user interface design to all phases of the product development including data definition and system modeling. It is not only the design of the user interface that requires bridging representational gaps. As has been highlighted with most recent statements of object-oriented analysis and design (e.g., Jacobson's Object-Oriented Systems Engineering), as well as other system design methods, systematic and traceable transformations from analysis, to design, to implementation, and testing are hallmarks of mature software development. User-centered design generally extends these methods through its focus on representations of user-centered data.

Using customer data as the source for analysis, and then consciously addressing what elements of system behavior should be revealed to the user and what elements should not, helps make the resulting system usable and useful by linking user-centered design practice with a software development discipline. For example, most Object-Oriented methods use class representations as part of a design. In these diagrams the user-visible objects can be separated explicitly from objects only visible within the software. Mapping an object analysis model onto the user view may indicate the need for mediating classes in order to preserve the user view. These mediating classes define requirements on the system design in support of the user interface and overall system usability, much as was shown in the discussion of conceptual models earlier. In this manner a unified object model (itself a representation) that links into the end user's view of the world and the implementor's analysis and design view can be created.

5. THE PSYCHOLOGY OF THE DESIGNER: TOWARD USEFUL AND USABLE REPRESENTATIONS IN DESIGN

Thus far the focus of this chapter has been on how the design process supports the creation of a representational system to bridge the gap between user-centered data and a concrete design. Moreover, it has been suggested that creating a representational system requires the transformation — coding and recoding — of information, and this process has necessary conditions for success. This section first takes this notion one step further and suggests some reasons for design success and failure — of best practice and of inadequate practice — that have their analog in other areas of cognition. The section concludes with recommendations for how to match design practice with the cognitive nature of the design problem.

5.1. DECISION MAKING IN DESIGN: WHY "TRADITIONAL DESIGNERS HAVE BAD INTUITIONS ABOUT USABILITY"

In his recent book Landauer (Landauer, *The Trouble with Computers*, 1995, p. 216) looked at "the trouble with computers" and considered the issue of why they are so difficult to use. Part of the problem may lie in the design practices of the people traditionally responsible for the bulk of the programs written. Landauer suggests some of the problem is that traditional designers take a software and hardware system point of view as they strive to decide how a program should "work". Unfortunately, the user of the program is not interested in how the program works, but rather in how well it will help them do a particular task. This difference results in a mismatch in both knowledge and method between the designer and the end user.

The notion that traditional designers have "bad intuitions about usability" can be analyzed in view of the model for design discussed thus far. Recall the three key steps identified in the creation of the representational system: selection of the aspects of the represented world to be modeled, selection of the aspects of the representing world to do the modeling, and development of the correspondences between them. In this view, the designer is making decisions in the course of forming representations. Research on human judgment shows interesting patterns in how people make decisions. It suggests there are systematic biases in their intuitions resulting from the heuristics they use in everyday situations. Here the term heuristic is used *descriptively* to mean the rules of thumb guiding human judgment. Experts as well as novices are subject to these biases (Tversky and Kahneman, 1974). In effect, "Bad intuitions" may be thought of as the misapplication of a rule of thumb. Tversky and Kahneman have studied a variety of biases, in which individuals are shown to have ignored useful normative models of probability in their decision making. One example that might be germane is the availability bias. This bias is seen when people use the ease of recall of examples of events as an indicator of the likelihood of that event. Factors that normally enhance recall such as salience and familiarity come into play in the estimation of probability. In the case of system design, the essentially different bodies of knowledge possessed by traditional designers vs. their end users is a powerful source of misinformation. ("You didn't know that alt-tab brings up a view of processes currently running? I use that all the time.") When the traditional designer taps into the only data they have for decision making, they use what is familiar or salient and therefore inaccurately estimate the skills, knowledge, goals, and intentions of the end user. While not all design decisions relate to inappropriate sampling of data, the point is that informing the design process with the appropriate data is central to design success. When taken to its extreme the failure to use end user data fallaciously equates expertise in the development of programs with expertise in the task domain. Finally, most fundamental may be the problem that traditional designers do not usually have access to disconfirming evidence for their own theories of user behavior.

In summary, there are critical pieces of information missing in the representational system of the traditional design scenario and key process steps missing from the traditional design process. User-centered design prescribes developing a representational system that includes (1) an adequate statement of the represented world and (2) a robust set of mediating abstractions to guide the design process. Iterations in user-centered design provide repeated refinement and validation, ensuring design judgments are guided by reasonable samples of the end user population.

5.2. HEURISTICS AND METAHEURISTICS: GUIDANCE IN DECISION MAKING

User interface design heuristics, as guiding principles, have been accepted as one way to assess and shape systems to make them more usable (Nielsen, 1994). In this usage heuristics are *prescriptive* rules of thumb that correct for biases rather than *descriptive* of the biases that produce errors. User interface design heuristics typically concern the decisions about how the "representing world" should be structured to be more usable. For example, there are heuristics concerned with ensuring the user is informed of what is going on in a system. The analysis presented in this paper suggests there may be a larger context for describing heuristics in user interface design. This larger context has to do with "metaheuristics" that are the rules of thumb governing decisions about the transformations required of designers. Such metaheuristics pertain to two broad areas in creation of a representational system: the choice of design processes and the choice of representational models. The next three sections describe three groups of rules of thumb. These metaheuristics reflect the experience described in this paper and echo the perceptions of authors within this volume, as well as others.

5.2.1. Defining the Represented World: Start Off on the Right Foot

The thrust of this metaheuristic is that it is critical to obtain the information needed to define the represented world and that this information needs to be cast into forms amenable to the larger goal of user-centered design (a point argued as well by Monk in this volume). In particular, the work on this project suggests the following rules:

1. *Make the represented world sharable* — One of the strengths of the scenario approach is that it retains the overall information and structure of end user experience. This enables multiple diverse audiences to share this representation and work with it throughout the course of the project. The scenarios serve as the context for storyboard walkthroughs, usability goal definition, and other design activities.
2. *Preserve the end-user view in the represented world* — Though usually an intrinsic part of the scenario form, it is worthwhile to isolate this particular idea. Specific words and end user experiences are extremely important in selecting aspects of the represented world to be modeled and for choosing details in the representing world. Essentially, key data must be kept alive through the course of the design cycle.
3. *Define the represented world at an appropriate granularity* — One size does not necessarily fit all for design. This project used both scenarios and use cases as complementary forms for the represented world. Under other circumstances, simply using scenarios may be adequate and because they are so robust they may be the preferred option if a single representation must be chosen. Alternatively other representations of end user work may work well for specific tasks. This application was complex enough to require the disciplined decomposition provided by use cases, while others may not require it. In any event, it is useful to appreciate the relative strengths and weaknesses of alternative representations as they are brought to bear during a design cycle.

5.2.2. Minimizing the Gap: Help the Magic Happen

Part of the pleasure of design is watching the *magic* happen. Nevertheless, part of the goal of a skilled designer or design team should be to create the conditions for the magic to happen, and not to leave it to chance (hence a notion like "Systematic Creativity", Scholtz and Salvador, Chapter 9, this volume). One way to accomplish this is to build a process that supports the coding and recoding of information necessary for success.

1. *Consciously create mediating abstractions* — As work progresses objects, models and metaphors should be the blueprint guiding the use of the bricks and mortar determined by the user interface syntax. This principle is based on the belief that it is difficult to go from user-centered data to an implementation without some mediating ideas; thus, explicitly defining them makes the process more efficient. In effect, part of solving the problem of design is creating different representations.

2. *Make iteration work for you* — This and the next principle go together. Often iteration is looked upon as the failure to get it right the first time. Here the opposite is advocated. Do not expect to get it right the first time. Early progress can be measured by the number of questions asked, rather than the number answered. Use rapid cycles in iterative design to test alternative views and designs, knowing the gap is bridged incrementally. However, be disciplined enough to get the information needed to resolve the questions and refine the design by creating paper prototypes, quick high-fidelity prototypes and other approximations of the representing world.

3. *Design is a bootstrap operation* — If the answer was clear, then the design work would be finished. Expect early iterations to be fragmented and imperfect. The goal of early iterations is create mediating representations that lead to the finished product, not create the finished product itself.

5.2.3. The Right Tools for the Job: Using Converging Operations

Design of a system seems to require knowledge of all the system elements in order to begin the design, otherwise how can you correctly design any one element? Part of the answer to this dilemma lies in using multiple approaches to refine a design. Using iterative design with a variety of techniques puts special demands on the design process, and the next principles help guide the operations.

1. *Use the strengths of different approximations of the representing world* — Pick tools (e.g., low-fidelity prototypes) so that early work is mutable at low cost, and expect it to change. Use techniques such as storyboard walkthroughs to validate broad issues of organization and modeling, because they are capable of representing whole subflows of a user interface at one time. Later in the process focus on high-fidelity prototypes to look at detailed issues in user interface structure.

2. *Infuse the represented world into the entire design and development cycle* — In moving from one representation to another, and from one step in the process to the next, it is helpful to have some thread of the represented world that links design artifacts and process steps. The end user via either actual involvement or extension is key. In this project, scenarios were used to generate content at all steps, and approximations of the representing world were tested with end users at each step. In the larger system context, this point was discussed previously with regard to object-oriented design and the reuse of use cases for analyzing event flows within a software system, as well as for testing. Here the use case is the unit of value and the context of application execution.

6. CONCLUSION

This chapter has reviewed one example of how the gap between user-centered analysis and concrete design can be bridged. Essentially, it suggested in both broad process terms, and in detailed data analysis, that the gap is bridged by transforming alternative representations for the end user's world within a representational system. The process for creating this representational system can be facilitated by systematically creating mediating representations that reveal and link the represented world and the representing world. Placing the user at the heart of the process corrects for inherent biases in the designer as they go about the cognitive task of deciding what aspects of the represented world to model and how to model them in the representing world. In this way the magic of design is grounded in knowledge of the world and repeatedly tested with the people from whom that knowledge was derived.

7. ACKNOWLEDGMENTS

I would like to thank Betsy Comstock, Peter Nilsson, Kevin Simpson, Colin Smith, Dennis Wixon, and Larry Wood for comments on this chapter.

8. REFERENCES

Anderson, J. R., *Language, Memory and Thought*, Lawrence Erlbaum Associates, Hillsdale, N.J., 1976.

Carroll, J. M., *Scenario-Based Design*, John Wiley & Sons, New York, 1995.

Jacobson, I., Ericsson, M., and Jacobson, A., *The Object Advantage*, Addison-Wesley, Reading, MA, 1994.

Lakoff, G. and Johnson, M., *Metaphors We Live By*, The University of Chicago Press, Chicago, 1980.

Landauer, T. K., *The Trouble with Computers*, MIT Press, Cambridge, 1995.

Microsoft Corporation, *The Windows Interface Guidelines for Software Design*, Microsoft Press, Redmond, WA, 1995.

Miller, G. A., The Magical Number seven, plus or minus two: some limits on our capacity for processing information, *Psych. Review*, 63, 81-97, 1956.

Monk, A., Lightweight techniques to encourage innovative user interface design, in *User Interface Design: Bridging the Gap from User Requirements to Design,* Wood, L, Ed., CRC Press, Boca Raton, FL, 1998.

Nielsen, J., Heuristic evaluation, in *Usability Inspection Methods*, Nielsen, J. and Mack, R. L., Eds., John Wiley & Sons, New York, 1994, 25-64.

Norman, D.A., *Things That Make Us Smart*, Addison-Wesley, Reading, MA, 1993.

Palmer, S.E., Fundamental aspects of cognitive representation, in *Cognition and Categorization*, Rosch, E. and Lloyd, B., Eds., Lawrence Erlbaum Associates, Hillsdale, N.J., 1978, 262-300.

Scholtz, J. and Salvador, T., Systematic creativity: A bridge for the gaps in the software development process, in *User Interface Design: Bridging the Gap from User Requirements to Design.,* Wood, L., Ed., CRC Press, Boca Raton, FL, 1998.

Shepard, R.N. and Metzler, J., Mental rotation of three dimensional objects, *Science*, 171, 701-703, 1971.

Simon, H., *The Sciences of the Artificial*, MIT Press, Cambridge, 1981.

Tversky, A. and Kahneman, D., Judgement under uncertainty: heuristics and bias, *Science*, 185, 1124-1131, 1974.

Wixon, D. and Ramey, J., *Field Methods Casebook for Software Design*, John Wiley & Sons, New York, 1996.

CHAPTER 4

Model-Based User Interface Design: Successive Transformations of a Task/ Object Model

Frank Ludolph
Sun Microsystems, Inc., Mountain View, California
email: frank.ludolph@sun.com

"Design is the conscious and intuitive effort to impose meaningful order."
(Papanek, 1984)

TABLE OF CONTENTS

ABSTRACT

There is a large gap between a set of requirements and a finished user interface, a gap too large to be crossed in a single leap. This gap is most easily traversed by using various sets of guidelines, based on patterns of human perception, cognition, and activity, to transform background information first into an essential model, then into a user's model, and finally into a user interface design. Scenarios form the primary thread in this process, keeping the designer focused on the user's activities. Rough sketches are used throughout this process, but sketches cannot represent the dynamic nature of the interface in a comprehensive manner. The designer must build interactive visual prototypes to better understand the actual interactions, test the design before it is coded, and communicate the finished design to developers and customers.

1. INTRODUCTION

The project is underway. There is a clear problem statement, the requirements have been gathered, and the users have been interviewed. Now it is time to design the user interface. How does the user interface designer transform an abstract list of requirements into a concrete design?

The goals of a user interface are daunting: for the novice user it should be easy to learn and recall; for the experienced user it should be flexible and efficient; and it should extend every user's abilities, enabling them to accomplish tasks that they otherwise could not. However, all too often the resulting application is difficult to learn, tedious to use, and forces people to focus on the computers and applications rather than on their work.

Why do so many user interface designs fail? Because the goals are diverse, the complexity is great, and we may fail to apply our knowledge of how people communicate and interact with the world around them. However, there is a way.

By combining complexity management techniques, guidelines on human interaction and communication, a bit of insight and creativity, and a good development process, it is possible to design user interfaces that meet these goals. This chapter describes one way to bridge the gap between requirements and a completed design using modeling to manage complexity and a series of transformations that take us across the gap a step at a time. This process is illustrated using a portion of an application builder as a case study.

1.1. USER INTERFACE DESIGN: CREATIVITY, SENSITIVITY, CRAFT, AND ENGINEERING

It takes a much more than just creativity to design a good user interface. In fact, it may be the least important aspect. Wroblewski (1991) argues that user interface design is a craft because the complexity and variation of each interface design require that at least some portions be implemented and tested to be understood, similar to the methods used by craftsmen in the past. There is also an engineering aspect to design in that the design should be efficient in presentation, use, and implementation, with a logical, understandable structure. However, a well-crafted, efficient, and logical design is not sufficient.

Developing an interface between person and machine is much more difficult that a machine-to-machine interface. The machine side of an interface can be known with precision and the functionality it supports is limited and well defined. On the other hand, people exhibit great variations with respect to behavior, experience, knowledge, temperament, needs, wants, and manual and mental dexterity; the tasks a person needs to complete are usually quit complex. A good designer molds the design with a sensitivity to these individual variations and an understanding of how people think, communicate, and interact with the world around them.

The activity of user interface design involves many skills: interviewing, modeling, interaction design, presentation design, graphic design, and usability evaluation. This chapter focuses on modeling, interaction, and presentation design. It describes how modeling can be used to manage complexity, the development of the initial model, the transformation of one model into another then into a finished design, and the guidelines that are used to perform these transformations.

1.2. THE ROLE OF END USERS IN DESIGN

Designing a user interface without involving users is as impossible as designing one without pencil, paper, and computer. They are the main source of information about how things are currently done, the problems they face, and how those problems are dealt with. The designer must watch the users work, talk with them often, and give them the opportunity to try out early versions of the developing design. They will express needs and concerns about how the job should be done. When an end-user suggests a certain way of doing something, consider it carefully. Dig deeper to understand the problem that triggered the proposal. The suggestion may be indicative of larger issues.

As the design develops, users can provide valuable comments at all stages. They can help the designer select a preferred interface from among several alternatives and polish the rough edges as the design is refined. However, end-users should not be asked to design the interface or to participate directly in design sessions. They are intimately involved in the details of the current system and are only vaguely aware of the viewpoints of other users. They do not have the designer's knowledge of design, human interaction, and technology. Once they have participated in creating a design, they are biased and their evaluations of subsequent designs are suspect.

2. MODELS AND TRANSFORMATIONS

People use models to explain the operation and underlying concepts of systems that are too complex to be otherwise understood. A model is an abstract representation of a portion of a system that consists of the concepts, objects, relationships, capabilities, and reactions that are important to the perspective addressed by the model. The key to modeling is to find the right abstractions that explain the desired aspects, and the careful weeding out of the irrelevant details. By reducing complexity the designer can focus on what is significant, simplifying the resulting design.

By intent a model ignores portions of a system so it cannot be used to explain those portions or to describe the system at a more detailed level. Additional models are required to address those areas. As a result, a system is often described by several related models that together illuminate all the facets of interest.

The process of design by transformation utilizes two task-based models, one extracted from background information and the second a transformation of the first. The second is then transformed into the final design. In all, the design progresses through four distinct stages:

*   *Background Information* — The requirements, real-life scenarios, and other information gathered before beginning the design.
*   *Essential Model* — A high-level description of the application's fundamental functions without reference to technology or how the user will actually perform them.
*   *User's Model* — The concepts, objects, and tasks as seen from the user's perspective, free of presentation and interaction elements.
*   *Completed U/I Design* — How a person will see, think about, and interact with the application.

Several sets of guidelines and patterns of human behavior are used to guide the transformations including metaphor; patterns of human interaction with the

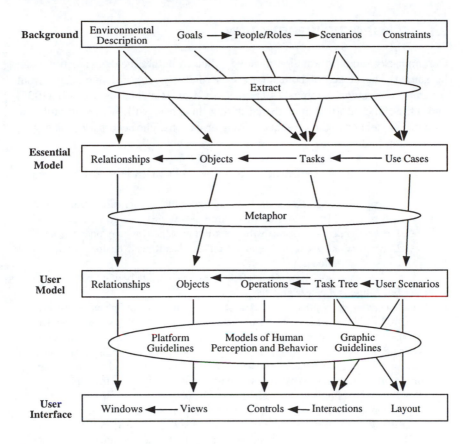

Figure 4.1 Stages, models, transformations, and guidelines.

physical world, information processing, and social interaction; and guidelines for high-level U/I design, visual and audio presentation, and platform/toolkit specific layout and widget use. Figure 4.1 summarizes the design stages, models, and transformation steps described in this chapter. The arrows indicate which elements at each stage are transformed into elements at the next stage and the information used to guide that transformation. Arrows within a stage indicate that some elements help to define other elements at that level.

Design by transformation promotes "pipeline" design, i.e., as soon as the central elements at one stage have been defined, work can begin on transforming them into next stage. Usually several alternative transformations are possible. The designer can determine the most promising alternatives by using the structure of a stage to identify and define its central elements and then try out trial transformations into the subsequent stage. When difficulties are encountered, the design focus returns to the prior stage and other alternative transformations are tried. The details of each stage are completed later as confidence in the trial design increases.

2.1. BACKGROUND INFORMATION

Certain background information must be collected before the design activity can be started. The means of collection are beyond the scope of this chapter, but several user-centered approaches are described by Holtzblatt and Beyer (1993) and others. The information gathered during this phase will be used to build the essential model and in the subsequent transformations. The necessary background information includes:

- *Goals* — There are many kinds of goals, several of which may conflict. These include
  - *System and application goals* — the purpose of the application and what it will be used for, in terms of the environment it will be used in.
  - *Business goals* — how this will affect the way the company does business.
  - *Organizational goals* — the affect on the department, business unit, and cross-organizational groups.
  - *End-user goals* — how it will affect things such as daily work patterns, job flexibility, and career growth.
- *Environmental description* — A description of the computing and real-world systems in which the application will function. What is the physical environment in which the application will be used? What function does the system perform? What are the objects in the system? How does the application being designed fit into the system, i.e., what are the tasks, in terms of the system and system objects, that it will be used for? What are the inputs to and outputs from the application?
- *People* — A description of the various roles that people assume when they use the application: end-users, customers, administrators, managers, auditors, etc. Which tasks does each perform? What information do they need to perform those tasks? What is the range of their education, experience, and physical abilities? What other activities are they involved in, especially those that they perform concurrently with the proposed application?
- *Constraints* — What parts of the environment can be changed and which cannot? Consider the physical environment, people, organization, current systems and equipment, rules and regulations.
- *Real-life scenarios* — How are the tasks identified in the environmental description currently performed? What are the frequencies and volumes associated with each task? What obstacles and errors occur while performing the tasks and how are they dealt with? Describe any external artifacts and their use within a scenario. What improvements have been suggested?

Even when designing for a new kind of application, there are usually real-life examples of how people currently perform the tasks of interest, however, it may be necessary to augment these with additional, made-up scenarios depicting new tasks to be supported by the application.

2.2. A BACKGROUND EXAMPLE

It is common in software development groups to hear that it takes too much time and effort to develop new applications so a software tools company decides to develop a product that better supports application development. The following is a very abbreviated example of the background information that might have been collected.

Goals — Shorten application development time; fewer bugs in the resulting application; more predictable development cycle; applications more easily adapted to changing business needs.

Environmental description — This is a corporate MIS shop. The computing environment is fully networked. Many different kinds of computers are used. Programs are written in C and incorporate routines from C-based libraries purchased from outside vendors.

People — Some developers have degrees in computer science but many have degrees in other fields and have taken a few computing courses. New programs are developed in small teams consisting a systems analyst, a couple of developers, a tester, and a documentation writer. The analyst, tester, and writer are usually involved in a couple of projects. Old programs are maintained and updated in response to end-user needs, leaving less time to develop new applications.

Constraints — C will continue to be used unless a very strong argument can be made for another language.

Scenarios — "We use libraries of routines that we buy from outside vendors. Each library has maybe 100 to 200 routines in it. To find routines that could be used in a new application, we look in the documentation and read about what they do. Usually there are some examples of how the routine is used. There is much to look through in a new library and it takes a lot of time to find ones that we might be able to use. Sometimes I'll ask other people I work with for suggestions. Once I find something that might work, I have to find it on disk so that I can include it into my code. I think that we would share more of the code that we write, but it is too hard to document and figure out where to put it so others can find it..."

3. THE ESSENTIAL MODEL

The purpose of the essential model (Constantine, 1995) is to define the tasks a user will do without describing how the task is actually performed. It describes the user's intentions, not activities. The model consists of the tasks a user is to accomplish, the objects and operations that comprise those tasks, the relationships among the those objects, and one or more use cases for each task. The tasks should include information on required inputs, outputs, volumes, frequency of execution, problems and their current solutions, who performs it, and constraints, e.g., processing time.

3.1. CREATING THE ESSENTIAL MODEL

The essential model is created by extracting it from the background information. The focus of the extraction process is the real-life scenarios. Embedded in each scenario are one or more goals. These goals typically state what the scenario is trying to accomplish and often refers to objects and information in the environment. These goals, restated as actions involving one or more objects, are the tasks of the essential model. Information in the scenario about inputs and outputs, problems and solutions, and constraints should be listed with the related task. Information in the scenario about how the user currently performs these tasks, usually the bulk of the real-life scenarios, can be ignored for now. If there are multiple user roles, each role should have its own task list. It may be appropriate to design separate interfaces for each user if their tasks vary significantly.

A preliminary list of objects is generated by extracting them from the background environmental description and the essential model tasks. The relationships between the various objects should be identified. Is one object really part of another? Perhaps they should be combined. Are sets of similar objects constantly used together? Perhaps a container object should be defined. Is there something that links the objects? A drawing is often the best way to indicate the relationships between objects and highlight inconsistencies. When the list of objects is finalized, the tasks should be revised accordingly.

The use cases are generated by restating the real-life scenarios using the tasks and objects, removing all references about how the user currently performs these activities. The resulting use cases should be quite brief in comparison to the original scenarios.

The essential model should be reviewed with the person(s) responsible for establishing the functional requirements and some of the users who provided scenarios. They should focus on the use cases, comparing them the with current environment in order to identify missing tasks.

3.2. AN ESSENTIAL MODEL EXAMPLE

The real-life scenario provided by a developer when the background information was gathered is restated here for easy reference:

"We use libraries of routines that we buy from outside vendors. Each library has maybe 100-200 routines in it. To find routines that could be used in a new application, we look in the documentation and read about what they do. Usually there are some examples of how the routine is used. There is much to look through in a new library and it takes a lot of time to find ones that we might be able to use. Sometimes I'll ask other people I work with for suggestions. Once I find something that might work, I have to find it on disk so that I can include it into my code. I think that we would share more of the code that we write, but it is too hard to document it and figure out where to put it so others can find it..."

This scenario describes a few goals: locate some routines that might be used, evaluate each, and include the useful ones in the new application. Rewriting these as tasks yield:

- Find a set of candidate routines within a library.
- Evaluate a candidate routine using its documentation.
- Include the selected routine in the application.

The objects mentioned in these tasks are:

- *Library* — a collection of routines.
- *Routine* — code that could be included in a new application.
- *Application* — the program being built.
- *Documentation* — the description of what a routine does.

A use case is constructed by recasting the real-life scenario using the tasks and objects of the essential model and discarding all references to how the activity is currently performed:

Developers build applications, in part, by including selected routines from libraries. They select the routines by finding a candidate set of routines and evaluating
each of them using its documentation.

Note that this use case does not include the information needs or specific problems. This makes it easier to discern the underlying structure. The information needs and problems are listed with the appropriate tasks and will be used later in the process to evaluate the alternative metaphors and to insure that the user's needs are met. The information needs and problems in this simple example are:

- Finding candidate routines can take a long time.
- What does a particular routine do and how is it used?
- Where is the routine located?

4. THE USER MODEL

A user model is the model the designer attempts to convey to the user through the user interface. It consists of the tasks, objects, operations, relationships, and the underlying concepts that tie them all together. User scenarios describe the sequences of user actions needed to accomplish a task. As with the essential model, the user model does not include anything about how a person interacts with the application or how the application is presented.

There is a temptation to design the user interface directly from the essential model; however, this is usually not possible since the actions specified in use cases are at such a high-level functionally that they typically cannot be accomplished by a single user action. In addition, the essential model does not necessarily have any underlying conceptual basis. Without this conceptual basis, a user must learn how to use the application by rote and remember it rather than using the underlying concepts to regenerate action sequences when needed, to solve problems, and to make educated guesses about how to perform unfamiliar tasks. As a result there is often a large gap between the essential and user models that the designer can attempt to bridge in several ways:

- Base the user model on the existing solution, altering it just enough to address the current problems. No big leaps, no big improvements, same training requirements.
- Refine the essential model by developing an underlying conceptual basis and defining a sequence of atomic user actions for each high-level function specified in the use cases. This requires much effort to create and structure. It is not so much bridging the gap as building a city in the wilderness.
- Base the user model on a metaphor. Possible big gains with potentially low effort, risk, and reduced training costs.

The author has a strong bias toward creating user interfaces based on metaphors. Over time, people have developed relatively efficient methods for dealing with commonly occurring situations. Ideally, these typical solutions are easily recognized, reducing the need for training, but even in those situations where a metaphor is not widely known among potential users it can still provide the structure of a time-tested solution. It has been the author's experience that once a metaphor has been selected, the user model can usually be fleshed out quite rapidly. The metaphor also provides a structure that can be easily extended to incorporate new requirements as they arise.

4.1. SELECTING A METAPHOR

A list of candidate metaphors can be generated by matching up elements of the essential model with things our target users already know about. The best place to start is to look for parallels to the objects, tasks, and terminology of the scenarios and use cases. Users will often use terms in their descriptions that are not part of the current environment yet somehow better convey how they think about it. If no obvious metaphors can be identified this way, the designer can always fall back on the basic metaphor of the physical world and concrete objects, assigning concrete representations to objects in the essential model that respond to similar kinds of actions.

The appropriateness of each of the candidate metaphors is tested by restating the objects and tasks of the essential model in terms of the metaphor. Not everything may fit exactly, but small differences can be ignored at this point. If a metaphor fits the essential model reasonably well, some trial user scenarios can be generated by restating the primary use cases in terms of the metaphor. These scenarios should still be functionally oriented, free of interaction specifics. This process or restating should be reiterated, using the metaphor as a guide to add details, until each task seems to be atomic, i.e., it seems likely that the user will be able to perform the task with a single action. This process will likely identify new, metaphor-specific objects needed by these atomic tasks. The metaphor is checked further to see that it provides the information needed to perform each task and ways of dealing with the problems that have been identified. What additional problems and limitations might the metaphor introduce?

Some simple sketches should be drawn that illustrate the trial user scenarios using metaphor-based visuals and the styles of presentation and representation common to other applications on the target platform. The intention is to get a feel for how the metaphor might be presented, not to define the user interface. This activity should be repeated with several alternative metaphors. The generation of several alternatives at each step is an essential part of the design process.

A metaphor seldom fits exactly right so some adjustments may be necessary. Parts of the metaphor may not be needed, although these unneeded parts may indicate missing functionality in the proposed application. More typically, parts of the scenarios cannot be mapped into the metaphor. Perkins, Keller, and Ludolph (1996) suggest that a metaphor can be extended in plausible ways by adding functionality that people wish existed in the real environment from which the metaphor is drawn. For example, the physical world imposes limitations such as an object can only be in one place at a time. A plausible extension would allow two geographically separated people to see and work on the same object on their computer displays while talking on the phone.

The preferred metaphor should be reviewed with the developers illustrating the primary user scenarios with a couple of line drawings or short storyboards. The intent is to keep the developers informed, giving them adequate time to consider implementation problems that might arise rather than surprising them later. It is the developers who will bring the design to life.

At this point the basic user model has been defined by remapping objects in the essential model and restating some of the use cases into the metaphor. The rest of the user model can be fleshed out by restating the rest of the use cases, making necessary adjustments to the metaphor, and generating the task tree (described below).

4.2. A USER MODEL EXAMPLE

We begin generating alternative metaphors by considering the use case in our example:

> Developers build applications, in part, by including selected routines from librar-
> ies. They select the routines by finding a candidate set of routines and evaluating
> each of them using its documentation.

Since this use case uses programming terminology, it doesn't immediately suggest other metaphors so we consider its underlying structure. Building applications by including selected routines suggests the assembly of something from parts. The library is a collection of these parts. The "assembly" and "collection" elements of the example's essential model suggest several metaphors including:

- Parts can be picked from a drawer of a parts cabinet.
- Semiconductor data handbooks contain information about electronic components. For each component there is a data sheet that describes it purpose and uses, often with an example circuit that demonstrates its actual application.
- Companies distribute catalogs that describe their products and provide a means to order and obtain the products.

The alternatives are then checked against the information needs and problems listed in the essential model:

- Finding candidate routines can take a long time.
- What does a particular routine do and how is it used?
- Where is the routine located?

The parts cabinet metaphor doesn't include any support for describing what the parts are or how they are used, and the only mechanism for finding candidates is by grouping similar parts in labeled drawers.

The catalog and data handbook metaphors each contain descriptive information. They both also have an index that supports locating items using keywords. The data handbook also has example use information while the catalog metaphor suggests that it can be used to obtain the items it shows. Each of these metaphors could be stretched a little to cover all these points. This example will develop only the catalog metaphor, but it is preferable to pursue a few alternatives to better highlight the strengths and weaknesses of the favored choice.

We check the fit by restating the objects and tasks of the essential model in terms of the metaphor:

- Tasks
  - Find candidate routines — turn to a section or look in the index.
  - Evaluate a routine — read an item's documentation.
  - Include a routine — copy an item to the application.
- Objects
  - Item — an item in the catalog, a "component" (routine).
  - Catalog — a collection of components (library).
  - Description — a component's documentation.
  - Application — what we're building.

Now that a preliminary mapping between essential model and metaphor has been developed, a user scenario can be generated by restating the primary use case:

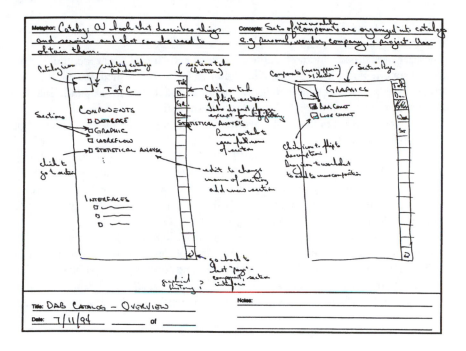

Figure 4.2 Preliminary sketch of catalog.

Developers build applications by including components selected from a catalog. The catalog is divided into sections that list similar components. The developer can browse the components in a section, reading their descriptions that include information about how they are used. If developers cannot find a desired component in a section, they can look in the index for other terms that might describe it. When the desired component is found it can be copied to the application.

The information needs and problems listed in the essential model should be addressed if possible in the user scenarios using elements of the metaphor. In the scenario above, sections in the catalog and the catalog index are used to address the problem of finding candidate components, and product descriptions provide information about the components.

A preliminary sketch of a catalog is shown in Figure 4.2. The sketch is an approximate visualization of the real-life metaphor objects and points out the elements needed to perform the various tasks. Unneeded elements of the real-life objects can be ignored. The sketch is not a serious proposal for a user interface but rather just "placing some puzzle pieces on the table" that can be rearranged later. The sketch is also a useful aid when reviewing the candidate metaphors with end-users and developers. Recording the metaphor and user-level concepts makes them explicit and is useful later when reviewing many sketches.

4.3. THE TASK TREE

The user model has a hierarchical tree of tasks and subtasks that the application must support. Each task specifies an action to be accomplished and the objects involved, expressed in the language of the user model. The tasks should include the obstacles that can arise and the information and subtasks needed to resolve them. It is this task tree that will drive much of the layout and interaction design of the user interface.

Much of the tree can be extracted from the user scenarios — the use cases restated in terms of the metaphor — but these scenarios typically illustrate only the primary functionality of the application, often missing secondary but necessary functionality, e.g., the setting of user preferences. The task tree on the other hand ideally should include everything a user can do.

Generating the complete task tree can be tedious and sometimes difficult because the lower levels may involve significant design effort. Typically it is sufficient to enumerate all the high-level tasks and flesh out their subtasks as the design for the primary tasks solidifies. Use the structure and patterns of the metaphor and platform standards as guidelines in designing these parts of the task tree.

4.4 A TASK TREE EXAMPLE

The portion of the example's task tree might look like this:
> Build an Application
>> Get a component
>>> Locate candidate components
>>>> Locate in Group (or)
>>>>> Turn to section of catalog that might contain similar components
>>>>> Turn to subsection — repeat for nested subsections
>>>> Locate in Index, if name is known (or)
>>>>> Turn to Index
>>>>> Scan names — may be more than one found
>>>> Find by description
>>>>> Indicate attribute — enumerate set of attributes
>>>>> Enter value
>>>>> Query — may find more than one
>>> Find a suitable component among the candidates
>>>> Select a component
>>>> Show its description
>> Copy selected component to application

At this point it is a good idea to review the task tree and reduce the marginal functionality either by folding it into other tasks or by eliminating it. In our example, the "Locate in Index" could be folded into "Find by description" if one of the supported search attributes is a component's name. This is a good choice since it eliminates an object, the Index, while only adding another simple use for an existing attribute, a component's name. It is likely that a user would rather query-by-name than by scrolling through a potentially long list.

4.5. OPERATIONS ON OBJECTS

Each task defines an operation involving one or more objects. As the task tree is refined, the operation of each atomic task and its description should be added to the list of operations for the appropriate object. The user model objects are the nouns that appear in the task tree; the operations are the verbs. These operations will appear in the user interface as some form of command or gesture. From the example:

Objects	Operations
Section	Turn (displays the candidates)
Attribute	Indicate kind, type-in value, query (displays the candidates)
Candidates	Select one (a component)
Component	Show description, copy to application
Description	—

As mentioned above, it is likely that some of the objects and operations may not occur in the metaphor. When possible, these should be cast as plausible extensions to the metaphor. As these extensions are not part of the metaphor and prior user experience, they must be clearly delineated and defined.

5. THE USER INTERFACE

A user model can be used to generate many different user interfaces. This step from user model to user interface can be one of the most intimidating. How are the concepts embodied in the user model going to be represented and how is the designer to choose from all the choices?

The basis for any user interface designed to fit within an existing environment will be the platform-specific guidelines for that environment, e.g., Macintosh (Apple, 1987), Windows '95 (Microsoft, 1995), or OS/2 (IBM, 1992) for desktop computers, or PenPoint (GO, 1992) or Newton (Apple, 1996) for pen-based computers. They describe, in varying levels of detail, both general design principles and the presentation and interaction elements for their respective platforms. These guidelines are used to map elements of the user model into views, windows, controls, and various standardized data representations. While these guidelines are similar, they differ in their emphasis on the general design principles and/or their use of different input and output devices.

Necessary as the platform-specific guidelines are, they are not sufficient for mapping from user model to user interface. Designers also need a deep understanding of how people perceive, think about, and interact with the real world. This knowledge is used in all phases of the design process, from initial interview to final usability studies and redesign. The author structures this knowledge for his own work as a set of models used to guide the transformations as a design progresses from step to step as shown in Figure 4.1. These models and the areas they affect include:

- *Perceptual* — Grouping of visual elements; task layout; use of color, sound, and animation.
- *Cognitive* — Response times; short-term memory; task flow.
- *Learning* — On-line reference materials; use of prompting queues.
- *Interaction* — Use of direct manipulation vs. language; social patterns.
- *Work* — Purposeful activity, collaboration.

Perceptual, learning, and cognitive processing models suggest how information is best presented so that people can recognize and utilize it most easily, while models of work and interaction with the physical world and with other people provide guidelines for direct manipulation and the use of social cues during collaboration. These models provide a number of patterns that can be used to structure the overall design, fill gaps in the platform-specific guidelines, design for nonstandard environments, and anticipate the consequences of design decisions.

The design of the user interface proceeds in three overlapping phases based primarily on the representations used in each phase: rough layout, focused on transforming task flow into simple sketches of proximate window layouts; interaction design, which transforms the task tree and objects into interactive prototypes; and detailed design specification, which defines the final graphics, terminology, menus, messages, and dialogues. Just as with the earlier design stages, these phases can be pipelined, and the completed portions checked for usability and communicated to the engineering and documentation teams as the design elements firm up.

5.1. ROUGH LAYOUT

The goal of this phase is a set of rough layout sketches of the screens and windows that support the primary user scenarios. There are five steps in constructing the sketches:

- Choose the basic interaction paradigm, procedural or object-oriented.
- Select the user scenarios that are central to the application's use.
- Extract the important objects in these scenarios and choose their representation.
- Layout the views and add the controls.
- Check the flow of the scenario using the sketch.

When the underlying metaphor has a strong visual appearance an alternative design approach is to mimic the visuals and interaction elements of the metaphor. Use this with care as it often leads overly cute, cluttered graphics that are difficult to visually parse and whose controls, such as tabs, are limited in comparison to the graphical widgets in platform-specific tool kits. On the positive side, this type of design often leads to a very distinctive visual appearance that can be quite appealing to casual users, though it can also become tiresome when used day after day.

The sketches of the layouts should follow applicable platform-specific guidelines and show the different view areas, their essential content, and the controls, while eliding unnecessary details. They can be shown to potential users and members of the development team for comments and used in preliminary usability studies. The quality of the comments however is limited because the study participants must use significant mental effort to visualize the dynamic operation and feel suggested by the static sketches, forcing a logical and intellectual consideration of an interface intended to be used in an intuitive manner.

Readers are encouraged to develop their own sketches as the example evolves in the following sections, or refer to Figure 4.3 which shows some of the alternative layouts that were prototyped for this example.

5.1.1. Procedural or Object Oriented

The first design decision is whether the windows should be procedurally or object-oriented. Procedural design focuses on the task, prompting the users at each step in the task, giving them few options to do anything else. This approach is best applied in situations where the tasks are narrow and well-defined or where users may be inexperienced, e.g., automated tellers and order entry. Object-oriented designs focus on the objects, allowing the user a wide number of options, and should be applied to situations where experienced users will use them as tools in a range of situations. The searching, reviewing, and selecting tasks described in the example's scenarios indicate that the more flexible and adaptable object-oriented approach would be best.

5.1.2. The Central User Scenarios and their Objects

The elements in an application should be laid out in the same way that any physical workspace would be, by designing for the most important tasks. The primary user scenarios should be selected and grouped based on the objects they involve and the likelihood that their tasks will be performed together. These objects are mapped into views that show either multiple objects or a single object's content, depending on the needs of the tasks. Sketches of the views should show only the essential structure and content; details should be suppressed. For example, a sketch of a view of unread e-mail messages might show only a list of lines where each line represents some information about a message. Details

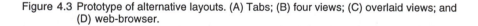

A   B

Figure 4.3 Prototype of alternative layouts. (A) Tabs; (B) four views; (C) overlaid views; and
(D) web-browser.

should be added later only as the need becomes apparent. If possible, use the types
of views defined in the platform-specific guidelines since users will likely be
familiar with their appearance and use, and it will save implementation effort.

The primary task from our example is "Get a component". The subtask
"Locate candidate components" generates a collection of candidate components,
so we need a view for that collection. One way to generate that set is to "Turn to
a section" so we need a view that shows the set of sections. Another way to
generate the candidates is to "Find by description" so we need a view for the
query. The second subtask is "Find a suitable component from the candidates".
There is already a view for the candidates. The next level subtasks are "Select a
candidate" — the "candidates" view again — and "Show the data sheet", a new

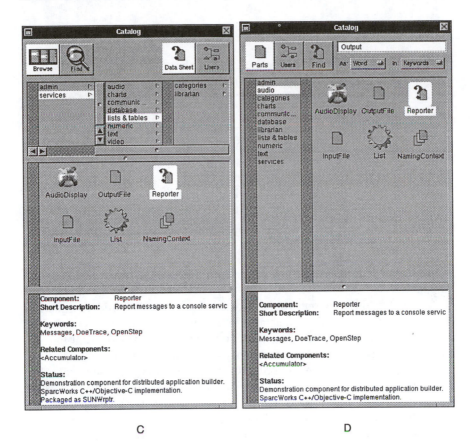

C   D

Figure 4.3 (Continued)

view. The other subtasks in the scenario don't suggest any new views. The example has four views: query, components, sections, and data sheet.

The type of each view depends on the objects and/or data it contains. Reviewing the environment and metaphor for existing representations that might be appropriate, we find that the data sheets generally show some text and maybe graphics. The "candidates" view is a collection of components, i.e., objects, and objects are generally rendered either iconically (spatial) or by name (list). The typical pattern of a query is a form: a collection of type-in fields, and a "find" button. The "sections" view is the most interesting. The catalog metaphor suggests a set of tabs but the number of sections is likely to be large if the catalog contains thousands of components. Typically large numbers of categories, the sections, are organized hierarchically, so some sort of hierarchical view seems appropriate.

5.1.3. Layout

Once the object views have been defined they can be grouped into windows. Each window should represent an object, with its views representing either that object's content or other objects that have a clear relationship to the window's object. At one extreme each object view could be in its own window, but this is likely to lead to a busy interface that involves much window opening, closing, moving, and resizing that is otherwise unnecessary. At the other extreme, all the views could be placed in one window either side-by-side, resulting in a very large window, or the views could be overlaid, forcing the user to switch views to begin a new task. Small applications should be able to fit into a single window, large applications in just two or three. Overlaid views should be used primarily to allow a user to configure a desired style of interaction, e.g., the "spatial" and "list" views for Macintosh folders allow the user to either manually group related icons spatially or to have the computer maintain an ordered list. They can also be used to begin a new scenario, as in our example below, provided the need to switch views is infrequent.

Views should be laid out within the window in "reading" order such that, as the user performs the series of subtasks in a scenario, the next items needed are where the next words would be. For western languages this would be left-to-right, top-down. Information within a view should also be laid out the same way. A person's eyes see only a small portion of the screen at any one moment, often failing to note related items only a few inches away. Poorly placed information will be missed by casual users and even by experienced users when they are deeply focused on the task or in a hurry.

Controls used to initiate each action are added to the layout as needed by the user scenarios. Use restraint when adding buttons and task bars to windows; while users have shown a preference for buttons over pull-down menus, large numbers of buttons are confusing and take valuable screen space. Platform-specific guide-lines usually indicate appropriate uses and locations for each type of control.

In our example there are two high-level, independent objects: the application under construction and the catalog. This suggests two windows, one for each, both of which will likely be on the screen at the same time. A frequent task is copying a component from the catalog to the application being built, so the windows should not overlap if possible. Since the application construction window will likely be large, the catalog window will fit best if it is tall and narrow.

Arranging the four views based on the scenario flow, the starting views, "sections" and "query" are first, the "candidates" next, and the "data sheet" last. Since the catalog window is tall and narrow, the views would be arranged top-down. Initial sketches suggest that arranging four views vertically will make them short so that they won't be able to display very much content. Since the scenarios always begin with either the "sections" view or the "query" view but never both, they can be overlaid in the same space and a button added to switch between them.

5.1.4. Scenario Flow

The scenario flow through the sketches is checked by drawing arrows to indicate the sequence of user actions for a given scenario. Usually a single sketch is sufficient to illustrate a single scenario, though a complex one involving many subtasks may require a storyboard, i.e., a sequence of sketches showing how a window changes as the scenario proceeds. As additional subtasks are added, secondary windows can be created for tool palettes and non-modal dialogues as necessary; modal dialogues should be avoided when possible in object-oriented designs.

5.2.   INTERACTION DESIGN

Human-computer interaction designs should be based on how people interact with things and with other people. These patterns are sometimes considered "natural" because they are so ingrained due to physics, physiology, and continuous repetition. Interaction can be modeled as a kind of dialogue, a sequence of actions and responses. In a human-computer dialogue the computer presents to the user what is possible, the user makes a request, and the computer acknowledges the request, makes the change, and responds with the results or confirmation. As with dialogues between people, the dialogue must be at the right level: too high and it is difficult to understand, too low and the extraneous detail becomes tedious. In either case the user must divert attention from the task to the dialogue itself, resulting in wasted time, effort, irritation, and reduced task performance. The challenge for the designer is to select the right dialogue level, i.e., the tasks, objects, and actions; to chose the most appropriate form of human-real world interaction; and then to map that interaction into the very limited set of interactions supported by the user input and output devices attached to the computer.

5.2.1. Four Kinds of Human Interaction

People interact with the world around them in four ways depending on what they are interacting with and the purpose of the interaction. They are:

* *Direct manipulation* — Handling physical things.
* *Language-based communication* — Conveying information via abstract symbols.
* *Demonstration* — Conveying information via a performance.
* *Social interaction* — Conveying information implicitly, usually about explicit activity, usually via body language.

The important aspects of direct interaction with the physical world are an object's immediate response to a person's actions; a wide range of sensory inputs: sight, touch, pressure, heat, sound, and smell; and the use of two hands, arms, feet, body, head, etc., with six degrees of freedom of movement. Support for these aspects of physical interaction within human-computer interaction continue to be very limited, typically: single-handed input with two degrees of movement, two pressure levels (the mouse button), and visual feedback that is often too slow. There are many development efforts to enhance the means of interaction, but they remain cumbersome and uncommon.

The lack of physical interaction techniques with the computer requires the designer to map many real-world actions into a different form with the computer. This changes the nature of the interaction, usually for the worse. For example, a scroll button maps distance to time; the longer the button is held down the farther the displayed information moves. The reader should compare the use of scroll buttons to move about a graphic document with the use of the "hand" cursor, common in graphics applications, that moves the document the same distance as the mouse cursor moves, a distance-to-distance mapping. The performance of the "hand" with its direct distance-to-distance mapping is superior to the scroll button's time-to-distance mapping for all ranges of movement: short, medium, and long. The designer must carefully consider the nature of each interaction to understand the consequences of such a substitution.

Command-lines, menus, and buttons are the primary computer representations of language-based communication, limited for the most part to simple sentence structures such as noun-verb. Since people converse only with other people, this experience causes people to treat dialogues with machines similar to conversations with people. One aspect of this conversational experience is timing; people get uncomfortable after a pause of 2 to 4 seconds in a conversation whether with person or computer. The use of language with computers also appears to trigger social responses in people (Nass, Steuer, and Tauber, 1994). This social response should be taken into account in designing messages, help, and other language-based situations in the interface.

Demonstration is used when direct manipulation and words are either too abstract or not sufficiently descriptive, such as when showing someone how to slide into a base in the game of baseball. This style of interaction is used with computers primarily for the "watch me" style of scripting in which the user performs some actions that the computer will later mimic. The difficulty with demonstration is in showing all the alternative actions to be used in different situations.

Social interaction deals with the use of cues, signals outside the main communication channel, that help to direct the dialogue. Without them the interaction between people is much more difficult and understanding suffers. For example, just as the listener nods his head or frowns to indicate his reaction to what the speaker is saying, computers need to acknowledge user input with some sort of feedback, otherwise the user is uncertain that the input was accepted. In applications where the computer serves as a communication channel between two people, the computer is most effective when it supports the transmission of the common social cues that people would use if they were face-to-face, e.g., facial expression and hand movement and position.

5.2.2. Reviewing Scenario Flow

The rough layouts should be reviewed with respect to these interaction patterns. The interaction style should feel right for the task and the controls should support the chosen style of interaction. Particular attention should be given to items not covered by the platform guidelines, e.g., the use of transitional animation or the support of social cues. The number of explicit actions that the user must make to accomplish a given task should be minimized, particularly those that just shuffle things around, e.g., opening and closing windows, scrolling, and view changes. After the sketches have been revised, it is time to prototype the primary user scenarios and any interactions that have been developed specifically for this interface.

5.2.3. Visual Prototyping

Sketches cannot be used to adequately evaluate the dynamics of an interface, nor can they be used to determine the exact sizes and placement of windows, views, controls, and information. For this, the designer must abandon paper and pencil and turn to the computer. While it is standard practice for designers to use drawing and illustration programs to create screen images of the visual elements, it is less common for a designer to create an interactive visual prototype though it takes only a little more time and effort. A visual prototype mimics the intended appearance, interaction, and feedback of the proposed application. The author finds it to be a far more effective design aid than a plain graphics program, often revealing missing details and rough areas in the interaction. It may be the only way to accurately evaluate alternatives. Visual prototyping is also the most effective way to validate the actual feel of the interaction, obtain pre-development, high-quality comments from users, and communicate the design to developers, marketing, and potential end-users.

Too much time and effort are needed to prototype an entire user interface so it is best to do only the primary user scenarios and those interactions that the designer has little personal experience with such as those developed specifically for this application. If a platform-specific GUI builder will be used to develop the application, it might provide a good prototyping environment though it will be difficult to prototype invented interactions and views and to fake the data needed to run the prototype. A GUI builder also enables a designer to contribute directly to the implementation, insuring that the finished application matches the design. When the design contains significant invention or when a GUI builder will not be used in the implementation, a number of commercial tools can be used for visual prototyping such as Macromedia's Director or Allegiant's SuperCard. Ideally the prototyping application should run on the same platform as the project application, but this is not necessary if the prototyping platform has adequate performance and the same user input and output devices, e.g., mouse, tablet, display resolution, etc., as the target platform.

Prototypes range from slide shows, which are quick to build but of limited use, to tightly scripted, which can mimic task interaction quite realistically, to fully interactive, which can support many arbitrary interaction sequences. The tightly scripted prototypes generally provide the best information for the least time investment while fully interactive prototypes are used to gain deeper experience with more radical designs.

Since the purpose of the prototype is to gain information about sizes, layouts, and interactions, the initial graphics used in the prototypes should be first approximations created from screen dumps of the target platform to save time, and revised later as the design solidifies. The next step is to create a slide show sequence that shows the screen appearance before and after the completion of each subtask. User actions, such as clicks and drags, are then added to initiate the transitions from one slide to the next. Finally, interaction feedback is inserted at the proper points to provide a fully realistic experience. A tightly scripted prototype of a high-level task or two can usually be built in a couple of days.

When the designer is satisfied with the prototype, it can be used to run low-cost user studies, with revisions as needed between sessions. The prototypes are also the best way to convey the design to the developers as they fully demonstrate the designer's intentions with little chance of misinterpretation. If the prototype will not run on the developer's platform or if the prototype is to be used as a specification, a screen capture facility can be used to create a narrated, platform-independent QuickTime movie that the developers can replay on their own computer as many times as needed.

5.2.4. An Example of Visual Prototyping

During the layout step it was determined that our example application needed a single tall, narrow window containing four views: candidates, sections, query, and data sheet. Based on the subtask flow within the scenarios, the "sections" and "query" views are the starting points, the "candidates" next, and the "data sheet" last. Since the catalog window is tall and narrow, the views would be approximately arranged top-down. Initial sketches suggested that arranging four views vertically will make them short so that they won't be able to display very much content. Since the scenarios always begin with either the "sections" view or the "query" view but never both, they might be overlaid into the same space with a button added to switch between them.

The representation for three of the views, based on platform standards, was straightforward:

- *Candidates* — Collections of objects are usually represented either spatially, with large icons, or in a list, with small icons and additional information. The spatial view was chosen since there was no additional information to display and since users prefer large icons for both easy visual identification and drag-and-drop operation.

- *Query* — Query views typically consist of a type-in field, a "Find" button, and some option buttons for indicating additional query criteria if any.
- *Data sheet* — This view contains a text description. The background information included statements about the kinds of information that is important to selecting an appropriate component so a simple format was designed on that basis.
- *Users* — An added view that would show the components that used the selected component in their own implementations; an additional form of documentation. Another "collection of objects" view and again a spatial view was selected.

It was unclear how to best represent the "sections" view. One member of the development team thought that a "tab" view would be best while another suggested some sort of "web-browser" approach. The author thought that a multicolumn browser, typical for this platform, was the best representation based on the likelihood that there would be a large number of sections and the use of this kind of view elsewhere on the platform for similar tasks. Some members also questioned the idea of overlapping the query and section views although they agreed that it seemed logical.

The designer developed a layout for each alternative, four in all as shown in Figure 4.3. Layout "A" shows the tab-style "section" view and "D" shows the web-browser alternative. Layouts "B" and "C" are straightforward layouts based on appropriate platform-standard views and controls. "B" shows all four views while "C" overlays the "section" and "query" views. The views were laid out top-to-bottom based on the sequence of tasks in the user scenarios as described above with a couple of exceptions. Based on an earlier design by one of the developers, in layout "A" the data sheet opened in a separate window and the "users" and search results shared the same area. In layout "B" the query area was moved below "candidates" to save space and the "info" and "users" views were overlapped.

The prototype could be quickly switched to show the different views allowing for easy comparisons. Each layout supported the basic tasks of locating candidates by turning to a section or by query, selecting a candidate, and reading its data sheet. The prototype supported clicking on buttons and typing into the query field to simulate performing these actions although there were no real data behind the prototype.

The prototype took a few days to develop and was used for just a few minutes by each developer. It was clear that violating the top-down flow caused much confusion. Overlapping the "sections" and "query" views saved space and made it clear which was the source of candidates. Consensus was reached on layout "B" in those few minutes and the developers bought-in to the design, avoiding repeated questioning as the project progressed. Quick user studies could have also been run using the prototype, but in this unusual case the developers were members of the target user group. The artwork and interaction of the selected design were also reused in a subsequent visual prototype of the application editor.

5.3. DETAILED DESIGN

By this point in the design, all the main windows have been laid out and all the primary high-level tasks and questionable interaction sequences have been prototyped. Only the final graphics, terminology, a stack of dialogues, and a myriad of small interactions remain to be designed. These can all be recorded and communicated to the development team through a Graphics and Interaction Specification that contains the full menus, a picture of each window, a description of all mouse actions on each responsive element of each window, a list of dialogues including a picture and description of each non-standard dialogue, and a set of target response times for each type of interaction.

The metaphor and platform environment are the best source of graphic ideas. The graphics should capture the essence of what they represent, the most important element, rather than being just crude images of real world objects. Mullet and Sano (1995) contain much practical advice on graphics and layout. The metaphor, platform, and real-life scenarios should be reviewed for terminology that presents a consistent view of the application.

The remaining interaction mechanisms necessary to support the remaining tasks in the task tree should be added. Take care not to clutter the design with seldom used elements. Much of what remains will likely be added as menu items and dialogues. Organize the menus according to platform guidelines. Menus are typically organized by selection and function. For example, a "Text" menu will contain formatting options for text selections. The same-kind-of-object guideline can be broken when the same functionality crosses many kinds of objects, e.g., "Format". Task-based menus, where all the items are subtasks of some higher-level task, should be avoided as users have a great deal of difficulty locating the menu that has the desired command.

All platform guidelines describe dialogues in some detail. After a careful review to insure that each dialogue is needed, task flow, spatial grouping, consistent terminology, and platform-standardized layouts should be used to help make dialogues clear and compact.

6. SUMMARY

There is a large gap between a set of requirements and a finished user interface, too large to be crossed in one leap. This gap is most easy traversed by developing two intermediate models: essential and user. Modeling strips away the irrelevant details, freeing the designer to focus on the central issues. It is this focus on the essential that often leads to significant insights and inspiration.

The design proceeds in four steps:

- Collect requirements and background information.
- Extract that information into the essential model.

- Transform the essential model into the user's model.
- Transform the user's model into a finished user interface design.

Scenarios form the primary thread in this process, keeping the designer focused the user's activities as the background scenarios are first extracted and then transformed across these steps. Patterns of human perception, behavior, and activity guide these transformations; metaphor is central to the essential model-to-user's model transformation while an understanding of human perception, cognition, and interaction is central to the user's model-to-interface design transformation. Platform-specific guidelines also aid in the selection of representations and controls used in the interface design.

Rough sketches are used throughout this process as an aid to visualizing the current stage of the design, but sketches cannot represent the dynamic nature of the interface in a compressive manner. The designer must build interactive visual prototypes to better understand the actual interactions, to test the design before it is coded and more difficult to change, and to communicate the finished design to developers and customers.

Design is not a straight-line activity that moves smoothly from step to step. It is messy, requiring the generation of many alternatives at each step and many iterations as ideas are developed and tested, returning to users time and again to check earlier decisions. This is what makes designing for people so much fun.

7. REFERENCES

Apple Computer, Inc., *Apple® Human Interface Guidelines,* Addison-Wesley, Menlo Park, CA, 1987.

Apple Computer, Inc., *Newton User Interface Guidelines,* Addison-Wesley, Menlo Park, CA, 1996.

Constantine, L. L., Essential models, *Interactions,* 2(2), 34-46, April, 1995.

GO Corp., *PenPoint™ User Interface Design Reference*, Addison-Wesley, Menlo Park, CA, 1992.

Holtzblatt, K. and Beyer, H., Making customer-centered design work for teams, *Communications of the ACM,* 36(10), October, 1993.

IBM, Inc., *Object-Oriented Interface Design*, Carmel, Que Corp., IN, 1992.

Mullet, K. and Sano, D., *Designing Visual Interfaces*, Prentice Hall, Englewood Cliffs, N.J., 1995.

Nass, C., Steuer, J., and Tauber, E., Computers are social actors, *Proceedings of CHI'94*, Boston, MA, 1994.

Papanek, V., *Design for the Real World*, Academy Chicago Publishers, Chicago, 1984.

Perkins, R., Keller, D., and Ludolph, F., Inventing the Lisa Interface, *Interactions*, 4(1), 40-53, January, 1997.

Wroblewski, D.A., The construction of human-computer interfaces considered as a craft, in *Taking Software Design Seriously*, 1-19, Karat, J., Ed., Academic Press, San Diego, 1991.

CHAPTER 5

Lightweight Techniques to Encourage Innovative User Interface Design

Andrew Monk
University of York, York, United Kingdom
email: am1@york.ac.uk

TABLE OF CONTENTS

0-8493-3125-0/98/$0.00+$.50

1. INTRODUCTION

This chapter describes four representations for recording and reasoning about the users' needs. It is argued that the gap between understanding the need of the user and an initial design can be minimized by using these informal techniques:

- A "rich picture" identifying the major stakeholders and their concerns to make sure the software fits the needs of everyone who will be affected by it.
- A Work Objective Decomposition to help the designer think about the reason for each step in the work.
- An exceptions list to reason about things that may go wrong, both for the application and the user.
- Some fictional scenarios of use that can be utilized to evaluate the task fit of the software design.

In each case there are sections describing what it is for, what it looks like and how to do it. A further section describes how to use these representations to produce an initial design.

2. THE DESIGN CONTEXT

2.1. PROVIDING A FIRM PLATFORM TO BRIDGE FROM — GETTING THE REPRESENTATION RIGHT

The problem introduced in Chapter 1 is how to bridge the gap between (1) an understanding of the needs of the user and (2) the first prototype design. The "understanding" referred to in (1) will include information about the work the system is to support, the kinds of skills the user will have, and so on. The initial design referred to in (2) may take the form of a paper prototype of the screens to be used with some verbal description of how they behave. It may be a software prototype of some kind or alternatively some more abstract specification of how the user interface will work (see Gould et al., 1987, for examples of the many forms a prototype design may take). After the gap has been bridged there are many practical techniques for refining the initial design (e.g., Monk and Curry, 1994; Nielsen, 1993). Techniques for use before the gap are also available (Whiteside et al., 1988). The gap to be bridged then is the large step between an understanding of the needs of the user and the first prototype.

In almost any design context documents will be produced to record the results of the deliberations of the parties concerned. These documents will contain diagrams, tables, lists, and other textual devices. Some of these representations have known mathematical properties (e.g., state transition diagrams); others are much more informal. The message of this chapter is that the gap can be made more bridgeable by the way we write down the results of our activities under (1). To stretch the metaphor somewhat, the argument to be made is that by using the right representation to record and reason about our understanding of user needs we can provide a firm platform from which to build the bridge, thus making it more likely that we will arrive safely at the other side.

Documentation, and the representations used within documents, have two important functions in addition to those usually given of providing a record for management, software maintenance, or whatever. The first is to communicate. Design is rarely a solitary occupation. Members of a design team need to communicate and negotiate their understanding of the design. In some organizations the "before the gap" activities will be carried out by different individuals to the "after the gap" activities and so the findings of the former group have to be communicated to the latter. Even in design teams where everyone takes part in all activities there is still a lot of communication to be done. Different team members will have different viewpoints and a common vocabulary, of the kind provided by a representation, makes it possible to negotiate an agreed understanding. The second function of a document is to facilitate reasoning. Writing down your conclusions makes it possible to reflect on and reason about them. Has everything been considered? Representing conclusions about one thing will remind you of other things yet unconsidered. Are the conclusions drawn consistent? Writing down one conclusion may make you realize that an earlier formulation about something else can be improved.

There are very good reasons then for documenting the design process. However, to be really useful as tools for communication and reasoning, the representations used need to be tailored to the context they are going to be used in. Different representations have different properties. First, they capture different aspects of what they are used to describe. For example, representing an organization in terms of a reporting hierarchy would make explicit different aspects of organizational structure than a sociogram recording who communicates with whom. Let us say that by making some additional assumptions it is possible to infer one representation from the other. Even if this is the case, so that one representation implicitly contains the information in the other, it is still the case that one representation may be most useful for one purpose and the other for another. We say that each representation "makes explicit" different kinds of information. Second, different representations have different cognitive properties (Green, 1989). For example, diagrammatic representations are generally more difficult to create and change than textual representations but if well designed may be easier to read. Third, different representations require different skills and effort from the people using them. Many of the techniques devised by academics for software engineers, for example, require such a large investment in training and effort during use that they unlikely to be justified in terms of the payback they produce (Bellotti, 1988; Monk, Curry, and Wright, 1994).

2.2. THE NEED FOR LIGHTWEIGHT TECHNIQUES

Software design methodologies prescribe a set of representations that have to be produced and methods for deriving those representations. These formally defined methods tend to be used when the design team is large, i.e., 20 or more people, and may serve a management function. Very large projects, e.g., military command and control systems or off-the-shelf word processors, can only be coordinated through the application of well-articulated and strictly adhered-to procedures. This chapter, however, is not concerned with large projects. Rather, it is hoped to offer something to the smaller low-profile design projects that make up so much of the everyday work of software developers. These projects may only involve teams of two or three people working for a few months or even weeks. The developers we have in mind probably work for software houses or within user organizations. In the latter case they might be part of a management information service or computer department. Much of the software they use is bought in and most of their work is to use the options provided to customize it for different subgroups within the organization. For example, a particular department may request a Windows interface onto the company database for some very specific data entry task that is then implemented using Excel or Visual Basic.

The main difficulty faced by the small design team, in comparison with a large project, is that the resources they have for recruiting people with special skills or for learning new skills are very limited. Any technique they may apply must be lightweight in the sense that it can be easily picked up and easily applied. If a project has a total effort of a few man-weeks then the process of understanding the user's needs can only be a few man-days and the effort required to learn techniques for doing this must be even less. Nielsen (1993) draws an analogy with shopping to illustrate this requirement for lightweight techniques. He describes his techniques as "discount" techniques: techniques that cost less than their deluxe versions but nevertheless do the job, cost being measured in terms of how much effort it takes to learn and then use them.

The techniques described here fit Nielsen's requirements for discount techniques. They are lightweight procedures that can be learned in a day or so and only take man-days to apply. One of the reasons that this is possible is that they assume that there is a well-specified and accessible user population doing some well-defined tasks. The developers in one of these small projects can be very clear about who their users are and the work to be supported. Potentially, it should be easy for the developers to talk to these users and observe how they work. Compare this situation with that faced by the designers of a word processor, for example. Their users will all have very different skills and expectations, for example, some may be scientists others secretaries. The work to be supported will also vary a great deal, potentially, from typing a memo to producing a book. As will be explained, being able to specify a small user population and a small set of tasks to support makes it easier to guarantee task fit, the most important attribute of a usable system.

The representations described below were originally developed in a collaborative research project. The partners were Data Logic, a software house and System Concepts, a human factors consultancy and the human computer interaction research group at the University of York. The work most relevant to this chapter is described in (Curry et al., 1993). As a part of this project the techniques developed were applied in a case study of a warehouse handling food products for a large group of stores in the UK. This study will be used as an example in the sections that follow. The techniques have also been taught to, and used by, several "generations" of computer science students at York University and to this extent they are well tried and tested.

The body of this chapter is divided into four sections, each of which describes a different representation that may be used to think about some aspect of the user's needs. In each case there is an introduction to the purpose of the representation, an example of what it looks like, and some instructions on how to produce it. Finally there is a section on how to use these representations when bridging the gap. The representations described are: (1) a rich picture to capture top level concerns; (2) a work objective decomposition (WOD) that serves a similar purpose to a hierarchical task analysis (HTA) but is easier to produce and use; (3) a user exceptions list of possible interruptions and mistakes, and (4) fictional scenarios of use generated from the WOD and user exceptions list.

3. REPRESENTING TOP-LEVEL CONCERNS — THE RICH PICTURE

3.1. WHAT IT IS FOR

A large number of the computer systems developed for use in specific contexts are delivered but never used. The most common reason for this is that they prevent someone from doing their work. It may be that they support some aspect of the work of the person operating the computer but force them to adopt a new way of working which is incompatible with some other aspect of the job. Another common story is that the work of the person operating the computer is well supported but the design requires changes in work procedures that are incompatible with someone else's responsibilities.

Implementing a new computer system is going to change the way people work. If it does not there would seem to be little point in providing that support in the first place. All too often the changes in work practices implied by a computer system are not properly thought through. Designing a computer system implies the redesign of existing jobs. This should be done explicitly at the start of the project rather than as an accidental by-product of system design when it is too late to change the new computer system. The developer has a responsibility to alert the user organization of the implications of the new computer system and to work with all relevant parties to ensure the system allows them to work in the way they need to. This is only possible if the developer has some understanding of the broad context of the work being carried out. It also requires that all parties who may be affected by the new system and procedures are consulted right at the start of the development process. The rich picture is a representation that serves the purpose of identifying these "stakeholders" their concerns and responsibilities. We have also found that developing a rich picture is a very effective way of getting all the developers in the design team up to speed with the aims of the design project.

3.2. WHAT IT LOOKS LIKE

The rich picture provides a very broad but high level description of the work context to demonstrate that you have thought about the impact of the new system on everyone who might be affected by it. The representation consists of a diagram, a picture, with some supporting text. The idea comes from Checkland's soft systems analysis and is a simplification of his scheme.

Figure 5.1 is the actual rich picture generated in the warehouse project. At the top left is the gate house where suppliers' vehicles come in. At the bottom left is the loading bay where the vehicles taking food products to the stores are loaded. The central character whose work is to be supported is the computer operator who logs the flow of products in and out of the warehouse, represented here by the fictional name Jenny. Jenny's job is to take the delivery notes from the drivers and enter them in to the computer. Tally cards are then printed and a checking procedure is carried out by the warehouse men with Jenny's help. In this drawing the warehouse men are signified by stick figures wearing black hats.

The procedure as described this far is represented by the arrow from Drivers to Jenny and the two arrows between Jenny and the warehouseman on the unloading bay. Once the goods have been moved into cold or ambient storage (they claim this is the biggest fridge in England) there is another procedure using a second copy of the tally note used to record where the goods are. Picking notes for the loads to be taken to stores are automatically generated by the company computer.

The arrows then record the work in sufficient detail to act as a visual aid when explaining the setup to someone else. Thus far, drivers, warehousemen, and operators have been identified as stakeholders. Further stakeholders identified in the drawing are Jenny's supervisor and fellow operators and directors of the company owning the stores. The clouds in the top right indicate a complex situation that arises because the storage facility is not owned by the same company as the stores. In fact, there were two computer systems involved, one belonging to each of these companies and the data all had to be entered twice. This made it seem an ideal candidate for redesign utilizing a PC that could communicate with the two mainframes.

The final feature of note is the thought bubbles coming from some of the stakeholders. These can be use to indicate "concerns" they may have. Clearly the

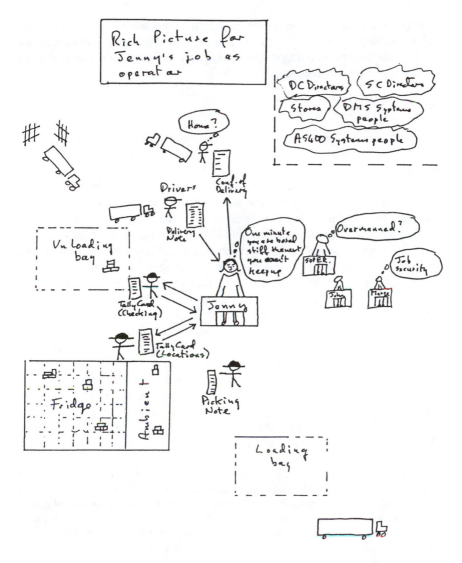

Figure 5.1 An example of a rich picture.

primary concern of the drivers is to get home, also the supervisor was under some pressure to decrease the number of staff in the office. Concerns like these can be very important. Had the new procedures significantly delayed the drivers, for example, it is quite possible that suppliers would have refused to cooperate. The rich picture serves as a reminder of figures peripheral to, but possibly critical in, the specific operation one is designing. It is also a useful basis for identifying the stakeholders who need to be consulted about the final design. It served as a compact notation for recording and reasoning about the wider context of the job within the design team and also for checking with our informants that we had understood what was going on. For some purposes the drawing on its own may be a bit too compact and we recommend that three short paragraphs are generated for each stakeholder specifying, respectively, their responsibilities, an outline of their work, and their concerns.

3.3. HOW TO DO IT

The information needed to construct a rich picture is obtained by talking to the stakeholders identified. In most projects there will be a designated contact to represent the user's needs. While you should start by talking to them it is important to talk to other people as well, particularly people who will end up working with the system. It is a good idea to interview people in their place of work. Here they will have access to documents, computer systems, etc. that can serve as prompts and examples. You may like to tape record what they say and it is always a good idea to go with a prepared set of questions to get you going (for practical advice of interview technique see Clegg et al., 1988).

A rich picture is informal enough to be presented to the stakeholders themselves so that your first stab at a rich picture can be taken back to your most useful informants. The process of explaining it to them will often elicit important new information and point up misunderstandings and errors of fact. Like all the other representations described in this chapter a rich picture may go through several iterations before the end of the design process.

The following steps should be taken to construct a rich picture. It is not necessary to be good at drawing to do this, the crudest figures will suffice (as is clear from Figure 5.1!). A drawing package has certain advantages given that you are going to have to change and add to the drawing. It is probably a good idea to use a different color for steps C and D.

A. In the middle of a large sheet of paper, draw a figure of some kind to represent each of the kinds of people who will actually interact with the system. These are the *user roles* (actors in Checkland's terms). There will probably be more than one; for example, there may be computer operators who enter data and managers who use summary displays.
B. Add further figures for people who might be affected by the introduction of the system even though they don't have to operate the system themselves. These *nonuser roles* (other "clients" and "owners" in Checkland's terms) may include, among others; supervisors, supervisees, and peers of the user roles; also customers, management, and the IT department who supply the relevant hardware and software services.
C. Indicate the flow of work on the diagram with labeled arrows. Try to keep this description at a fairly high level and avoid getting bogged down in too much detail. For example, a customer may make an enquiry which is entered into a database by an enquiry clerk and which then results in some action by a repairman. A supervisor makes summary reports using the same database and gives them in printed form to a manager who uses them in his reports to the board of directors.

D. Indicate the major concerns of all the roles represented by writing a short phrase next to each e.g., management are often concerned with cutting costs, operators with losing their jobs or being "deskilled".

E. On a separate sheet list each of the roles defined as drawings on the diagram and write for each a concise definition (not more than two or three sentences) of:

   1. Their responsibilities (people are responsible *to* someone *for* something).
   2. Their work (this is simply an amplification of the work flow arrows, step C, for that role).
   3. Their concerns (this is similarly an opportunity to explain and add to the concerns indicated in step D).

Each of the steps A to E will suggest changes and additions you want to make to what you recorded in the earlier steps; this is a good thing to do. You will almost certainly have to redo the whole thing to make it presentable anyway. The diagram and these descriptions should stand on their own but may be supplemented by a short paragraph of explanation.

You will generally need to prepare a "before" and an "after" picture, i.e., a rich picture of the situation before the introduction of the computer system and a rich picture of the situation after it has been introduced. The before picture is needed when interviewing informants, to play back your understanding of the situation. The "after" picture is the basis of the design and used in the next stages. It should also serve to alert management in the user organization of the broader implications of the design.

4. REPRESENTING WORK AS OBJECTIVES — THE WOD

4.1. WHAT IT IS FOR

The description provided by the rich picture should be very high level because one is aiming for a broad scope. The WOD and exceptions list, specify the work of the target user population in more detail. WOD stands for Work Objective Decomposition. Alternative approaches to representing this information tend to be (1) very time consuming and (2) focus the designer on what happens at the moment rather than the opportunities for creative and innovative design. The advantages of the WOD over these alternatives will be illustrated by representing the "work" of making a cup of tea.

Most people when asked to describe this task will generate a numbered list such as in Table 5.1. This does not easily code conditionals (what if the kettle is already full) or hierarchical structure (1 and 2 are part of the same subtask). The commonest response to this, in human factors, is to use a Hierarchical Task Analysis (HTA) as in Table 5.2. HTAs separate processes (the numbered items) from control (the "plan" in italics). Designers with a systems background tend to

Table 5.1 Making a Cup of Tea, Represented as Numbered Steps

1.   Fill kettle
2.   Switch on kettle
3.   Get out cups
4.   Put tea bag in cup
5.   Wait for water to boil
6.   Poor water in cup
7.   Get out milk
8.   Remove tea bag
9.   Add milk
10.   Add sugar
11.   Stir

Table 5.2 Making a Cup of Tea Represented as a Hierarchical Task Analysis

1. Boil kettle
   1.1. Add water to kettle
   1.2. Remove water from kettle
   1.3. Switch on kettle
          1.3.1. Plug in kettle
          Plan: 1.3.1 if not already
   Plan: 1.1 OR 1.2 as necessary then 1.3
2. Prepare cup/tea
   2.1. Get cup
   2.2. Get tea bag
   2.3. Put tea bag in cup
   Plan: 2.1 and 2.2 in any order then 2.3
3. Poor water on tea bag
4. Add milk
5. Add sugar
6. Stir
Plan: 1. and 2. in parallel then 3; 4. 5. and 6. as necessary
(HTA)

get deeply into specifying plans in great detail when this is really irrelevant to the design. It is irrelevant as the purpose of design is to change (and improve) the way the task is done. Focusing on processes has a similar unfortunate effect of emphasizing what is done now rather than how it might be done better. A WOD describes the task in terms of required states of the world, and avoids considering the processes by which these are achieved and the order in which they are achieved. This forces the designer to think clearly about the purpose of each process rather than the interdependencies between them. An example is given in Table 5.3.

A comparison of Tables 5.2 and 5.3 illustrates how different representations of the same thing can make different information explicit. It may seem a small change to redescribe the process "boil kettle" as the state of the world "have boiling water" but in our experience it can lead to significant insights concerning

Table 5.3 Making a Cup of Tea Represented as a WOD

(Have cup of tea)
1. Have tea bag and boiling water in cup
    1.1. Have boiling water
        1.1.1. Have right amount of water in kettle
        1.1.2. Kettle heating water
    1.2. Have cup
    1.3. Have tea bag
2. Have milk and sugar to taste
    2.1. Have milk
    2.2. Have sugar
        2.3. Tea stirred

Table 5.4 A WOD for the Warehouse Example

1. Delivery logged
    1.1. Delivery note recorded in system
        1.1.1. Have delivery note obtained from driver
        1.1.2. Gate house record number entered
        1.1.3. Supplier details entered
        1.1.4. Products entered with quantities
        1.1.5. Printing of tally cards requested
        1.1.6. Warehouse men have tally cards
    1.2. Delivery note validated
        1.2.1. Quantities agree
        1.2.2. Printing of confirmation of delivery requested
        1.2.3. Driver has confirmation of delivery
    1.3. Locations of delivery logged
        1.3.1. Locations entered
    1.4. Delivery record sent to DMS for allocation to stores
2. Goods allocated to stores [normally accomplished by DMS]
3. Picking notes generated

how procedures can be redesigned. Stretching this example a little, one can see how formulating the objective "have tea bag and boiling water in cup" might lead one to think of alternative methods of boiling the water such as boiling the water with a heating element placed directly in the cup. Without the restriction to write down the objective of each step it is too easy simply to use the name given to the process in the old procedure without really thinking about what that process is for.

4.2. WHAT IT LOOKS LIKE

Table 5.4 is the WOD generated to reason about the design of a computer system for logging goods in and out of the cold storage facility described above. The objectives 1.1, 1.2, 1.3, and 1.4 come from the rich picture. Note that the top level objectives 2 and 3 are not expanded. This is because it was not anticipated that the design would be concerned with this part of the operation. The analysis suggested possible changes to 1.1 and 1.2. The delivery note (see objective 1.1) could be obtained from the supplier in electronic form. It could be sent by e-mail or carried on magnetic media by the driver. If this were not possible various short cuts could be provided for entering the data. Quantities (see objective 1.2) were currently agreed by the warehouseman shouting them through a window. This process could potentially be simplified if the information in the tally card were on a portable data recorder.

4.3. HOW TO DO IT

Start from the rich picture. You may have to return to some of your informants to check on details. Like the rich picture, the WOD should stand on its own and will only need minimal supportive text. You will need to create a WOD for each user role. The following instructions may be used. As with the rich picture you will probably need to prepare "before" and "after" WODs, though sometimes the objectives will remain the same even though the processes have changed.

A. A work objective describes a state of the world the user would like to achieve. Examine the steps taken by the user and ask yourself why each step is carried out, i.e., what is the objective of that part of the work. Make a list of these "states of the world".
B. Next organize the list into objectives and subobjectives. The top level objectives will probably correspond to the processes identified in the rich picture. A subobjective is an objective that has to be achieved in order to achieve a top-level objective.
C. Examine the hierarchy for objectives not in your original list. It may be useful to decompose some of the subobjectives into sub-subobjectives but avoid deep hierarchical structures. You will often only need to go to subobjectives, it should not be necessary to go further than sub-subobjectives. Also, you can be quite selective in how deeply a top-level objective is decomposed. Those that are to be supported by the computer system will be decomposed in some detail, while those that are not will not. Notice that the objectives given above are still fairly abstract and stop short of specifying how the system will work.
D. Number the objectives for reference. Note this does not imply they have to be carried out in a specific order. There is no need to consider the order in which things are "normally" done or the logical constraints on the order in which objectives have to be achieved at this stage. Indeed we would advise against thinking about this at all at this stage as it may impede creative solutions at the design stage.

Some developers with a mathematical training may find the above process arbitrary and informal. It is. The WOD is not a formal notation and the method specified above will result in different representations when it is applied by different people. This is not a problem. Design is a creative craft and this analysis is a part of that creative process. The representations described here are better thought of as artists materials than engineering tools. The representations make it possible for the developer to create something new and useful by taking a new view on an old problem.

Table 5.5 Exceptions List for the Warehouse Example

Application exceptions
    Queries from DMS in 2
    Invalid Gate House Record No., Supplier details or Product in 1.1
    Printer off-line at 1.1.5., 1.2.2, or 3
User exception — interruptions
    Interrupted in 1 to do 1.1 or 1.2 for more urgent new delivery
    Wait for warehouse man to return with new count in 1.2.1
User exceptions — problems/mistakes
    Allocation by hand in 2
    Notice error in data during 1.1.2 to 1.1.4
    Quantities changed during 1.2.1
    Repeat printing of Tally Cards at any point
    Repeat printing of COD at any point
    Repeat printing of Picking notes at any point

5. PROBLEMS AND INTERRUPTIONS — THE EXCEPTIONS LIST

5.1. WHAT IT IS FOR

The WOD is an idealized view of the task. It needs to be supplemented by what might go wrong, the exceptions list. Application exceptions are things that can go wrong for the system; user exceptions are things that can go wrong for the user. Engineers are used to anticipating application exceptions, such as power failure or the system being unable to recognize a password. They are less used to thinking about user exceptions.

User exceptions are usefully categorized as interruptions and problems/mistakes. An example of an interruption in the cup of tea example would be "being called away while the tea was mashing". Interruptions imply the need to save work. If this problem were serious one might think of some way of automatically removing the tea bag and keeping the tea warm. Problems/mistakes imply the need to undo something. Adding sugar when it was not wanted would be an example of a mistake, though it is difficult to see how this could be undone.

5.2. WHAT IT LOOKS LIKE

Table 5.5 is the exceptions list for the warehouse case study. All the exceptions listed were mentioned as being disruptive to the flow of work by the operatives questioned. Most particularly, the current system did not allow the operator to save the work if interrupted while entering the details from a delivery note. This commonly happened when they were working on a delivery note of goods for the ambient storage and then a delivery for the cold storage arrived and began to defrost on the unloading bay. Naturally, the cold storage took precedence in such a situation and the former work was abandoned and hence lost.

5.3. HOW TO DO IT

Go back to your interviews with the users and note where they mention events that were disruptive to the flow of work. Then go through the WOD and try to think of all the things that could go wrong. Finally, gather together your thoughts under the three headings described below.

A. List the *application exceptions* — These will include physical breakdowns and 'correct' behavior (e.g., an unacceptable ID when the user is logging in to a system). Work out where these exceptions could occur, i.e., which objectives might the user be working on when they occur.
B. *Problems/mistakes* — List user exceptions due to the users making mistakes or changing their minds. Take each subobjective to be computer supported in turn. Ask yourself whether the user having achieved that objective might want to "undo" it at some later stage and if so where such a decision is likely to be taken, i.e., which objectives might the user be working on at that point.
C. *Interruptions* — List user exceptions due to interruptions. Most people interleave several tasks in their daily work. Ask yourself when they could be interrupted and what implications this could have for design. The higher level work objectives and the rich picture will suggest what these interruptions are likely to be. Again work out where in the WOD these interruptions could occur.

6. ILLUSTRATIVE STORIES — SCENARIOS

6.1. WHAT THEY ARE FOR

The rich picture, WOD, and exception list will capture most of your understanding of the work context that is to be supported by the computer system. However, these representations are relatively abstract and may seem rather cryptic to someone who has not been in on their development. The purpose of the scenarios is to put back a bit of detail and make the understanding more concrete.

Scenarios have been used widely in HCI design (Campbell, 1992). In this chapter the word is taken to mean a fictional but nonetheless typical story describing a user's work. Scenarios are to summarize and illustrate your understanding of the work so fictional scenarios are more useful than real accounts of user behavior because it is possible to make several points in the same scenario in an efficient way. Another reason for using fictional scenarios rather than real transcripts is that you need to illustrate the new way of working, after the system has been introduced.

Scenarios flesh out a WOD and exception list by including sequences of actions and some detail. They contain examples of typical data associated with real use. It is particularly valuable to attach samples of the actual documents used such as delivery notes or invoices. The stories should highlight crucial sections of

Table 5.6 Scenario of Work When There are No Exceptions

Scenario 1: ideal case
1. Driver Dave Hodges gives Jenny gate house pass 7492 and delivery note (see sample documents)
2. Jenny enters gatehouse no. "7492", supplier code "Smith34", product codes and quantities (see sample delivery notes)
3. Jenny request printing of tally cards (see sample documents) for 7492 and gives them to warehouseman John
4. Warehouseman Mike comes in with tally card for 6541 with locations (see sample documents)
5. Jenny recalls delivery 6541 to screen and enters locations.
6. DMS prints store picking notes for cv49w to cv52z; Jenny gives these to warehouseman George
7. Warehouseman John comes to window with tally card for 7492
8. Jenny recalls delivery 7492 to screen and checks quantities with John — OK
9. Request printing of COD for 7492 (see sample documents)
10. Jenny gives COD to driver Dave Hodges
11. Jenny sends delivery record for 7492 to DMS

the users tasks. Scenarios are the first representation to be used in checking a design and the best representation for describing the work to someone who has not seen any of the representations before.

6.2. WHAT THEY LOOK LIKE

Two scenarios developed for the warehouse case study are given here. Table 5.6 was constructed directly from the WOD in Table 5.4 and represents the ideal case where there are no exceptions. This illustrates how the work involves interleaving different jobs in a way that is much less apparent in the WOD. Table 5.7 was generated by adding two of the exceptions from Table 5.5 to the ideal scenario in Table 5.6.

Note that these scenarios are very selective in what they illustrate. There are many ways an ideal scenario could have been generated from Table 5.4. Nevertheless, the scenario illustrates well how the work proceeds. Similarly, only two exceptions were selected from the list of 11 in Table 5.5. These were judged to be most important as it was known that the existing system handled them very poorly.

6.3. HOW TO DO IT

It is useful to include sample documents and other data with a scenario, e.g., photocopies of delivery notes and invoices, printout, and so on. Wherever possible these should be real documents and data. If real data are not available it is still useful to make something up and show it to users and ask how it could be made more realistic.

There is no need to be exhaustive in this exercise. It is unnecessary to have more than five or six scenarios in total. Also, there is generally no need to have

Table 5.7 Scenario of Work with a Data Entry Mistake and Interruption when Entering Data from the Delivery Note

Scenario 2: exceptions

1. Driver Dave Hodges gives Jenny gate house pass 7492 and delivery note
2. Jenny enters gatehouse no. "7492", supplier code "Smith34", and half of the product codes and quantities (see sample delivery notes)
3. Warehouseman Tim informs Jenny of priority cold storage delivery and hands her gate house pass 7581 and delivery note from driver
4. Jenny enters "7581", supplier code "Browns67", and the product codes and quantities
5. Jenny request printing of tally cards (see sample documents) for 7581 and gives them to warehouseman Tim
6. Warehouseman Mike comes in with tally card for 6541 with locations (see sample documents)
7. Jenny recalls delivery 6541 to screen and enters locations
8. Jenny recalls partly entered delivery 7492 to screen and enters remaining quantities and product codes
9. Jenny request printing of tally cards (see sample documents) for 7492 and gives them to warehouseman John
10. DMS prints store picking notes for cv49w to cv52z; Jenny gives these to warehouseman George
11. Warehouseman John comes to window with tally card for 7492
12. Jenny recalls delivery 7492 to screen and checks quantities with John; one product code was mistyped but the quantities correspond
13. Jenny changes product code and requests printing of COD for 7492
14. Jenny gives COD to driver Dave Hodges
15. Jenny sends delivery record for 7492 to DMS

scenarios illustrating the situation before the system is implemented; the intention is to illustrate what will happen with the new system. To generate the scenarios

A. Use the WOD to write one or more best-case scenarios. Use the sample documents and your knowledge from interviews to flesh out the extra detail. Choose orders of events that you think will be good tests for the new system, e.g., those that are at present reported to be difficult to deal with.

B. Select the most important exceptions from the exceptions list. These might be exceptions that are reported as being most disruptive to work at present or that you have other reasons for thinking will be difficult for the new system. Another criterion to think about is the frequency with which exceptions occur. Clearly, something that happens very infrequently would not need to be considered unless it is likely to have very severe consequences. Write these exception scenarios by adding to the best-case scenarios described in A.

7. BRIDGING THE GAP — THE NEED FOR A DIALOGUE MODEL

The four representations described are to reason about and record the needs of the user. They allow developers to communicate and develop their understanding as a group and to check their understanding with their informants. They also serve to record that understanding in a form that facilitates making the bridge to an initial design. The only additional information required is some sort of characterization of the users. A good user interface takes account of the previous experience of the user, their skill with mouse and keyboard, their knowledge of different operating systems, and their use of other computer systems (for "upward compatibility"). There will also be constraints imposed by the hardware and software available. This should all be written down and agreed among the design group and with the customer. One is then ready to "bridge the gap" to a first design. This section describes how to do this and then how to use the representations described above to evaluate that initial design.

Again we wish to argue that the gap can be made easier to bridge by choosing the right representation at the other side of the gap. The representation suggested is a dialogue model. This is a description of the high-level structure and behavior of a user interface. A common form of dialogue model is a rough sketch of screen outlines and a flow diagram to indicate how the user can change parts of the screen or move from one screen to another. The reason for starting with a high-level description of the behavior of the system is that this is the same level of abstraction as is provided by the WOD, exceptions list, and scenarios and these representations can thus provide inspiration for this part of the design.

Returning to the warehouse case study, the first step was to decide which objectives in the WOD (see Table 5.4) it would be most useful to support. *2. Goods allocated to stores* and *3. Picking notes generated* are already well automated as is *1.4 Delivery record sent to DMS for allocation to stores*. Therefore, objectives 1.1, 1.2, and 1.3 were identified as the crucial work objectives to be supported. As these objectives are essentially data entry tasks the next step was to specify a data structure for storing the information to be entered. This took the form of a list of the data fields associated with each delivery.

The first really creative step was to decide how these data fields should be distributed across screens. It was decided that one basic screen, a form, would suffice for all three tasks. This form would gradually be filled in as the objectives were accomplished. The reasons for this were as follows:

1. It makes the dialogue model very simple, there is only one screen layout.
2. The commands needed would mainly be the standard commands for editing a form and this would be familiar to the users who were all experienced Windows users.
3. The additional commands needed to create a new blank form and two others to hide or display existing ones could again be made similar to the commands they already new for creating, hiding and revealing documents.

This central screen, the form, was sketched in pencil. This allowed various details to be glossed over. Similarly, no commitment was made about how the commands, hide_form, display_form, and make_new_form would be implemented. This lack of commitment is important as it allows one to get the top level structure of the design right. If the first design had been produced using a software prototyping tool or user interface generator the developer would have been forced to make decisions about low-level detail, such as the names for fields, menu items, etc. before the overall structure of the design has been worked out. These details can pre-empt the top-level design and are also difficult to get right without the overall picture presented by a more abstract dialogue model.

A good dialogue model constrains the order in which operations are carried out only where absolutely necessary. It is dangerous to constrain the order of operations according to what you as a designer consider to be "normal" or "logical". You may have missed something in your analysis or the work situation can change. In some applications there will be legal constraints on the order in which things are done, while in others, constraints may by imposed by security considerations. However, in office systems, order constraints are rarely this fundamental. As the dialogue model is primarily concerned with such constraints, this is the time to consider these issues.

This principle of minimizing constraints on the order in which things are done was followed in the warehouse case study. Operators were allowed to change anything up to the moment the data was sent to HQ (objective 1.4). Data cannot be changed then because the consequences of making those changes would be very expensive. The resulting dialogue model is thus very simple, any form can be accessed at any time and any field on it changed, up to the point it is sent to DMS where upon it becomes read only.

Having produced an initial dialogue model, the next step is to check it against the scenarios. This is done by going through each step in the scenario "simulating" or "walking through" what the user would have to do. This will probably identify some problems such as points where the user cannot access the relevant commands or where access is unnecessarily laborious. When the dialogue model has been modified to cope with these problems, more exhaustive checking should be undertaken using the WOD and then the complete exceptions list. The reason for working from the most simple (scenario) to most complex (WOD) is to make the process more tractable. There may be some exceptions that would be just too expensive to deal with. These should be noted to be discussed with the customer.

The scenarios for the warehouse case study were checked against the dialogue model, then the exceptions, and WOD. Because it was so simple and unconstrained no serious problems were detected. Most dialogue models are more complex than this and the process of checking them against scenarios, WOD, etc. is thus more complex. There are software tools for producing dialogue models. The author has developed Action Simulator (Monk and Curry, 1994) This allows a designer to build simple models of the high level behavior of the user interface that can be executed to give a dynamic view of the design. StateMate is another tool that allows modeling using Harel diagrams (Harel, 1987). There are also multi-media tools such as MacroMind Director that can be used to make prototype user interfaces that "behave" without requiring the designer to fill in low-level details.

After all this work considering the needs of the user, filling the missing detail needed to turn the dialogue model into a full design should be very straightforward. A style guide for the platform being used, such as the CUA guidelines

(IBM, 1991) or the Apple Human Interface guidelines (Apple Computer Inc., 1987) should be followed at this stage. The full design may take the form of a paper simulation or a bare-bones simulation using an interface generator. There may still be a few improvements that can be made in the wording of items, layout, and graphic design to make the screens communicate what is required to the users. These improvements are best identified using a technique that brings representative users in contact with the design such as Co-operative Evaluation (Monk et al., 1993).

8. AFTERTHOUGHTS

The techniques described here do not require extensive training to use and the effort required to use them has been minimized by using informal common sense representations. Despite their informality the representations can help a design team to communicate and to reason about the needs of users. They will result in designs that take account of many usability problems that might arise if no analysis of user needs had been carried out. However, they do not guarantee the exhaustive identification of all such problems. This may be more closely approached by formal techniques though these will certainly require more effort to apply and learn.

It is also important to recognize that these representations were developed for use in a very specific design context. It is assumed (1) that the number of people developing and using the representations is small so that all will have a great deal of shared background knowledge, (2) that the users of the system can be readily identified, and (3) that the development team will have access to them.

Assumption (1) makes it possible to use concise representations, even though they lack a formal syntax or semantics. The analysis for a typical project may be expressed in a few pages. This is only possible because of this assumed shared understanding within a small design team. Assumptions (2) and (3) are also essential for the ease of use of these techniques. Getting designers to see their designs from the point of view of a user is the central point of user-centered design. The more often that developers can get together with users, see them operating their systems, and understand their work, the better the designs that will result. While this is the normal modus operandi in many companies, in many others there are obstacles to it. Developers may feel threatened by the process, management may not be confident in the ability of developers and there may be "political" objections from other groups. These problems are more often imagined rather than real, and once developers and management have seen the advantages of techniques such as those described above, they quickly come around (Haber and Davenport, 1991).

While the techniques described are tailored to a specific design context and so make these important assumptions, the reader may see elements of the approach that can be adapted to other contexts. More generally, it is hoped that this chapter has illustrated the value of developing representations for reasoning and recording users' needs and that the form those representations take can either facilitate or hinder the development of the understanding needed for effective design.

9. REFERENCES

Apple Computer, Inc., *Human Interface Guidelines: The Apple Desktop Interface*, Addison-Wesley, Reading, Massachusetts, 1987.

Bellotti, V., Implications of current design practice for the use of HCI techniques, *Proceedings of HCI'88: People and Computers V*, Jones, D. M. and Winder, R., Eds., University of Manchester, (September 5-9): Cambridge University Press, 13-34, 1988.

Campbell, R. L., Categorizing scenarios: a Quixotic Quest?, *ACM SIGCHI Bulletin*, 24, 16-17, 1992.

Checkland, P., *Systems Thinking, Systems Practice*, John Wiley & Sons, Chichester, 1981.

Clegg, C., Warr, P., Green, T., Monk, A., Kemp, N., Allison, G., and Lansdale, M., *People and Computers: How to Evaluate your Company's New Technology*, Ellis Horwood, 1988.

Curry, M. B., Monk, A. F., Choudhury, K., Seaton, P., and Stewart, T. F. M., Enriching HTA using exceptions and scenarios, *InterCHI'93 — Bridges Between Worlds*, Adjunct Proceedings, Ashlund, S., Mullet, K., Henderson, A., Hollnagel, E., and and White, T., Eds., ACM Press, Amsterdam, 45-46, 1993.

Gould, J. D., Boies, S. J., Levy, S., Richards, J. T., and Schoonard, J., The 1984 olympic message system: a test of behavioural principles of system design, *Communications of the ACM*, 30, 758-769, 1987.

Green, T. R. G., Cognitive dimensions of notations, *Proceedings of the HCI'89 Conference, People and Computers V*, Sutcliffe, A. and Macaulay, L., Eds., Cambridge University Press, Cambridge, 443-460, 1989.

Haber, J. and Davenport, L., Proposing usability testing to management - an "It works therefore it's truth" approach, *Human Factors in Computing Systems: Reaching Through Technology, CHI'91 Conference Proceedings*, Robertson, S. P., Olson, G. M., and Olson, J. S., Eds., ACM Press, Amsterdam, 498, 1991.

Harel, D., Statecharts: a visual formalism for complex systems, *Science of Computer Programming*, 8, 231-274, 1987.

IBM, *Common User Access (CUA). Systems Application Architecture, Basic and Advanced Interface Design Guides*, IBM technical publications, 1991.

Monk, A. F., and Curry, M. B., Discount dialogue modelling with action simulator, *HCI'94 Proceedings: Computers and People 9*, Cambridge University Press, Cambridge, 327-338, 1994.

Monk, A. F., Curry, M. B., and Wright, P. C., Why industry doesn't use the wonderful notations we researchers have given them to reason about their design, in *User-Centred Requirements for Software Engineering*, Gilmore, D. J., Winder, R. L., and Detienne, F., Eds., Springer-Verlag, Berlin, 195-188, 1994.

Monk, A. F., Wright, P., Haber, J., and Davenport, L., *Improving your Human-Computer Interface: A Practical Technique*, Prentice-Hall, BCS Practitioner Series, Hemel Hempstead, 1993.

Nielsen, J., *Usability Engineering*, Academic Press, New York, 1993.
Whiteside, J., Bennett, J., and Holtzblatt, K., (1988). Usability engineering: our experience and evolution, in *Handbook of Human-Computer Interaction,* Helander, M., Ed., North-Holland, New York, 791-817, 1988.

CHAPTER 6

Interaction Design: Leaving the Engineering Perspective Behind

Peter Nilsson and Ingrid Ottersten
Linn Data, Frolunda, Sweden
email: pn@acm.org   ingrid.ottersten@lig.linnedata.se

TABLE OF CONTENTS

ABSTRACT

In this chapter we will address the intricate issues that arise while performing interaction design. Our view of design is that it is a mental process. Therefore, we will not focus on individual activities in the interaction design process. Instead we will try to communicate the designer's experiences while performing interaction design. In doing so, we will give the collection of user data and usability evaluation activities less emphasis.

Often the literature on usability issues focuses heavily on the process of collecting user data and on usability evaluation activities. Also, in descriptions of design work, the artifact itself is emphasized, rather than the process of creating it. In this chapter we attempt to remedy this by attempting to help the reader bridge the gap between collected user data and a designed artifact.

This chapter describes a journey that passes through the designer's concerns and experiences, the actual bridging of the gap, the design process as a whole, the techniques used by interaction designers, and the demands placed on them. All these topics contribute to the description of bridging the gap. We have chosen not to describe one specific design case, because we do not believe this will help in communicating the various aspects of design work. Describing one case also tends to draw attention to details, thus clouding the more important issue of the design process as a whole.

A word of wisdom from Albert Einstein has inspired us. He said, "In order to solve the problems created by the former way of thinking, one must find a new way of thinking."

1. A DESIGN STORY

I (Peter) just received an assignment to perform the interaction design in a software development project. I have engaged in some informal discussions with the project leader and the Context and Requirements (C & R) analyst. These discussions have focused on the customers' ways of expressing themselves, the assignment as a whole, and the customers' organization.

My first step is to team up with a co-designer. When I began as an interaction designer, it was difficult to convince project leaders that I should work with a co-designer, because they were convinced that I would "burn" both time and money.

Fortunately, I had the opportunity to try co-designing on one project because one of my colleagues was training to be an interaction designer. Therefore, the managers were willing to assign her to work with me to gain some experience. The result was that we produced three good design alternatives in half the time required for me to produce one design alternative on the preceding project. Following that success, the value of co-designers working together has never been questioned by our project managers.

On one project I worked with Linnéa, a colleague that usually works with multimedia productions because the system was a product aimed at the home market, at schools, and at libraries. Linnéa was able to spend $1\frac{1}{2}$ days per week for the following 3 weeks, helping me out with the interaction design. We agreed to spend most of our time together sketching, discussing, and hopefully having a wonderful time. We searched for a room that suited us both, equipped with a whiteboard that we could have exclusively for our use. During the time I spent working independent of Linnéa, I reflected on the design at hand and discussed its technical aspects with other members of the project team.

To acquire an understanding of the design space as a whole, Linnéa and I began our work by reading the report produced by the C & R analyst. This helped us understand the business goals of the system, situations where the system would be used, the characteristics of users, and the overall character of the system and technical limitations. We were aware that we would make incorrect assumptions while reading, but design is a process of continuous learning, where those initial errors would be corrected.

While reading the report, I actually started the process of designing. I made some sketches on paper, and wrote down some of the most important things, from a design perspective, that I found in the report. I also noted design issues related to them.

After reading the C & R report, I had a basic understanding of the design space, but I also had many questions. My next activity was a 2-hour discussion with the C & R analyst to gain an even richer understanding of the design space. My intention at this stage was to understand how the potential users of the system think about the tasks which the system will support, which goals they have, and what their professional concerns are. In this case, I found that the two most critical goals for the users were (1) avoiding "losing face" and (2) having the potential to generate decision alternatives quickly. This understanding helps me to appreciate the perspective of a potential user as I reflect on alternative designs.

Some designers use detailed descriptions of user tasks, but I have never found them critical in my work. In the design of systems for use in offices, homes, and public places, I find concentrated descriptions of users, situations, and usability goals to be sufficient. I do strive to understand the situation as a whole, rather than being concerned with details.

Although I now have a preliminary understanding of the design space, I'm aware that I still don't have a coherent picture of how things fit together. Therefore, I feel overwhelmed by the difficulty of the task. This was particularly prevalent during the early part of my career, but now I am filled with anticipation because I am confident that some hard work and creative thinking will lead to significant progress on the design. A feeling not unlike what I felt as a child on Christmas just before opening the presents.

It is now time for creativity and reflection. Linnéa and I use our conception of the design space and our experience with similar design problems to begin generating ideas. As we work together, ideas begin to flow and we reflect on them as we go. My method for capturing the results of this activity is to draw interaction sketches (not screen shots) on a whiteboard. For this I use a visual language with arrows. The specific technique is not as important as being able to visually represent the ideas. Even more important is the ability to clarify the ideas for myself and my co-designer. Presenting ideas visually helps us reflect on the design ideas to evaluate them and to generate new ones.

When working with a whiteboard, I quickly shift from idea generation to reflection and back again. For this I use techniques such as "Bubbling" (described in a later section), but I never carry it out in detail or for very long, and I only record it if I find something critical for the design. For me, recording design paths, suggestions, alternatives, and decisions are vital, but must not hinder my progress.

When designing, I generate conceptual, functional, and graphical suggestions simultaneously. This is a result of reflecting on ideas from all aspects in the design space. However, I am careful to never lose focus on the design space as a whole. At the conceptual and functional level of design, I try to generate directives for the graphical design and leave the graphic design details until later. Later, when doing the graphic design I can then follow those directives as I attempt to generate an effective graphical representation of the user's mental model.

Linnéa first was very surprised, when after some hours of intense, productive work, I took a step back and said, "Well, this is quite good, but I don't know if I can defend this design." At first, she thought I was joking, but as we discussed my comment, we came to two interesting conclusions. One is that a designer must be able to justify every design decision, whether it pertains to a detail or to the design as a whole. If someone questions a part of a design or proposes something that hasn't been considered, a designer should carefully evaluate it. Therefore, one of the core abilities of designers is to be critical of their own designs. The other thing Linnéa and I concluded is that designers should be aware of their particular styles of designing if they are to improve them.

Because I can never be certain of how effective a design is, I conduct user-driven evaluations to determine how well the design matches the way the users think and act. In this case, we found that our conceptual foundation didn't match the users' way of thinking about their tasks. As a result, we abandoned that particular design in favor of others.

In a previous project, my co-designer and I had used the conceptual metaphor "Swedish smorgasbord" to communicate our design to the users. Linnéa and I began searching for a metaphor for our current design space. However, we limited our search time to 4 hours because there is little benefit in constructing a mediocre metaphor just for the sake of having one. Time is better spent searching for an effective design representing the user's mental model.

Our co-design sessions at the whiteboard are our most efficient activities, but it is impossible for all design work be that efficient. It is intense, tiring work, and if all our design efforts were carried out together, there would be no time for individual reflection. We would then miss the opportunity for some other creative ideas. The time that we are not working together we both do individual design work. Because creative ideas and potential difficulties can occur at the most unexpected times, I am careful to write them down or record them on my digital recorder. As we discussed our activities together, we concluded that co-designing on the whiteboard can be compared with children playing, combined with the adult analytical abilities.

After three hectic weeks of design sessions, user driven evaluations, and technical considerations, it was time to implement the design. After a few weeks of implementation work, we found that the programmers had omitted some vital details of our design. My experience is that, even if the design idea is communicated to the developers, they do not retain it throughout the implementation. Therefore, it is important that I verify the external design throughout the course of the project. It is also important that I coordinate the work of the graphical designers and system developers so that their decisions will be consistent. It's my responsibility to insure that the initial design concepts are implemented. This coordination cannot be accomplished simply by writing down all design details. It is impossible to capture all the design specifications in writing.

In this case, the design was accomplished without using a formal information model because there were few classes and their structure was relatively obvious. However, this is not something I recommend. A "map" of the data to be presented is usually necessary. As a designer, I've had experience with most ways of presenting data (e.g., business documents, ER-diagrams, and OO-models). However, when performing conceptual design I prefer business documents or simple ER-diagrams rather than detailed ER/OO-diagrams. The diagrams include detailed implementation considerations of which I am totally indifferent as a designer. At Linné Data, we use an object-oriented technique to create declarative enterprise models. It allows us to easily capture important issues such as the case of a person occupying the roles of salesperson, customer, and buyer all at the same time.

On each project that I work, when I finally decide on a design and implement it, I am always concerned that I haven't considered everything in the design space. Also, invariably I will think of an excellent design idea after the project is completed. Even though it may be too late to incorporate this idea on the recently completed project, these reflections are helpful for future projects. Linnéa also reminded me that there is no single correct or ultimate solution to a design space. On the contrary, there are many ideas that are never even considered.

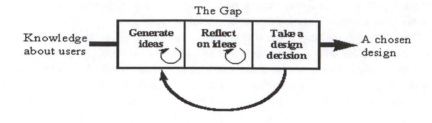

Figure 6.1 Bridging the gap.

2. BRIDGING THE GAP

To us the "design gap" is between having knowledge about the users and choosing a design based on that information. The design can be the design of the whole system or a detail such as which colors to use on the screen for a part of the interface. The gap consists of three parts: generating ideas, reflecting on ideas, and making a design decision, as shown in Figure 6.1.

The gap is bridged not once, but many times. As a designer you create one or several ideas, reflect on them and make a decision. Then you generate more ideas, reflection on them, and make more decisions. This is a rapid, iterative process. In this process you also ask yourself more and more detailed questions about the users, thus increasing your knowledge about them. It is important to separate the three parts (generation of ideas, reflection on ideas, and making design decisions). By so doing, you allow yourself to be truly creative thus saving reflection for later. When reflecting, it is important to reflect on as many aspects of the design space as possible before making a decision. This is especially true when working with a co-designer, because one of the most important benefits of working together is stimulating each others' creativity while not hindering one another with reflections. Therefore, instead of reflecting on your ideas, you should use them as a stimulus to generate more ideas. When working together, reflecting on ideas is also effective, because you can view the design ideas from different aspects of the design space much faster.

2.1. GENERATION OF IDEAS

Generation of ideas is a creative step best done by two or more designers sketching on a whiteboard. To begin this process, the technique of Bubbling (described later) can be used to generate ideas based on the design space. Here the designer uses experience from previous design work along with pure creativity. It is important to visualize through sketching, which makes it convenient for all other project members to evaluate the ideas.

2.2. REFLECTING ON IDEAS

Reflection on ideas can be seen as filtering the ideas through the one's understanding of the design space (from reading the C & R report), knowledge about human factors, and experience with former designs. The result of the reflection should be an understanding of the relative advantages and disadvantages of the various design alternatives, with the ultimate goal of choosing among them.

When reflecting, a designer should view the proposed design from the following different perspectives:

- The users — what will it be like to perform the task with this solution? Will the user get the right feeling when using this design?
- Human factors — does it give the user cognitive overload?
- The business organization — does it follow the business rules and contribute to relevant business goals?
- The entire system — does this design fit well into the design of the rest of the system and other systems that the users are to use?
- The hardware platform — will this design work as suggested by the guidelines of the platform?
- Feasibility — is it possible to implement this design at reasonable cost?

It is important that the designer has a good general picture of the design space. It is necessary because she will never be able to systematically filter all design ideas through all facts and details in the design space. Rather she will make judgement calls under way.

2.3. MAKING A DESIGN DECISION

One of the most challenging tasks of design is deciding among the plausible alternatives. This is because there is seldom *one* correct solution to a problem and choosing one design means rejecting many others. Making the decision often means striking a reasonable compromise among users' needs, technical considerations, the context of use, and the business situation. If reflection suggests that none of the ideas are acceptable, it is necessary to return to generating ideas.

2.4. AN EXAMPLE OF BRIDGING THE GAP

We will present a short example to demonstrate how we usually bridge the gap several times. The example is a GUI system for apartment administration. The users needed to search for and access information about apartments (e.g., availability, rates, size). We had decided on a design where a window on the left contained a list of apartments and a window on the right listed detailed information about an apartment selected from the list (see Figure 6.2).

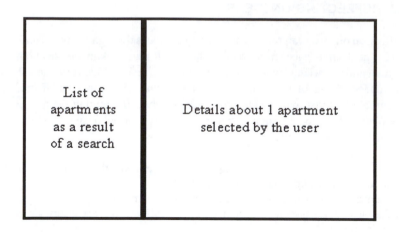

Figure 6.2 Apartment system design.

The focus of the design work was on the user's ability to view and work with details of one apartment. We knew that:

- There is a considerable amount of information stored about each apartment (more than could fit on one screen).
- The overall goal of the design was to minimize the total number of windows.

Idea generation gave us two main ideas:

1. Show detailed information about the selected apartment in one window and provide buttons in that window to open modal dialogue boxes containing further details.
2. Show all details about the selected apartment in one window, and organize the information using tabs.

The results of reflection about the first main idea were:

- The user will experience fast initial access to details about the apartment because a small amount of data is loaded from the database on any particular request.
- It will constrain the users into a sequence for information access and require them to perform the following two actions to view additional items of information: cancel the open dialogue and open the next one.

The results of reflection about second main idea were:

- The user will be able to access all object data in one window instead of being required to open secondary windows. The desired information is only one "tab-click away".
- Loading all object data from the database will require a relatively long time, and the user may become frustrated while waiting.

Decision result:

- Neither of the two ideas were acceptable, so we decided to return to generating ideas.

New idea generation:

- We felt that our first idea was the least acceptable, so we concentrated on improving the second one. Its main weakness was the technical constraint of the time to load data. The alternatives for improvement were:
    1. Create separate operating system processes for each tab so that they will be filled while the user is working with some other tab.
    2. Delay reading the information related to each tab until the user selects that tab.
    3. Load all the object data and show the tab with the most preferred information first. The user could then view, but not interact with, the information for that tab while waiting for the remainder of the apartment information to be loaded.

Reflections about alternative 1:

- This idea was impossible to implement with the development tools used in this case.

Reflections about alternative 2:

- The user may be frustrated by the delay when switching between tabs.

Reflections about alternative 3:

- If we could be certain that the most preferred information rarely changed and that the user required time to read it before interacting with it, the solution might be acceptable.

Decision result:

- We chose alternative number 3 because we believed that the user would be more willing accept an initial delay, rather than having occasional delays later. We also found that the most preferred information took the longest to load from the database, so the other parts could be loaded sequentially. Choosing alternative number 3 also required choosing main idea number 2, because that idea was the basis for alternative number 3.

We later asked the users to perform real work tasks to evaluate our choice between design alternatives 2 and 3.

3. DESIGN CONTEXT

As interaction designers we have found that two key questions need to be answered before design can begin. (1) "What are the desired effects of this system?"

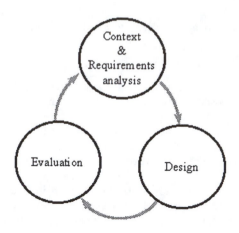

Figure 6.3 The iterative process of external design.

and (2) "What attributes are needed for the system to produce those effects?" We are convinced that the C & R analysis must be performed prior to the start of the interaction design (see Ottersten and Bengtsson, 1996; Nilsson and Lachonius, 1996). Otherwise, those questions will surface later, during the system development process. Therefore, we have developed a method that ensures that these key requirements are defined before interaction design begins.

Interaction design and C & R analysis are two of the activities in what we call *external design* (see Figure 6.3). The other activities are:

- Information modeling
- Design evaluation
- Technical writing
- User training and support

We use the term *internal design* when discussing activities contributing to a good technical realization of the system. The contents of external design are contained in our two methods for usability work, AnvändarGestaltning©,[1] and VISA©.[1]

3.1. CONTEXT AND REQUIREMENTS ANALYSIS

The Context and Requirements (C & R) analysis includes interviewing the customer, who is seldom a user. A structure is followed that ensures that the system's effects on the enterprise (business, humanitarian, and organizational) and the

---

[1]   Registered trademark of LinnéData Management AB.

system's qualities (information, technical, and what we call character) are clearly described. Often the customer has not realized that the system will affect peoples' way of working. The customer has seldom defined the desired effects of the system, other than those related to automation, efficiency, or costs. Effects on business relations and individual values, work load, and stress are often unanticipated. The goal of the C & R analysis is to explore issues that might have been overlooked previously.

We use the term "customer" to refer to the person who is responsible for those in the organization who will use the system. Sometimes this person has transferred the responsibility to a project leader or to someone else in the organization, but still it is that person who is the recipient of our design work. Among the issues addressed by the C & R analysis are the following:

- The desired degree of individual customization.
- The importance of the system to the organization.
- The importance of the system to the user(s).
- The characteristics of tasks to be supported (e.g., reflective or active, free or controlled, simple or complex, or boring or engaging).
- The physical context in which the task(s) are performed.

The C & R analysis can also include interviewing and observing users while they are conducting their work, following a structure that ensures the descriptions of:

- Work tasks and their structure.
- Work load.
- General characteristics of users (e.g., age, sex, education).
- Users' experience with computers, the work to be performed, and the organization.
- Users' motivation and values and their cultural and social environment.
- Existing support systems, either manual or automated.
- User goals and mental models.

The results of the interviews are described in a report delivered to the customer, the users, and the interaction designers. Distributing the report allows both the users and the customer to be involved in the design process and provides them an opportunity to react to any misunderstandings. C & R analysis, when interviewing and observing users, involves activities similar to those of Contextual Inquiry and Contextual Design (Holtzblatt and Beyer, 1993). Some differences are that in our C & R analysis:

- (Usually) only two people from each user group are selected.
- Very few formal modeling techniques are used — primarily just written and spoken language.
- The same people conduct all the interviews and write the report.

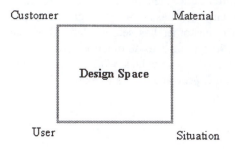

Figure 6.4 The design space.

3.2. DESIGN

3.2.1. The Design Space

The design space is created by the boundaries of the design (see Figure 6.4). These boundaries are the customer, the user, the material, and the context of use (situation). In addition, there are always some practical and "political" constraints. For us, building information systems for customers on a contract basis always means that the time and funds available for usability work are limited.

3.2.1.1. Customer, the Organization
The customer's intent is one limitation for the design space. The customer is, however, very seldom a single person. Furthermore, customers belong to an organization, and they share the organization's values and "mentality". This is seldom something conscious or explicit and therefore something the customer usually cannot reflect upon without some assistance. Our experience shows that customers have great difficulty explaining their concerns and wishes. We have developed a technique to explore possibilities with them and to help them express these needs.

To us, the word "customer" also represents the business rules that exist in the organization. These business rules can easily be captured with information models of business objects. We create information models as soon as a decision is made to begin a system development project. LinnéData uses a declarative, object-oriented technique, which captures the enterprise objects and the rules assigned to them. However, the details in this model are used for the internal design. For the external design, the object classes and their structure are the most important because they specify the relevant business objects and their interactions.

3.2.1.2. User Values and Goals

The users have values, skills, goals, and particular experiences, all of which influence our design. The design should provide users with the capability to perform their tasks while promoting the appropriate effect (e.g., a system for care of elderly people should promote a feeling of seriousness and accuracy in the user).

For us, the term "user" also embodies the tasks or actions they would want to perform. Our experience shows that only rarely does a designer need to analyze the users' work in detail. Instead, it is sufficient to capture the potential activities through interviews and observation, along with rules connected with the use of the system (e.g., sequential rules, rules of access). This provides sufficient background for designing the user interface. We seldom create detailed models of tasks. On the contrary, we suspect that detailed modeling could interfere with a designer's being innovative. This arises because the external designer is trained to think in terms of such human characteristics as cognitive workload, stress, and learnability.

3.2.1.3. Material

Designers are limited by the materials with which they have to work. We have found that in many system development projects the material limitations are not explicit. By "material" we mean all hardware and operating system limitations as well as any functionality related to the internal structure of the system, such as performance, adaptability, security, and maintainability.

3.2.1.4. Context of Use (Situation)

The physical and psychological context in which the system will be used is very important. When the external designer considers situational issues (e.g., time of use, placement of users, frequency of use, personal integrity, and ethics) important design information is obtained.

3.2.2 The Design Process

It is very important for the designer to focus on the right things at the right times in the design process. For example, the manner in which users will perform their tasks in the system (flow) must be considered prior to considering the exact placement of buttons on the screens. This may seem obvious, but our experience has shown that design work often begins with a heavy focus on graphical design. This may be an unintentional, but natural consequence of using GUI prototyping tools in early stages in the design process.

To help the designer focus on the right things at the right time, our design process is divided into three phases as shown in Figure 6.5 (see also Nilsson and Lachonius, 1996). With this approach it is possible to ensure the usability of the

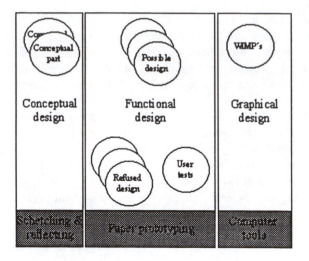

Figure 6.5 The design process.

design and to avoid being concerned about the need to change the concept of the design *after* doing the graphical design.

3.2.2.1. Conceptual Design

Design work should begin with conceptual design. At the conceptual stage, it is important to ask questions such as, "what are the components that users work with (from the their point of view)?" and "how do those components combine to fit the design space?" The work in the conceptual phase is preferably done on a whiteboard or with pen and paper. The result should be recorded in rough sketch form. Its purpose is to communicate the conceptual design of the future system and should reflect the user's mental model.

Figure 6.6 shows an example of a conceptual sketch from a travel reservation system, with the following parts:

- Journey, with journey plan, customer and "other".
- Resources, with means of transportation, hotel and "other".

These are, from the users point of view, the components upon which the system should be built. Note the that the arrow, "build journey", embodies the fundamental concept of the system: to build journeys from possible resources. In this case, one single sketch visualizes the entire fundamental concept of the design.

These sketches cannot be evaluated directly by a user trying to perform a task, because they are much more abstract than actual screen layouts. Therefore, it is

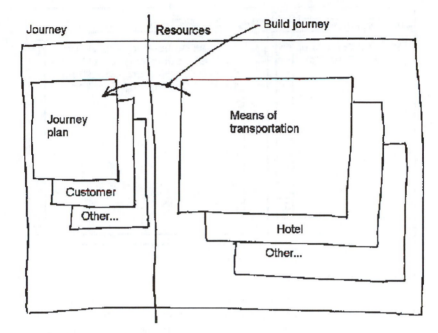

Figure 6.6 Conceptual design sketch.

often necessary to proceed to functional design (described in the following section) to evaluate the conceptual design and verify that the system reflects the user's mental model in an effective way. It is in the conceptual phase that the designer should begin thinking about how to provide the user with the desired emotional tone of the system. An effective way of doing that is to use the Bubbling technique described later.

3.2.2.2. Functional Design

Functional design is the second phase of the design process and is intended to make the conceptual design more concrete. In the functional phase, questions are asked such as, "how should the user interact with the system?" Rough screen designs are sketched in this phase, which are possible for the user to test in a user driven evaluation. Listboxes, buttons, and other controls are drawn, but their exact graphical placement or form is not a major focus. It is important to create a prototype with which the user can interact and perform real work tasks. Typically, we test several possible functional designs based on one conceptual design.

Figure 6.7 shows an example of a functional sketch with which the user can interact and perform the task of "selling a journey". The sketch consists of:

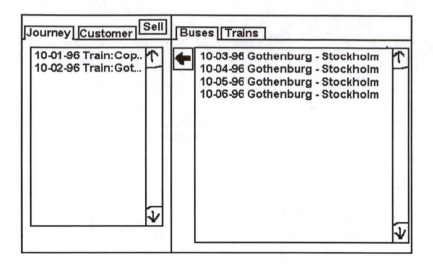

Figure 6.7 Functional design sketch.

- An area on the left, containing tabs for the journey that the user is planning (according to the conceptual design) and for customer information. The journey is shown in a listbox. The area also contains the button "Sell" which the user can press to actually sell the journey.
- An area on the right where the user can browse and select the transportation the customer requires (through tabs and listboxes). To move a selected item into the journey list, the user can press the button with the left-pointing arrow.

In this manner it is possible to evaluate the adequacy (for users) of the concept of "building a journey" *and* the means to build it (tabs, listboxes, and buttons).

Accomplishing functional design is never a simple transition from conceptual design. When constructing the functional design, all of the contextual issues are combined with information about the users and their tasks. The goal is to improve the users' productivity and feeling of satisfaction. One special case of functional design is a "quick and dirty" functional design. This functional design has only one purpose, which is to enable a user-driven evaluation of a conceptual design. Functional design does not focus on graphical form, which makes it suitable for low-fidelity (paper) prototyping.

3.2.2.3. Graphical Design

Graphical design is the third phase of our design process and refers to such items as the exact placement and grouping of controls and the choice of their colors, fonts, and sizes. This is best done using computerized tools appropriate for the situation (e.g., the development environment). The users are involved in the graphical design as well through user-driven evaluations.

3.2.2.4. Working in the Design Process

Keeping the appropriate focus when working within a design phase is important. This does not mean, however, that one should discard ideas and thoughts that are relevant to other phases. They should be recorded for later reference. It is natural for designers to have these out-of-focus ideas, but it is important for them to avoid getting caught up in graphical details, for example, during conceptual design. When we worked with creating the conceptual idea above, we generated both functional and graphical ideas. The functional idea was the use of tabs, which we recorded. Later, we decided to use the idea because it allowed us to maintain a great deal of information in one window. The graphical idea was to place the "Sell" button at the top left of the screen. We also recorded this idea and later decided not to use it, because it didn't fit naturally into the flow of how the user read the screen. "Sell" is the last action taken by users and is always performed after they scan the journey list to ensure its accuracy. Therefore, we placed it at the bottom right-hand corner of the left area.

3.3. EVALUATION

There are basically two types of evaluations: expert evaluation and user-driven evaluation. We conduct both of these evaluations with paper prototypes as well as computer prototypes. The expert evaluation is a method involving an expert in design guidelines (Skevik, 1994) which are based on principles of perception and cognition. The so-called user driven evaluation is a method based on cooperative evaluation with users (Wright and Monk, 1991). After years of performing these evaluations, we have developed a specific set of work roles for performing the evaluations and a question format for evaluating the design prototype afterwards.

We have also found it critical to formulate specific goals for the evaluations. For an evaluation conducted at a very early stage, the most important thing is to determine if the user can understand the conceptual idea behind the system. Later on, it is more important to determine if the user can perform a specific task, perhaps with a particular time constraint.

Following the use of our techniques, it is possible to determine if the system is appropriate for the users. This is our major goal for all evaluations performed, ranging from the first paper prototypes to the final delivery test. Some users are involved in the evaluations throughout the course of the project and some are involved only in selected evaluations.

4. BUBBLING TECHNIQUE

We have developed a technique called "Bubbling" that allows a quick launch into the design process (Nilsson and Lachonius, 1996). Bubbling makes use of a person's ability for quick associative thinking. All that is needed is a pen and paper. One begins by placing a key issue from the design space in a bubble in the

Figure 6.8 Bubbling with a key issue.

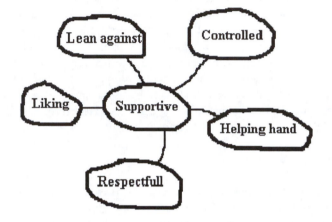

Figure 6.9 Bubbling associations.

middle of the paper as shown in Figure 6.8. That key issue can be a desired emotional response (from users) to the system, a user goal, a user category, a business goal, a task, or an information entity. For example, perhaps a goal is for the users to perceive the system as supportive.

After listing the key issue, the next step is to *associate* freely to that issue, drawing connecting bubbles as shown in Figure 6.9, until no further associations come to mind. Examples of possible associations to supportive are respectful, liking, controlled, helping hand, and lean against.

The next step in Bubbling is to generate ideas on how to create one or more designs for each of the associated words. It is helpful to ask questions such as "What can I do to make the user able to do/feel...?", "What should I do to counteract the users tendency to do/feel...?" (see Figure 6.10 for some Bubbling design ideas). The ideas can be conceptual, functional, or graphical. The important thing is to base the process of generating ideas on the design space. Examples of design ideas for the associated phrase "helping hand" are:

- Do integrate a guide, giving helpful hints based on the context by setting aside a small area of the screen
- Don't activate the guide automatically. Rather, provide the user the ability to ask for a helping hand when needed.

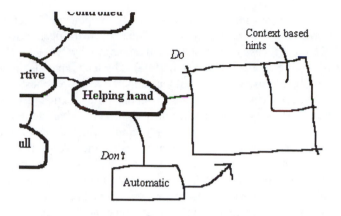

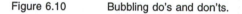

Figure 6.10   Bubbling do's and don'ts.

This technique should provide a list of desirable design ideas as well as things to avoid in a design. It is also helpful to place the items in a list with separate columns for desirable and undesirable ideas. They can then be compared for potential conflicts (an idea can be desirable in one situation but not in another) or for the possibility that several ideas support a similar concept.

To generate additional ideas, Bubbling can be used with other key issues. When ideas are no longer being generated, it may be time to combine them and to reflect on the alternative potential designs. It is important to avoid focusing too long on any particular detail. Instead, try to fit the design ideas into the design space in its entirety. Bubbling is most helpful in decomposing the design space into smaller components and getting started toward a useful design. It is also important to sketch during Bubbling. This will help to communicate the ideas and to generate even more.

Bubbling can be done alone or in cooperation with others. When doing it with others, a group can do it together or each member can take one key issue each and work with it by themselves. Group members can then trade issues after all associations have been generated with a particular issue. The Bubbling technique is part of one of our methods for usability work, called VISA.

5. OUR VALUES AND CONSIDERATIONS

We consider the computer system being designed as a future social actor in the organization (Stolterman, 1991). As Swedes, we have a culture of industrial democracy that demands participatory design or the "Scandinavian school" (Ehn, 1992; Floyd et al., 1989). We have also been highly influenced by thinking of interaction design as a process that begins at the very time a design assignment occurs and that the resulting system could be described as a social actor having a character (Stolterman, 1991). We do not believe there is ever an objective description of the real world. Modeling is therefore always an action where the modeler's knowledge and values are a necessary component. Therefore, at Linné Data we created an object-oriented technique to create declarative enterprise models, which are easily understood and managed by "nonmodelers" in the organization (Ottersten and Göranson, 1993). The technique also makes it possible to capture all business rules without imperative expressions.

Generally, design evaluation suffers from the limitation that there is never *one* correct design. However, for interaction design, alternative ideas are relatively easy to evaluate. This is why we strongly emphasize the need for continuous evaluation and co-design. The evaluations are performed to ensure that the development process is kept on course. Our experience shows that during implementation some design ideas are transformed, resulting in unintentional changes in the design. This is not the result of "dumb" programmers, but rather an effect of their different roles (from designers) in the development process. Their goal is to produce (design) elegant code. When they are faced with a technical problem, they will find a work-around that sometimes reduces the usability of the system. Therefore, it is advantageous to have the external designer working part time during implementation in order to maintain the integrity of the original design.

Traditional, formal design methods too often end up being no more than modeling techniques or ocedures that should or could be used. Furthermore, most formal methods do not explain the reasoning behind, or the values that lead to, the proposed actions. This results in methods that are even more difficult to use. Among system developers, in general, there is a widespread and justified mistrust of design methodologies (Stolterman, 1991). At the same time, some designers are seeking *the* method that will solve *all* problems. Our view is more pragmatic. The most important thing for us is not that the method is complete or 100% accurate but that it involves the users, and supports the designer in the design process. In fact, we strongly believe that there is no single method that can address all design questions.

External design could not be done without the co-operation of users. An experienced designer can usually generate desirable alternatives, but they are of little value until they are evaluated by users in the appropriate circumstances. This is a fact rarely understood by software designers and project leaders. Even customers tend to be insensitive to user issues. At LinnéData, we conducted a survey to assess the level of knowledge and interest in usability work among potential customers. Results showed that the major reason the customers have little interest in usability work is that they rarely, if ever, have the organizational responsibility for the people who are going to use the system.

There exist many techniques for generating a design. However, interaction design is more than just creating an artifact that appeals users. Interaction design is the very core of external design (i.e., producing an altered reality for people and contributing to the realization of an organization's goals). The difficult part in interaction design is focusing on human needs. It is the myriad of human considerations that separates interaction design and software design, in general. However, we do not agree with those that claim interaction design is an art form. On the other hand, it seems obvious that some aspects of interaction design could never be formalized.

We emphasize that design is a continuous learning experience. In a specific project, the designer learns more and more about the design space, making the design process iterative. Over time, a designer's knowledge is organized into larger chunks that consist of complex design issues and potential designs. The kind of learning that best describes interaction design is entertainment (i.e., the need of first-person-feeling and the urge to avoid interruption from the outside world or from thoughts that hinder the process) (Norman, 1993). This is consistent with our experience that interaction design is a social activity and is best done by people working in pairs (Winograd, 1996).

A computer system inevitably reflects a mental model of the way the users are believed to perceive the system's structure. The design should be carefully crafted to reflect the users' actual mental model. We use the term computer "interface" to emphasize the perspective of the human beings, not computers (Grudin, 1993).

6. CONCLUSIONS

We find effective external design, in general, and interaction design, in particular, to be a challenging and engaging activity. When developing computer systems for humans, it is the human-computer interface that embodies all opportunities, values, information, knowledge, and feelings that the user will experience when using the system. We claim that there are many issues to be considered when performing interaction design and "bridging the gap". We have called this the design space.

We are constantly striving to find new and better ways to collect the data needed for design. One difficulty lies in gaining access to all the implicit knowledge and the self-evident matters that exist in the minds of customers and users. This means that the design process can never be a simple transformation, because the customer and the users are never able to express all their needs in detail at the beginning of the design process. Therefore, the matter of design is to be able to collect enough facts to begin a discussion of the proposed design. We perform interaction design in this manner to ensure that important design decisions are made in cooperation with the customer and the users. This is important because those decisions effect costs in both the short and the long term and they affect users' everyday activities.

From the customer's and the users' points of view, it is critical that all work concerning external design is focused on satisfying their needs, rather than satisfying a formal system specification. We have been using our methods for external design with users for all types of applications (e.g., public information systems, multimedia production systems, production-planning systems, products for homes, and for World Wide Web access). It is important that the method used for project management can accommodate a process of continuous learning and revision of the original system specification.

There is a great challenge in the future uses of computers. We strongly believe that the area of interaction design will benefit from expertise in areas such as architecture and commercial advertising, where knowledge about how to meet human emotional needs are taken seriously. We also hope that the area of interaction design will develop better means to respond to cultural and social values.

7. ACKNOWLEDGMENTS

The work described herein has benefited from the contributions of several colleagues in many different ways. In particular the authors would like to acknowledge the efforts of Anna Skevik, who founded the usability program at Linné Data in 1989.

8. REFERENCES

Ehn, P., Scandinavian design: on participation and skill, in Usability: Turning Technologies into Tools, Adler, P. and Winograd, T., Eds., Oxford University Press, New York, 1992, 99-132.

Floyd, C., Mehl, V-M., Reisin, F-M., Schmidt, G., and Wolf, G., Out of Scandinavia: alternative approaches to software design and system development, Human - Computer Interaction, 4, 253-350, 1989.

Grudin, J., Interface-an evolving concept, Communications of the ACM , 36, 110-119, 1993.

Holtzblatt, K. and Beyer, H., Making costumer-centered design work for teams, Communications of the ACM, 36, 93-103, 1993.

Nilsson, P. and Lachonius, J., Internal Linné Data Handbook for interaction design using the VISA method Ver. 1.0, 1996.

Norman, D. A., Things that Make us Smart, Addison-Wesley, Reading, MA, 1993.

Ottersten, I. and Bengtsson, B., Internal LinnéData Handbook for context and requirements analysis using the VISA method, Ver. 1.0, 1996.

Ottersten, I. and Göranson, H., Objektorienterad utveckling med COOL-metoden, Studentlitteratur, Lund, 1993.

Skevik, A., Internal LinnéData Handbook for graphical and textual interface design using the AnvändarGestaltning method, Ver. 2.1, 1994.

Stolterman, E., The Hidden Rationale of Design Work, Umeå University, Umeå, 1991.

Sweden, Winograd, T., Bringing Design to Software, Addison-Wesley, Reading, MA, 1996.

Wright, P. and Monk, A., Co-operative evaluation. The York Manual, University of York, York, UK, 1991.

CHAPTER 7

Mind the Gap: Surviving the Dangers of User Interface Design

Martin Rantzer
Systems Engineering Lab, Ericsson Radio Systems, Linköping, Sweden
email: rantzer@acm.org

TABLE OF CONTENTS

ABSTRACT

The Delta Method is a systematic approach to usability engineering that is used within the Ericsson Corporation. The method has successfully supported usability work in a number of projects and continued to evolve during the process. We have managed to introduce usability engineering as a way to establish a solid platform of user data and to extend that platform to the other side of the design gap.

Based on a real-life case study we describe and exemplify the background information processes necessary to bridge the design gap. The central activities during the user interface design are two design workshops. During the first workshop we structure the services of the system into a conceptual model and during the second we transform the implementation independent structure into a paper prototype that reflects the future user interface.

The case study shows that a method such as Delta does not stifle the creativity that is needed to design good user interfaces. It helps to structure the work so that the combined force and creativity of a usability team can be used efficiently during the process.

1. INTRODUCTION

As usability engineering is making its way into the mainstream of software development at Ericsson, we face the problem of integrating usability activities with the design process and putting the results of the usability work to good use in the design of products. This difficult integration often becomes acute when we try to bridge the gap, transforming the user information into an effective user interface design. To bridge this gap we use a usability engineering method called Delta. In order to build an adequate bridge, the scope of the method spans from user and task analysis to conceptual modeling and to the design of user-interface prototypes.

The face of the telecommunications market is changing rapidly, and usability has become a very important factor in attracting new customers. Following the deregulation our traditional customers, the old, large, and skilled telephone administrations, are forced to change their operation to meet the competition from the new operators. They need powerful and flexible systems to support their experienced and skilled personnel in order to stay ahead of the competition. To continue to supply these customers with our products, our systems must evolve to support the new situation.

We also want to attract the new telecom operators who want to "turn the key on the new system and start earning money". They want a system that is up and running within minutes after delivery, that keep on running with no down time, and that can be managed by unskilled personnel. In this case we have to provide most of the relevant processes rather than being able to adapt existing ones within an organization. The business processes and the general technical requirements are the same in both cases, but the new context poses dramatically different usability requirements on the user interface of the system.

The typical context for our usability engineering efforts is large, complex technical computer systems within the telecom industry. It is often a technical support system used to manage the installation, operation, and maintenance of large telecom networks. We have used the Delta Method during the development of new systems and redevelopment of existing ones. The methodology is sufficiently scaleable to be used in small projects and it is also applicable outside the telecom domain. It is more doubtful that it would support experimental prototyping as described by Smith in Chapter 11.

This chapter presents the Delta Method and how it was used in the design of the next generation of a test and simulation tool for telecom equipment. As always in case studies the context and conditions are unique, but we believe that many of the problems are universal and that our experience can be used to bridge the design gap easier.

2. OVERVIEW OF THE DELTA METHOD

The Delta Method is developed as a framework for usability activities within software development projects. The method assembles existing usability tools and practices into a usability process (see Figure 7.1) that supplements the early phases of traditional system development. It is our experience that it is crucial to perform the usability activities at the early phases of a project and as an integrated part of the system to have an impact on the system design.

In large development projects, the requirements specification often represents the "absolute truth". If usability engineering is applied too late, i.e., after the requirements have been defined, there is an apparent risk that the usability requirements will be considered as "unfeasible proposals for late changes". It then becomes a matter of either approving the usability of a finished product or to "put lipstick on the corpse". The user interface might be aesthetically pleasing, but the system will not offer the appropriate services.

The Delta Method focuses on finding and eliciting the requirements of the future users. This is accomplished through interviews, observations in the workplace, and studies of users' interaction with prototypes. The tight integration of the method into the existing system development process raises the usability requirements to the same level as the technical and functional requirements. They are no longer optional or add-ons to the requirement specification. The Delta method is summarized in following inset.

The method is designed to be used by system developers and technical communicators with limited formal knowledge of usability work. Trained usability engineers and human factors specialists are still very scarce in Swedish software development companies, a situation that has led us to adopt on-the-job training. We supply a method that produces good results even if the work is performed by workers not trained as usability specialists. Selected system developers and technical communicators take part in basic usability training and then receive support from an experienced usability engineer during their first projects.

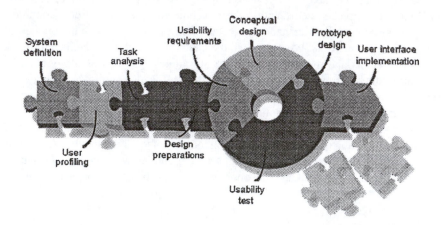

System definition: Define the scope of the proposed system and identify preliminary user categories and system services.

User profiling: Create detailed user profiles for each relevant user category.

Task analysis: Identify and record all relevant user activities of the current work practice.

Design preparations: Restructure and reinvent the current work tasks.

Usability requirements: Define usability requirements that the prototype and the finished system must meet.

Conceptual design: Create a conceptual model of the system services that support all future work tasks.

Prototyping: Design prototypes, using paper or computer, that reflect the conceptual model.

Usability tests: Observe representative users testing the prototype. Evaluate how well the system meets the requirements and redesign the prototype if necessary.

UI implementation: Support the system developers with user interface development skills during the implementation of the applications.

Other sources for information regarding the Delta Method are the Delta Method Handbook (Ericsson Infocom, 1994) and *The Delta Method — A Way to Introduce Usability* (Rantzer, 1996).

2.1. WHAT IS SPECIAL ABOUT DELTA?

The Delta method is a tool for improving the communication, both within the development team and between the team and the users. It is a way of performing usability engineering in which the system designers, technical communicators, and usability engineers are supported in carrying out the user and task analyses and in designing the user interface.

The *system designer* typically works with the definition of the system in the early phases of the project. He or she has the main responsibility for the design of the system's internal functions and the detailed design of the system services for the user interface. The systems designer usually has a background in (object-oriented) system modeling and as such is a key actor during the conceptual design.

The *technical communicator*, or technical writer, has the main responsibility for the enabling information, i.e., on-line help, user guides, etc. He or she also has to ensure that the user interface and the tasks performed by the system are designed in a way that is accessible to the user. The technical communicator plays an important role, deciding what information should be included in the system, and finding an appropriate structure for the user interface, system services, and enabling information. The technical communicator should also (together with the usability engineer) act as a link between the designers and the users since he or she often has both training and experience in how to explain complicated technical issues to inexperienced users.

The *usability engineer* will plan and lead the design of the user interface and ensure that it fulfills predefined usability requirements. This is accomplished through usability testing and evaluation of user interface prototypes. The usability engineer has formal training and/or experience in usability engineering or human factors. He or she will work together with the system designer and the technical communicator in the usability team.

Traditionally the user interface has been defined as the graphical layout of the program, as it is seen on the computer screen. The Delta Method expands this concept of user interface to have a wider meaning. According to the Delta Method a user interface consists of three equally important parts:

- The services offered to the user by the system (i.e., the functions directly supporting user tasks).
- The actual graphical presentation of the services on the screen (traditionally referred to as the user interface).
- The enabling information (e.g., the user documentation) needed by the user in order to be able to use the system efficiently.

All three aspects of the user interface are taken into consideration when the requirements on the system are defined. The process of defining the system functionality is influenced by how it is to be presented to the users and the knowledge and information that is needed to use the functions. Since the enabling information is a part of the user interface, it is important that the technical communicators and the system designers cooperate during the design process. This ensures that the different parts of the user interface are designed in a consistent way and that the services offer a comprehensive view of the system. In other words, working according to the Delta method means that system designers and technical communicators work side-by-side during analysis and design, with the aim of preserving the interests of the users.

3. THE CASE STUDY: TSS 2000

The case study describes a project to develop the next generation of a Telecom Simulation System, TSS 2000, a tool used during the installation and testing of switched and cellular communication equipment from Ericsson. TSS 2000 will typically be used to test the capacity of telephone exchanges and base stations for cellular phones. A sample test case would be "Shinkansen". Imagine the Japanese express train Shinkansen running at a speed of over 200 km/h, transporting hundreds of commuters between Osaka and Tokyo. All of them decide to call home at the same time to find out what's for dinner. TSS 2000 offers the possibility to generate a realistic traffic load and simulate how the calls are handed over between base stations along the track.

The goal of the TSS 2000 was to integrate the capabilities of two existing test tools and also offer additional services. The focus of the project was to merge the tools and rework them as necessary. It was believed that poor usability was a dominant factor in many of the user complaints about the old products. Some of the more technical problems would be addressed in the new system, but there was a need to address the usability problems in a more systematic way. During the spring of 1996 a group of system developers and technical communicators initiated a study to improve the usability of the new tool.

The purpose of the usability study was to produce

- An on-line, evolutionary prototype.
- A test specification for the user interface.
- A design specification that contains measurable requirements for both the user interface and the user documentation.
- Guidelines and recommendations for a conversion from Open Look to CDE/Motif.

Although the fact that usability had been identified as an important aspect of the new product, substantial lobbying and internal marketing was still required to get the usability study going. The effort to design and implement the functionality of the system was massive and, compared to the task of "getting the system up and running", usability was considered a minor problem. Once the study was approved we faced some restrictions:

- *Only a new UI* — The study was limited to "improving the user interface of the tool." At the start of the project there was very little understanding for the need of an "open-ended" usability study.
- *Just port it* — The old test tools ran on PC and UNIX platforms using a character-based user interface and the Open Look look and feel. Ericsson is in the process of migrating all development and test tools to Motif/CDE. The need for moving TSS 2000 to Motif/CDE was used as an argument taking the opportunity to make a complete redesign of the user interface.
- *Ready by yesterday* — The time schedule for the usability study was very tight. Everything that was not considered to be critical to the study was left for later, and every activity that we performed had to be trimmed to fit the deadlines. This has surely affected the quality of the study, but we simply had to produce the best result possible with the given limitations.

This case study is far from the schoolbook example of usability engineering; it is more of "Usability — shooting from the hip". The initial time plan for the usability study, roughly 3 months, was very short. In this time we had to perform all the necessary usability activities, and there was little background information that could be reused to help us shorten the time for the study. This meant that we had to cut every corner and constantly publish reassuring results in order to secure more time and resources.

Due to the limited resources, design decisions sometimes had to be based on results that were a bit incomplete or unfinished, but in those cases we had to trust our intuitions. A method for usability engineering has to survive in the real world, adapting to the changing characteristics of the projects. To us usability is an engineering in practice; we will never design the ultimate user interface, but we always strive to produce the best possible result with the given resources. Many times the industrial usability engineer has neither time nor interest to study exactly how unusable a product is. The mere fact that the users have problems is enough for considering a redesign.

4. BEFORE CROSSING THE GAP

The focus of this book is the actual bridge across the design gap, but in order to build the bridge we need a solid base of user data. In order to establish that base we perform a set of usability activities:

- System definition
- User profiling
- Task analysis

- Design preparations
- Usability requirements

These usability activities should result in a good understanding and description of the users, their tasks, and the environment in which they perform their work. In order to decide where to position the bridge on the other side of the gap, we also define usability requirements to describe how to verify that the new system is usable.

4.1. SYSTEM DEFINITION

The Delta Method does not address the reasons behind the decision to develop the system. This work has most often been carried out as some type of enterprise or business analysis. During the System Definition the focus is on the customer's idea of the system. It is important to make use of the customer's ability to see things from the viewpoint of the organization and to find out how the computer system fits into the company's business.

During the system definition the design group and customer representatives perform a rough analysis of the proposed system on an abstract level. The customer representatives are typically upper or middle managers, marketing people, and technical or organizational specialists. The intention is primarily to set a scope of the project, and users are not present during this activity. The purpose is to gather the customer requirements and set the stage for future, more user-centered work. The information is documented as a System Vision, a mix of the customer's expectations, concrete requirements, and preliminary user categories and system services.

The requirements on the system tend to differ a great deal, depending on whether information is gathered from the customers or the users of the system. The customers emphasize qualities such as low price, fast delivery and long life, whereas the users want a system that is fast, easy to learn, and effectively supports their work tasks. These differences in requirements are seldom observed in traditional systems design, and most often the users are completely cut off from the design work. The aim of the Delta method is to make sure that both parties are involved.

The usability team makes a rough draft of the categories of system users and their requirements on the system to create an Information Matrix. Preliminary user categories are placed on one axis and important work tasks on the other. The intersection describes what requirements a user category has on a specific task.

There was no formal system definition activity in the TSS 2000 usability study. Much of the work that is normally performed during the system definition had been conducted as internal usability marketing activities. This included seeking management support for the work, finding relevant background information, and planning the scope of the project. Therefore, when the study was approved there was neither a pressing need nor adequate time for a full scale system definition, although the scope and objectives of the TSS 2000 usability study were described in a manner similar to a system vision.

4.2. USER PROFILING

The Delta method uses questionnaires to investigate the current and future users of the system. The design group tailors a questionnaire to the domain and sends it to persons within the customer's organization who are to use the system and/or who have experienced similar systems. The results of the questionnaire are compiled and analyzed to distinguish different groups of users with different, or alternatively similar, requirements of the system. The questionnaires are used to get the big picture of the user categories. It is important to verify the results and add more details to the user profiles during the user interviews.

The questionnaire used in the case study was based on a general user questionnaire that was adapted to the target group. It included two parts: general characteristics such as age, gender, and level of education and a domain-specific part with questions regarding experience of certain work tasks and test tools. We also asked for a rating of the current tools and documentation. An excerpt of a user profile follows:

User Profile: Tester
Work experience
> The turnover for people working as testers is high. Testing is often used as a way to introduce new personnel into the organization. By performing the tests they learn all parts of the system. After some time they often move to other parts of the development organization.
> The questionnaire showed that 20% of the testers had been working in that position for less than a year, 60% between one and three years and 20% of the testers were veterans with more than five years experience.
> On the question of how long they expected to stay on as testers 40% expected they would move on within one to three years time, 40% expected to stay three to five years, and 20% planned to stay more than five years.

Work Situation
> The Testers work very independently and have a quite hectic work situation. A summary of the questionnaire shows the following characteristics:

Teamwork	To some extent
Individual work	Quite a lot
Enabling information	Possibly at hand
Time to prepare for test	Hardly sufficient
Time to conduct tests	Hardly sufficient
Time to summarize tests	Not sufficient

Existing Tools
> Most testers had no experience with the current version of the product. One that had some experience rated one of the tools as being supportive and easy to learn. The other tools received low ratings.
> None of the testers found the language in the manuals or the user interface hard to understand.

The users were also asked to describe their work tasks on a "keyword level". These general work descriptions were used to prepare the task analysis and as a basis for selecting representative users to interview. The questionnaire was sent to approximately 100 intended users, of whom 70 percent completed and returned it. To induce the users to help us, we promised them a small gift (a pen with the TSS 2000 logo) for returning the questionnaire on time.

The analysis of the questionnaire identified three user categories: test program developer, tester (as shown in the inset above), and support person. The user categories were created based on their work title, their description of their work, the tools they were using, and knowledge of the customer organization. Further analysis, after performing a number of user interviews, led us to eliminate one of the user categories, support person. The category of "tester" was split into two separate categories: system tester and function tester. The work tasks of these two categories were found to have different characteristics, which imposed some conflicting requirements on the system.

4.3. TASK ANALYSIS

Based on the user profiling, the usability team selects representative users from each category and they are asked to participate in an interview, including a task analysis session. The purpose of the interview is to identify all relevant work tasks and to study how the users perform them currently. The interviews are conducted at the workplace of the users, allowing interviewers to observe the users performing their present tasks and to capture the atmosphere of the workplace.

The observations of the users performing their tasks allow interviewers to capture the physical environment in which the work is carried out and to verify the descriptions from the interviews. The users often forget details regarding their tasks, especially when it comes to the information that is needed to perform it. In one case a user pulled down a binder, looked up something, and then returned it without a comment. Afterwards he was not able to recall what information he had accessed during the task. Spending more time at the workplace would increase the interviewers' understanding of the work climate, but usually there is little time to study this in detail.

During the interview, the user describes his or her work situation and tasks. The interviewers will try to capture the tasks in an activity graph (see Figure 7.2) which describes the user's tasks and environment. The activity graphs method of taking notes is described in a Swedish book *Verksamhetsutveckla datorsystem*

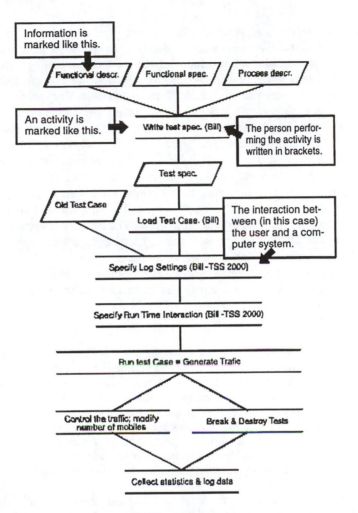

Figure 7.2 An activity graph showing part of the tasks of a tester.

(Enterprise Development of Computer Systems) by Goldkuhl (1993). To verify that the information in the graphs is correct and complete, the interviewers "play back" the description of the tasks to the user. This means that the interviewer describes the work tasks to the user as they are described in the activity graphs. It allows the user to listen and concentrate on correcting the description and adding missing information.

Eight future users of TSS 2000 were selected for interviews based on the questionnaire or after being suggested by key contacts within the customer organization. The users represented all the categories and the user characteristics found by the questionnaire. Each interview lasted approximately 2 hours and resulted in activity graphs, updated user profiles and general notes on the design of the future system.

The user interviews of the TSS 2000 project were conducted at the users' workplace. The actual interviews were conducted in an ordinary conference room, but the visit also included a guided tour of the facilities and an opportunity to observe the users performing their tasks. During the tour we also met and talked to other users that were not scheduled for the interviews. They were still very eager to tell us about their situation. The users taking part in the interviews had no problem mastering the notation and most of them actively took part in the drawing of the activity graphs. The graphs were a good way for the users to structure their story, and it helped them to recall the information needed to perform the tasks. It was also helpful in keeping the users on track. Some users were primarily interested in giving their opinion on the shortcomings of the current system and their wishes for improvement. Focusing the user on the graph helped to structure and control the interview. The activity graphs drawn in cooperation with the users were later merged into supergraphs representing a consolidated description of all the tasks of a user category.

The usability team also created general descriptions of the work tasks based on the interviews and questionnaires. The tasks of the System and Function Testers are described below:

Work Descriptions:
> **The System Tester** is handed a fairly complex test case from the Test Program Developer, with 5 to 8 test programs and a parameter set that is to be tuned during test execution. The system tests are executed over a long period of time, during which different parameters such as traffic load are constantly changed.
> **The Function Tester** writes the test programs, the test specification and the test instruction himself. The test programs are usually written from scratch. The function test programs are written to test a specific function in the telecom equipment. The Function Tester is not interested in observing the test tool while the test is running unless something goes wrong during the test set-up.

It is important to focus on the work tasks of the users and not to become involved in a discussion about the shortcomings of the current system. The expectations of the users can sometimes lead to difficulties. During a customer satisfaction survey in Japan, the users and customers reported a number of problems to the interviewer, expecting them to be fixed in the next release. Since this was not the focus of the survey, the problems remained in the next release, much to the annoyance of the Japanese customers.

4.4. DESIGN PREPARATIONS

The report of usability work so far has primarily focused on the current state of the workplace. The results reflect the users' current requirements, needs, and the shortcomings of the existing systems, but only vague ideas or hints of how the new system should support the work.

We now start the work of carefully restructuring the current work tasks and adding new tasks. The graphs are transformed into scenarios and/or new activity graphs that reflect the new way of performing the tasks. The activity graphs are often used as the starting point when writing the scenarios, but the scenarios also reflect the characteristics of the physical environment of the users. That is something that cannot easily be expressed in the graphs. The scenarios are also easier for outsiders to understand, and they are often presented to the users and customer in order to verify the services of the new system. Just as the scenarios are created to describe the future work tasks, the user profiles should be updated to define the skills and characteristics the future users will need.

One of the major mistakes of the case study was the decision to try to save time by not writing scenarios as part of the design preparations. The following inset contains a reconstruction of a potential scenario. The scenario illustrates how new tasks (in bold) are integrated into the current work.

Scenario for a Function Tester:
> The function tester Tom enters the test lab one Tuesday morning. He is a bit late since he stayed late last night **scheduling** a break & destroy test. He had estimated that the test program would crash the system when the load reached about 10 000 simultaneous calls. He therefore specified a number of **alternative tests** that should be run at such a breakdown. Just as he suspected the test had come to a halt halfway through the normal path sometime during the night. With TSS 2000 it is not difficult for Tom to analyze the log containing the relevant parameters and to **recreate the exact situation of the breakdown**. He fills in the **preformatted trouble report** and **attaches the relevant part of the log file** and **mails** it to whom it may concern.

The usability team also developed design recommendations to capture needs and requirements from the user and task analysis that had not surfaced through work with the scenarios. Two examples are:

> *Problem* — Generally the users do not work as Function Testers for more than a year or two. The personnel at some test sites consist of almost no regular testers, only consultants.
> *Recommendation* — The initial impression of using the test tool must be positive. It must be simple to learn and use; otherwise, the testers will be reluctant to use it. It is also important to provide documentation and training courses that are adapted to inexperienced testers.
> *Problem* — Many Function Testers are newcomers that do not have the skill or the time to develop extensive test programs. The time between when they get their assignment and when the testing is expected to be finished is very short.
> *Recommendation* — Offer context- and syntax-sensitive help or prompting and include good support for reuse of old test programs.

4.5. USABILITY REQUIREMENTS

The usability requirements for a system consist of test cases and requirements that the system has to meet in order to be judged minimally usable. The test cases are based on the scenarios from the design preparations, and the measurable requirements are based on tests of the current and competing systems or are based on theoretical estimates. The test cases describe realistic work situations but focus on *what* work should be performed, not *how* it should be carried out.

The Usability requirements are set to verify how well the system should support the users in their work (Gould, 1988). The Delta Method focuses on five aspects of usability: relevance, efficiency, attitude, learnability, and availability (Löwgren, 1993). An example of a requirement would be to specify the time for completion of a specific task. Another one would be to specify the number of errors allowed in completing a task. It is not always possible to find good measurements of usability for each single test case. A set of test cases is needed to extend over all parts of the system and all usability requirements.

The project manager and the customer negotiate the usability requirements in the same manner as when defining the functional requirements. The result of this activity is the usability requirements that are a part of the requirements specification and a usability test specification describing how to verify the requirements. In the usability study we began with five test cases with associated usability requirements. One of them can be seen in following inset. These test cases did not provide comprehensive coverage of the complete set of system services, but rather those available in the first paper prototype. More test cases were added later and some of the initial ones evolved during the prototyping and usability tests.

Usability Requirements:
> *Test case*: You have been enrolled in project Gizmo as a function tester. A number of test scripts have been prepared by a colleague. Use TSS 2000 to start the test script "Alpha" and increase the traffic load until the number of dropped calls reaches 100.
>
> *Relevance*: 90% of the users are required not to invoke more than one irrelevant command.
>
> *Efficiency*: 90% of the users are required to complete the task in less than two minutes.
>
> *Attitude*: All users are required to prefer the new system over the present.
>
> *Learnability*: The time spent using the documentation shall be less than 1 minute.
>
> *Availability*: 95% of the users are required to find relevant help in less than 20 seconds.

5. BRIDGING THE GAP

The actual bridge across the design gap consists of two activities: Conceptual Design and User Interface Design. During the conceptual design the system services found during the task analysis are structured into an implementation independent conceptual model. This model is transformed into a paper prototype describing the actual layout of the user interface on the target platform.

5.1. CONCEPTUAL DESIGN

The goal of the conceptual design is to create a conceptual model of the system that allows the users to concentrate on their work tasks instead of manipulating the system. Initially, this work is carried out on a comprehensive, abstract level, where decisions are made about which services the system should offer and how to present those services in ways that are logical to the users.

There are other important issues in connection with the conceptual design:

* What metaphors can be used to exploit the users' previous experiences from other areas?
* Which enabling information is needed for the users to be able to actually make use of the services offered?

These general issues are addressed iteratively during "time-outs" in the conceptual design work. At the start of the conceptual design it is very difficult to find good metaphors that support the services, but a good metaphor makes the work of structuring the services much easier. It is the "Catch-22" of conceptual design. The work of finding a metaphor is described in more detail later in this chapter.

5.1.1. The Workshop

The main work during the conceptual design phase is carried out as one or more workshops. The main task of the workshop is to define a structure for the services offered by the system. The background material, consisting of user profiles, activity graphs, scenarios, design recommendations, and a concept list[1], is used to cluster related system services, objects, and intentions into focus areas. The focus areas describe the actions a user might perform on relevant objects at a given time. The concept and notation of focus areas are based on the work of Holtzblatt and Beyer (1993).

Because of the large number of aspects that determine if a system is to be usable, the conceptual design tries to reflect as many of these aspects as possible by bringing together individuals with a variety of relevant skills in sketching an overall structure of the user interface. The work at the workshops is very intense, but it is the best way for a group to produce the blueprints for the user interface and to achieve a shared understanding of the users and their work tasks. It works well to run at least two workshops, with each workshop lasting two or three days.

---

[1]   The concept list is a collection of user terms and their meaning. It is continually updated during the run of the project.

The time plan for TSS 2000 only allowed for one 2-day workshop. This allowed time to design a basic service structure, but left very little time to discuss alternative solutions.

5.1.2. Participants in the Workshop

In order to make the workshop and the continued development run smoothly and efficiently, it is important that the participants represent the team that will design, implement, and test both the user interface and the intrinsics of the product. In large design projects it is impossible to have all designers taking part in the workshop, but since there are often several design teams working in parallel it is important to have key representatives present. It is also important to get "buy-in" from the developers who are going to implement the real user interface. The mix of skills also allows a more holistic approach to the design of the user interface by always having people present who know the different areas.

The participants of the case study workshop were

- A moderator
- A system designer
- A technical communicator
- A GUI-prototyper
- A system architect
- A system tester (of TSS 2000)

The workshop is led by a moderator who is responsible for the "flow" of the work, for effective management of discussions, and for keeping the group focused on the work process. In the case of the TSS 2000 workshop, the moderator had limited knowledge of the previous products and the work domain of the users. This proved very productive because it kept discussions from lapsing into unnecessary details. It also forced the participants to describe the tasks and problems of the users in a manner that made it easier to form a conceptual model.

The usability study was jointly led by a system developer and a technical communicator, both of whom were experienced in their respective fields, and also were knowledgeable with the Delta Method. The technical communicator had developed the user manuals for some of the previous tools and was therefore aware of the many difficulties involved in explaining the use the old system. She also provided most of the suggestions on how the user information should be divided among the on-line help, on-line documentation, and the user guide. The system developer had the best knowledge of the current users and their tasks because of having documented the results of the task analyses and the activity graphs earlier.

The GUI-prototyper had not taken part in the user and task analysis and therefore needed to quickly understand the most important aspects of the earlier work so as to effectively implement the computer prototype later in the study.

During the later stages of the conceptual design, he could also offer advice on how different concepts could be represented graphically.

The system architect had been one of the driving forces during the development of the current versions of the test tools. He was extremely knowledgeable on the design of the current test tools and on all the technical aspects of the equipment the users test, such as the operating system and communication protocols.

The system tester had long experience of testing and debugging the current version of one of the test tools. Several of these tests were performed at the customer's work sites in cooperation with the users of the system, so he had developed a good understanding of the characteristics of the users' tasks and their workplace.

5.1.3. The Design Room

The design room acts as a repository for all usability information that is gathered during the course of the project. We strongly recommend the Design Room approach suggested by Karat and Bennet (1991). In some projects, including this one, we have experienced problems enforcing the "sanctuary" of the design room. The reasons have varied from "No vacancies" to "I need the relevant information available at my desk".

In the usability study of TSS 2000 we did not use a permanent Design Room for the usability work. Instead the workshop was held at a small conference hotel away from the city. This arrangement allowed us to focus on the work without being disturbed. The walls of conference room were used for posting the background information and new information was constantly being added to the walls.

The moderator was constantly on his feet heading the discussion, moving between the different walls. All conclusions were first sketched on the white board; when the concept started to stabilize it was summarized on a flip chart; finally, when the subject was "closed", the paper was moved to the appropriate wall. This way of working allowed the concepts to gradually mature and then be added to the facts and assumptions concerning the users and their tasks or to the emerging design described in the User Environment Diagram.

5.1.4. Walk-Through of the Background Material

When all the background material has been posted on the appropriate walls, the team conducted a walk-through of the information. The walk-through during the TSS 2000 workshop developed into an interview where the moderator interviewed the participants, walking through all the background information that was visible on the walls. This gave all the participants a basic understanding of the facts, with more details available from the system developer and the technical communicator on request. The other participants offered their reflections on the data as they were presented, and relevant comments were added to the user profiles and activity graphs.

The walk-through has several purposes:

- It is an effective way to introduce the material to participants that has not been part of the user and task analysis.
- It is an effective way to check that the material is correct and complete. Participants can add their individual experience to the description. Note: It is a good idea to separate (by color coding) the facts from the user and task analysis from the information added during the walk-through. The assumptions of the group can then be verified before they are used as bases for major design decisions.
- It is an effective way of achieving consensus and a shared view of the users and their work tasks.

The main focus for the walk-through was the user profiles and activity graphs. We had more material visible on the walls (e.g., the design recommendations and screen shots of the old user interface), but time constraints forced us to leave them out of the discussion.

The important characteristics of each user category were summarized an a large paper sheet. For each category we tried to jointly answer questions such as, "Who is this user?" and "What is important to him or her?" Together we reassembled the users from the essential information we had collected about them so that they would appear as people we all knew and could relate to.

The activity graphs proved to be the first obstacle of the workshop. The level of detail was simply not sufficient. We needed more details, regarding the actual work, the information needed to perform each activity, and the information that would result from the activities. The system designer and technical communicator who had produced the graphs actually knew much more than was reflected in the graphs. It was simply a matter of extracting the information and having the system architect and the tester verify and supplement the information they had acquired themselves. Once again the moderator acted as an interviewer, leading the discussion and adjusting the level of detail in each graph.

During these discussions we noted several possible improvements to the work process. One user behavior that had been observed was refined by the group into new services for the system. The tests run by the system testers were often tedious and time consuming because of the need to simply wait for things to either break or to conclude in a normal fashion. The tests were often run overnight, but there was no support for this way of working. The test could run for hours before halting or could stop the moment the tester left. In either case the tester needed to be able to specify alternative test paths or what should happen in the test tool when an error occurred.

This rather detailed walk-through compensated for the fact that there were no scenarios prepared in advance. The activity graphs served as a guiding thread and we jointly created scenarios as needed. I would recommend that the design team have prepared scenarios to describe the future work tasks of the user. The scenarios are easier to verify with the users than are some forms of graphical work description.

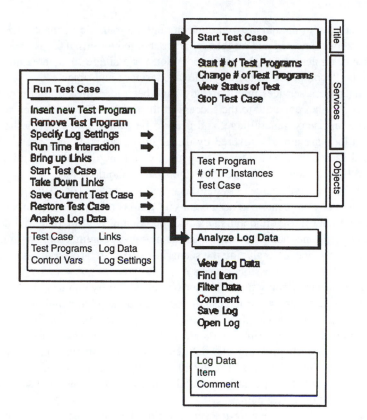

Figure 7.3 Turning an activity graph into a focus area.

5.1.5. User Environment Diagrams

The goal of User Environment Diagrams (UEDs) is to structure the services and objects of the system in a way that support the users' tasks without imposing a strict task order. The structure is implementation independent, even if in reality the choice of platform and "look and feel" is often obvious or not under the control of the design team.

A focus area describes what system services and objects a user requires to solve a defined task. The services might be simple, possibly corresponding to a single function in the user interface, or to a complex set of functions, where there is a need to decompose functions into new focus areas with additional but less complex services and objects. An example from the case study can be found in Figure 7.3.

The activity graphs are the starting point for identifying possible focus areas. Each activity in the graphs is a candidate for becoming a focus area. The team needs to be flexible and to keep an open mind when identifying candidates for the focus areas. There is not a one-to-one mapping between an activity in the activity graphs and a focus area in the user environment diagram. Several activities might be intimately connected and might need to be merged to form a focus area. On the other hand, an activity might be too complex for a single focus area and might need to be decomposed to identify relevant services and objects.

Some system services might already have been identified in the information matrix as services essential to the success of the system. These services are often described on a very general level and need to be analyzed to identify the extent to which they are already covered by the activity graphs. If they are vital, they should already be accounted for. If they are not present, the customer might have a very different view of what services the system should offer!

Another potential source of system services are scenarios describing the future work practice. The scenarios and the activity graphs reflect the same reality, but scenarios often offer more details and also include more of the potential difficulties and exceptions that the system must be able to accommodate. A simple and straightforward way of analyzing the scenarios is to search for verbs as candidate services and nouns as possible objects.

The process of finding possible user objects is tightly connected with identifying system services. A service usually operates on an object and, if a service is identified, the related object(s) are usually close by. The information objects in the activity graphs are often prime candidates for becoming objects or focus areas for managing the information objects (data entry, database management, etc.). Another source of information is the concept list, which defines the users' meanings of all terms. It is used to identify potential objects and to ensure that services and objects have appropriate names.

In most cases it is easy to describe the flow between the focus areas. They might be identified from the connections in the activity graphs or be quite obvious, for example, when a focus area has been decomposed into subareas. The situation can get more complex if several focus areas use the same system services or even the same subareas. This is an indication that perhaps further investigation is needed, possibly resulting in restructuring of the focus areas. There is no rule that prohibits this multiple use of services, but our experience is that the resulting user interface often becomes more complex. Therefore, it is easier to resolve the matter during the conceptual design.

5.1.6. Conceptual Design in TSS 2000

The conceptual design of the case study was highly interactive, involving the entire usability team. The moderator selected a central activity from the activity graphs and led the discussion regarding services and objects that would be relevant to the user when performing the activity. The session began with the design team suggesting the services and objects to include in a focus area. The suggestions were written on colored notes and added to the focus area on the white-board. Whether or not the group found it easier to identify the services or objects first was dependent on the problem domain. In practice, it did not really matter because the two sets were interdependent. If a service was identified first, it was usually easy to identify related objects and vice versa.

All system services (yellow notes) and user objects (white notes) were organized on the white-board under a suitable title for the focus area. If a service was complex it was decomposed into subareas, each of which consisted of more detailed services and objects. The flow between the focus areas was indicated by arrows on the white-board.

Once a focus area or group of areas seemed to be stable (i.e., no additional services or objects could be found and no system service was judged to be overly complex), it was copied from the white-board to a flip-chart and then posted on a wall. The white-board allowed the freedom to quickly add or revise services, subareas and objects. Moving the information onto paper was a natural way to accomplish a sense of closure to the work process, giving the structure greater stability, but still allowing further comments or revisions. This process allowed us to maintain some structure in the design process and to avoid excessive debate on issues. The moderator determined when the level of detail was sufficient and when it was time to consider a new focus area.

When an activity graph had been fully analyzed and converted into a number of focus areas, the scenarios were used to verify that the service structure described by the UED was correct and complete. Since we lacked explicit user scenarios in the case study, we used the user profiles and the activity graphs to create hypothetical scenarios. When they are the basis for the focus areas, it may seem circular to test the diagrams using scenarios from the activity graphs. Surprisingly, the hypothetical scenarios revealed several problems and inconsistencies in the design and were an excellent substitute for real scenarios, given our situation.

5.1.7. The Result

The mood of the design team after the workshop was a feeling of urgency mixed with weariness regarding the application being developed. We still managed to muster up enough enthusiasm to "publish" the results of the workshop. All material from the workshop was put on a wall in the hallway back at the office. We arranged a walk-through of the user environment diagrams for other developers, relevant management, and knowledgeable customer representatives. We felt it was important to continually communicate the status of the project, and it was an excellent opportunity to get buy-in and reactions from managers *before* the design. It was also important to quickly establish a common view of the outcome of the workshop, which could serve as a baseline for future discussions.

5.2. USER INTERFACE DESIGN

After the conceptual design has been completed and all relevant parts of the system have been structured as focus areas, we begin the prototype design. The structure described in the conceptual model is implementation independent, but during the prototype design we commit the design to the style, features, and limitations of the target platform. During the transformation we work extensively with low-fidelity paper prototypes. The visual design of the user interface is still of little concern. The first priority is to decide how the objects and services of one or several focus areas should be represented as user interface components. The structure and realization of the interface are gradually refined during the prototype design. The work of prototype design is highly iterative. We work our way through the user environment diagram, transforming focus areas into user interface elements.

When the paper prototype is judged to be adequate, the work proceeds by sketching the layout of "screen windows", using a prototyping tool. Parallel to this work, the structure and contents of the enabling information is outlined in a step-by-step process, using prototypes. We run usability tests on both the paper prototypes and the computer prototypes that are produced later. The prototype design work is completed when the usability requirements have been fulfilled or the planned number of iterations has been reached. The result of this activity is documented in a design specification, of which the prototype is a part.

Usually the design work is organized as a second workshop in a design room, but most of the work on the initial TSS 2000 paper prototype was actually conducted in the hallway outside the room of one of the designers. This approach of taking the work out in the open had several advantages:

- Unlimited workspace. All UEDs and activity graphs were placed on the same wall. The opposite wall was used for alternative screen layouts. It was easy to browse the UED, turn around, and turn the focus area into screen elements.
- High visibility. It was easy to show that we had made progress.
- Instant feedback. It was very easy for outsiders to comment on the work and the data.
- Quick test runs. The structure of the user interface could be verified instantly using the scenarios or the activity graphs.

Posting results in the hallway also proved to have drawbacks. When there was a need for closed discussion, all material had to be moved from the hallway into a conference room. When the meeting was finished, all the material had to be returned to the hallway. After a time the material was simply kept in rolls and piles between meetings.

5.2.1. Opening Screen — Main Window

One of the first and most important tasks of the prototype design is to find an effective way to introduce the users to the system. The main window is usually the first thing the users come in contact with, and it is a window that will continue to be the basis for their work. We basically look at three different aspects when designing the main window of the application:

- *Vital tasks* — those that are vital for the user to perform well, even under heavy stress. Example: A network supervisor continually monitors the traffic in a network. If something goes wrong (e.g., someone cuts off a cable), it is important that the user be able to asses the situation quickly and reroute the traffic.
- *Frequent tasks* — those tasks that users spend a majority of their time performing need to be done effectively, and the system should offer alternative ways of performing them. Example: Directory inquiries, or any similar data query application, need to offer good support for the limited number of tasks that the users perform during each call.
- *Navigational aid* — the users need to understand quickly and easily what the application is capable of doing and how they should go about accomplishing the tasks. Example: Information kiosks, which need to be easy to learn and use without instructions.

It is desirable to design a user interface that supports all these aspects well. In most cases this is not possible, and the characteristics of the users and their work tasks should be used to determine how to optimize the user interface for the most important aspects.

In the main window of TSS 2000, we focused on providing navigational aid by introducing the central concept or metaphor of a "test case". The system was to be used by several categories of users. All of them had a number of important (but not vital) tasks to perform, and none of the tasks were highly repetitive. With good navigational aid, each category of users would find it easy to find and work with their section of the application. We also wanted to offer good support for the frequently performed tasks, but these tasks were better suited to their own windows, depending on the different categories of users and their work.

5.2.2. Choosing a Metaphor

The purpose of a metaphor is to exploit the users' existing knowledge. The user can relate to the contents and operations of the user interface based on their earlier real world experiences through the metaphor.

The initial proposal for a metaphor in the case study was to visualize the test situation in terms of the physical connections of the test equipment. If a person connected something to the test tool he or she would see a representation of it on the main window. To configure a connection he or she would just click on it and fill in the relevant data. This metaphor did serve its purpose as a visualization of complex concepts such as mapping and configuration of physical and logical links. It was dismissed, however, because it supported only a small part of the task. It could not be used as a central supporting concept, but it was later reused in a window for configuring the test equipment.

The user interface of TSS 2000 needed a metaphor that could provide integration and structure to all relevant tasks. Setting up and running a test involves many different disparate activities often performed by several people. We needed a metaphor that would represent some central well-known concept that could unite the work of all users. The metaphor "test cases" was chosen as the main theme of the application. A test case is a collection of all the information that is relevant

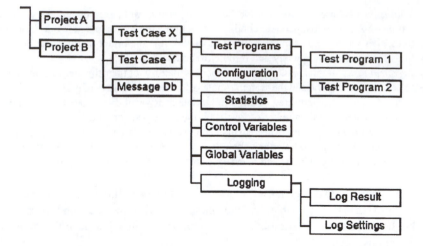

Figure 7.4 The hierarchy of a test case.

when performing a system or function test. The users of TSS 2000 either prepare the tests by developing the contents of a test case or execute the tests using the prefabricated test cases. The test case was an existing concept known to all users, but it was not reflected in any of the present applications. In order to visualize the test case we chose to impose a hierarchical structure that described its contents (see Figure 7.4). The lack of structure to the test data was a recurring comment during the task analysis, and by making the hierarchy of the test cases more explicit we aimed to solve this problem.

The metaphor also supported the testers when they reused test programs and data from old test cases or from each other. Reuse was not supported by the current tool. Instead it involved a very cumbersome procedure of making a complete copy of the database in use and then removing the irrelevant parts.

Previous experience outside this project provides a good example of how the choice of an appropriate metaphor is very important since it will affect many design decisions. During a preliminary study of what was to become one of the existing test tools, we used a prototype to help customers visualize the suggested capabilities of the system. The developers of the prototype had very limited knowledge of the domain and no usability activities had been performed. The target group for the prototype was in fact the customers and not the end users. The prototype could therefore show a very simplified view of two difficult areas that the tool needed to support — running the tests and presenting the test results.

The metaphor used to present the information during a test run was conceived from the layout of an audio mixer used to record music in studios. The channels of the mixer represented the eight test ports of the test tool. The status of the test ports was presented at run-time as "VU-meters" and test parameters could be changed dynamically by turning "knobs" on the mixer board. The execution of the test could be controlled by "play" and "stop" buttons on each channel. The metaphor supported a very simple and attractive visualization of the test execution, but it failed to support several important aspects of the task. Instead of making the system more usable, the metaphor became a liability and constricted the use of the tool.

The metaphor failed to capture the fact that most test cases would run for several hours, usually during the night. There would not be any tester to review the test results on the screen or to change the parameters during the test run. Furthermore, it did not include support for presenting or analyzing logs or other historical data that could reveal what had happened during the night. The easy operation of the tests and the instant visual feedback looked very impressive to the customers when they used the system only for a few minutes during the prototype demonstration but it did not support the work of the real users.

5.2.3. Transforming the Conceptual Model into a user Interface Design

The work of transforming the UEDs into user interface elements is a combination of straightforward mapping of the focus areas to window elements and sparks of innovation. In most cases the focus areas translate into a child window or a dialogue box with the services as menu items and with the attributes of the objects as GUI widgets (e.g., fields, check boxes, radio buttons, etc.).

It is often possible to use the metaphor or the content of the main window as a starting point for translating a group of focus areas representing a complete task into interface components. The relevant objects in a focus area are either visible in the main window or there should be a service to make them visible. The service of selecting an object is often implemented as a mouse operation or as the result of searching or filtering.

The services connected to the selected object should now be available as menu items or through some form of direct manipulation such as a double-click or as an item on a tool bar. A typical result would be a change of focus to a new area in the UED and the opening of a dialogue box or child window in the user interface. The window would display the objects of the new focus area such as lists, fields, or other means of data entry. The services might be accessible through menu items, buttons, or keyboard entry.

Sparks of innovation are needed to know when to depart from this general approach and to search for similarities between areas and services that can be combined into more complex windows or dialogue boxes. A typical example of merging two focus areas into the same window or dialogue box is the creation of an object and the editing of its contents. Initially two separate areas may result from the users having different foci during the conceptual design. However, when areas contain basically the same objects and services, they can often be merged. An example of the conversion of a focus area into a dialogue box is shown in Figure 7.5.

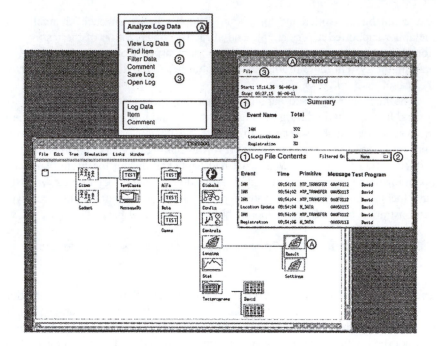

Figure 7.5 A focus area converted into a dialogue box.

Once a structure of windows and dialogue boxes start to emerge it is necessary to resolve potential conflicts between different screen elements. Elements often compete for screen space, and it is necessary to decide what aspects in the dialogue box that are most important to the user. The style guides and guidelines give some guidance when selecting and organizing the dialogue boxes, but it still requires training and experience to create an attractive and well-organized user interface.

In the case study we used the hierarchical representation of the test case as the central concept in the main window. To it we added a menu containing services to cut/copy/paste the elements of a test case. We also needed some way to edit the contents of an element, a way to control the execution of a test, and a way to represent the result. For this purpose we created a dynamic workspace where the content changed depending on what the user wanted to do.

In order to supply the users with relevant information connected to the task they carried out, we added an information area in the main window. The content of this area changed depending on what elements the users were working with. Connected to this area were services to change the information and to add private or public comments.

The initial layout for the TSS 2000 main window consists of three parts:

• On the left was the hierarchic structure of the test case.

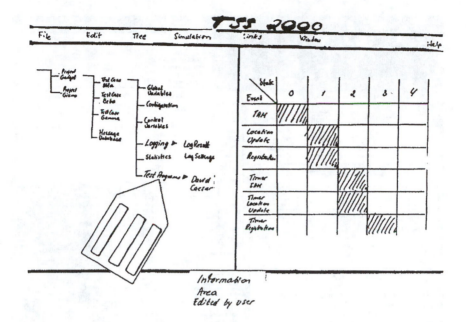

Figure 7.6 An early version of a paper prototype. Note the mouse/pointer that the users used to manipulate the interface.

- On the right was a dynamic workspace. The content of the workspace is dependent on the element that was selected in the left window.
- At the bottom was an information area. The information is connected to the element selected.

An early version of a paper prototype is shown in Figure 7.6. Note the representation of the mouse/pointer used to manipulate the interface. This paper prototype was tested by users performing realistic test cases. At this stage the prototype was too crude to meet any of the usability requirements, but simply observing the users work with it led us to make both major and minor changes to the design.

The main window was split into a new main window containing the test case tree, a separate child window for information, and several additional child windows. The child windows contained the services and objects to solve specific tasks, such as writing a test program or controlling the execution of a test. The split was generated by the users' need to have information relating to several focus areas available at the same time. A later version of the user interface with these windows can be seen in Figure 7.7.

We also developed a prototype of the user documentation for the system. In the initial prototype, it consisted only of a table of contents with an alphabetic index on the back. When the users needed help they turned to the manual and selected what they thought to be a suitable entry. One of the designers then acted

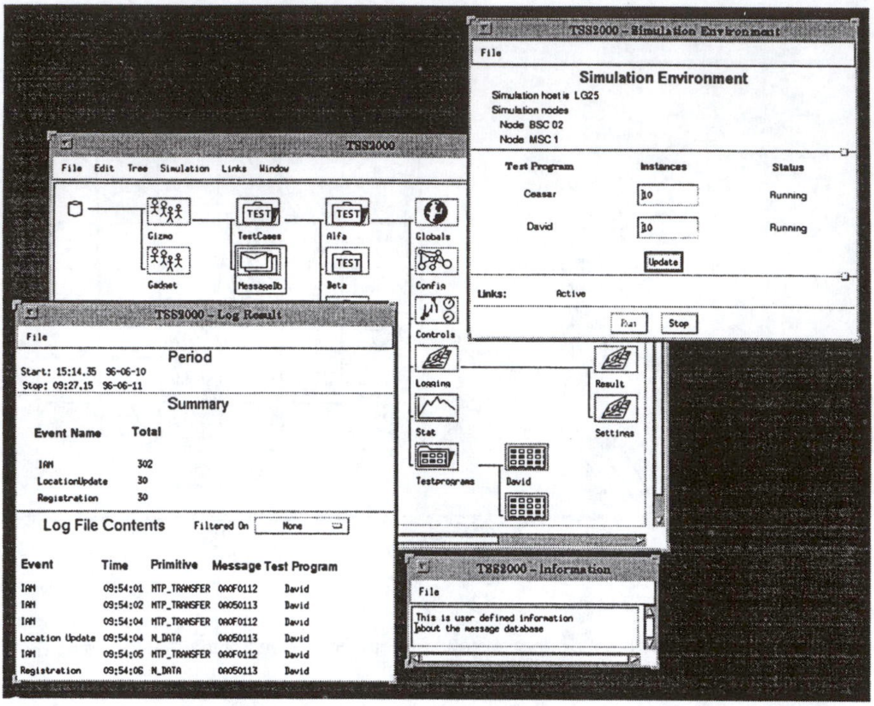

Figure 7.7 A computer prototype showing the main window.

as a "talking manual" giving the user the kind of advice they would find in the finished documentation. We tried to avoid making the talking manual overly interactive, thus avoiding excessive user support. We were interested in what specific enabling information the user needed to solve the tasks.

6. AFTER THE BRIDGE

It is difficult to determine at what stage the gap has been successfully bridged. The process of prototype design and usability testing is highly iterative, but once user testing is begun, even if with a paper prototype, the gap is crossed.

6.1. USABILITY TESTS

The activity of testing and evaluating the interface is intimately connected to the prototype design. By testing the prototype, the design group will find out how well it meets the requirements. Also, the users are given the opportunity to give their opinions about the proposed design. Representatives from the various user categories participate in the testing by being invited to carry out a number of tasks or "test cases". using the prototype.

The design group records how well users carry out their tasks and compare the result to the usability requirements for the system. All problems that the users experience during the tests are addressed in the subsequent prototype, which, in its turn, is tested and revised. This process continues until the usability requirements are met or until a specified number of iterations have been performed. The result of the test and evaluation activity are recorded for each user.

When we performed usability tests of the paper prototype for the case study, we ran short of prepared scenarios! This resulted from a combination of factors. The paper prototype did not implement the entire user interface, and we tried to steer the users away from those parts that were incomplete. The users also managed to solve the tasks too quickly. When the test cases were created, we were concerned that they would be too difficult and complex. As a result, we oversimplified them. Finally, we had too little time available for development of the tests. It is difficult and time consuming to design effective test tasks, and when the users arrive to participate in testing, it is necessary to use what is available, even if it isn't optimal. To gather additional usability information, we often used the debriefing session following the usability test for a more comprehensive interview. During these interviews, the users were encouraged to talk freely both about the paper prototype and the tasks that were not yet supported by the tool.

6.2. COMPUTER PROTOTYPE

A computer simulation or on-line prototype was developed using a user interface management system. The work with the computer prototype began before all parts of the user interface had been designed on paper. The two prototypes were developed in parallel, moving the stable parts of the paper prototype to the computer version. The computer prototype eventually "caught up" with the paper prototype and it was then abandoned. Figure 7.7 contains a computer prototype showing the main window of the application.

Additional problems with this version of the layout were discovered during the tests. The users liked the hierarchical organization of the test cases, but they had difficulty handling large numbers of test cases. The concept of "Test Suites", consisting of several related test cases, is currently being evaluated.

The usability tests of the computer prototype have been very successful, and the user interface has been viewed favorably by the users, the customers, and the responsible management personnel within Ericsson. Attention to usability issues increased dramatically following a series of demonstrations of the prototype. Using the computer prototype as visual proof of our work increased the understanding of what we attempt to accomplish, or as a colleague outside the project expressed it, "Now I understand the purpose of the questionnaires, interviews and graphs, but why didn't you start out with designing the prototype?"

7. CONCLUSIONS

The way of working that we have described does not eliminate the "magic" or creativity needed to bridge the design gap, but usability engineering enables us to structure the work and make better use of the skills in the design team. We believe that one part of the magic is the learning process that the individual designer and the usability team take part in during analysis and design. The joint discovery of the user information and the subsequent discussions within the team enable them to manage more complex information and to develop solutions that encompass more aspects of the work tasks.

One of the initial restrictions of the study was that the scope was limited to "improving the user interface of the tool". There was very little understanding of the need for an "open-ended" usability study. This turned out to be a smaller problem than one might expect. During the early phases of the usability work (user and task analysis), this constraint did not become an issue. During the conceptual design and prototyping we had gained enough credibility to be able to suggest changes that would affect the underpinnings of the system. Having one of the system architects in the usability group allowed us to suggest solutions that were inexpensive and easy to implement, but which improved the usability of the system considerably. Still, the unwillingness of project managers to allow us to design from "scratch" affected what services we chose to support and how we wanted to implement them in the prototype.

We believe that the need for a general usability questionnaire will diminish or change over time. As the Delta Method is used as an integrated part of system development, we will be able to build a repository of user information that can be reused in later studies. This will allow us to focus on other issues such as internationalization and localization of the user interface.

Producing effective activity graphs and scenarios has proved to be very important to the success of the usability work. They are very good ways to capture and visualize the tasks that the system is to support and an excellent platform for modeling a suitable user interface.

The central usability activities presented in this chapter are the two workshops to produce the conceptual model and the user interface design. Concentrating the work to a limited time and space (a few days in a design room) provides a number of benefits:

- The design room acts as a repository for all relevant information and reduces the disturbances from the outside world.
- There is a foreseeable end to the workshop that enables intense work, followed by a period of contemplation.
- The mix of skills allows for different views on a problem or design idea and it gives the team a broad knowledge base. Including people from later stages in the project (e.g., testers) also introduces a measure of concurrent engineering into the work.
- An outside moderator can concentrate on keeping the design process going, and can reduce low-level discussions.

The case study has provided us with valuable experience that has led to improvements of the Delta Method. Some of them have already been used in subsequent projects and have resulted in improvements of both the process and the result. An example of this is the work process of the workshops that has improved considerably in subsequent projects. Discussing possible metaphors during time-outs was introduced as a way to cool down heated design discussions, but it also proved to be an effective way to interleave high- and low-level design activities. During the walk-through of the background information, we now also identify one or two core activities for each activity graph. These activities are the first ones to be transformed into focus areas. This helps us address the most important, and often most difficult, parts first and forces the remainder of the design to conform. In later projects we have also added time (20 to 30 minutes) for the team members to work individually on transforming the activities into focus areas. The parallel designs are then presented on a white-board and merged into one solution, retaining the best ideas from all designs.

The most tangible result from the conceptual design phase is a structure of system services described with UEDs. Since it is based on the activity graphs, it generally reflects the order in which work tasks are carried out. However, the focus areas also include the user objects. This creates a more object-oriented user interface with greater freedom of choice of the order in which to perform tasks. So far the user interfaces have been object oriented rather than structured, but a heavier focus on the system services would allow for a more structured interface.

The second workshop, turning the model into a user interface paper prototype, has become much more structured as a result of the case study, and we have moved our posting of intermediate results from the hallway into a design room. The level of detail in the paper prototype has varied considerably across projects and also between different parts of the same prototype. We are still working to find the proper balance.

One of the most important conclusions from the study is that a method such as Delta does not stifle the creativity that is needed to design good user interfaces. Instead it helps to structure the work so that the combined force and creativity of a usability team can be used efficiently during the design of the user interface.

8. ACKNOWLEDGMENTS

I would like to acknowledge the members of the unofficial Delta Group at Ericsson Radio Systems in Linköping, with special thanks to Åsa Bäckström, Åsa Dahl, and Cecilia Bretzner. Thanks also to Jonas Löwgren of Linköping University Susan Dray of Dray & Associates and the members of ZeLab, The Systems Engineering Lab at Ericsson, who have made valuable comments on this chapter.

9. BACKGROUND TO THE DELTA METHOD

The Delta Method was developed as a joint effort by Ericsson in Linköping and Linköping University. The method development group consisted of technical communicators and system designers at Ericsson, and researchers within these fields at the Linköping University. The researchers represented the Department of Computer and Information Science and the Institute of Tema Research, Department of Technology and Social Change. The development was supported by the Swedish National Board for Industrial and Technical Development (NUTEK). The project was a part of the ITYP venture for increased efficiency and skill in the services sector.

The Delta Method is marketed and distributed outside Ericsson by WM-Data Education in Linköping, Sweden.

10. REFERENCES

Ericsson Infocom, *The Delta Method Handbook.*, Internal Ericsson Document, 1994.

Goldkuhl, G., *Verksamhetsutveckla datsystem*, Intention AB, Linköping Sweden, 1993.

Gould, J. (1988). Designing usable systems, in *Handbook of Human-Computer Interaction*, Helander, M., Ed., Elsevier, Amsterdam, 1988, 757-789.

Holzblatt, K. and Beyer, H., Making customer-centered design work for teams, *Communications of the ACM*, 36(10):93-103, 1993.

Karat, J. and Bennett, J.L., Using scenarios in design meetings — a case study example, in, *Taking Software Design Seriously: Practical Techniques for Human-Computer Interface Design*, Karat, J., Ed., Harcourt Brace Jovanovich, San Diego, 1991, 63–94.

Löwgren, J., *Human-Computer Interaction — What Every System Developer Should Know*, Studentlitteratur, Lund Sweden, 1993.

Rantzer, M., The Delta Method — A Way to Introduce Usability, in *Field Methods Casebook for Software Design*, Wixon, D. and Ramey, J., Eds., Wiley Computer Publishing, New York 1996, 91-112.

CHAPTER 8

Transforming User-Centered Analysis into User Interface: The Redesign of Complex Legacy Systems

Sabine Rohlfs
IF Interface Consulting Ltd., Ottawa, Canada

TABLE OF CONTENTS

1. INTRODUCTION

This chapter describes a pragmatic approach to building a bridge from user/system requirements to a reasonably polished user interface design. Managing the building process efficiently and effectively is of critical importance in bridge building and, therefore, usability project management issues are addressed throughout. The goal is to provide heuristics for scoping and estimating usability project tasks, the content of usability deliverables within a widely used framework for information systems architecture, and suggestions for managing user involvement. The emphasis here is on practical suggestions and solutions, because this reflects the author's experience developing and implementing such user interface designs.

The bridge from user/system requirements to a reasonably polished user interface design is built by carrying out a sequence of well-defined project tasks. For each task, building the bridge requires a carefully thought out project methodology, approach, and plan, appropriate tools, methods, and people. It also requires metrics to measure the quality of the results at each step.

The scalability of methods and their appropriate selection is a significant challenge; yet it is crucial to success. The author's experience has been that there is no one-size-fits-all set of user interface design methods, guidelines, and techniques that are applicable to all projects. Rather, each project requires a custom-tailored set of methods, guidelines, and techniques. When deciding which ones to apply and how to custom-tailor them, several factors shape the decision:

- Product for sale vs. in-house application.
- Product/application upgrade vs. new product/application (no manual or computerized system to accomplish the user tasks exists (i.e., "this has never been done before").
- Degree of novelty of the technology (e.g., Graphical User Interfaces (GUIs) are tried and proven, whereas an interface combining a small display and voice recognition technology is relatively new, with many unanswered questions and few guidelines for design).
- The availability of real vs. surrogate users.
- The nature of the user interface assignment: firefighting ("we have major usability problems, the project is already over budget, and the deadline for roll-out is x weeks/months from today") vs. fire prevention ("we want to integrate usability into the project right from the start").
- Size of the project in terms of function points, budget, staff, and number of stake holders.
- The budget, staff/consultants, and time available for the user interface work.

This chapter presents a pragmatic approach to redesigning the user interface for so-called legacy systems (by contrast, design for novelty products is addressed in the chapters of this volume by Smith, Chapter 11, and by Scholtz and Salvador, Chapter 9).

1.1. REDESIGNING COMPLEX LEGACY SYSTEMS: CHARACTERISTICS OF PROJECTS

Typically, these systems are a set of transaction-oriented, mainframe-based systems for administrative and/or customer service purposes. Systems for public administration, managing a financial/insurance portfolio for a customer, or managing supply, warehousing, and distribution are popular examples. In terms of the characteristics mentioned above, these projects can be described as follows:

- The project is an in-house application for several thousand users across one or many countries with a unilingual or multilingual user interface.
- The project is an application upgrade. Existing work flows and tasks are redesigned "a little" so that users become more sales and customer-service oriented: users become advisors to customers about a wider range of products and services offered by their organization. In fact, the new technology serves as a vehicle to introduce a major shift in organizational culture, including changes to required staff expertise (the new system requires generalists rather than specialists; the system provides the specialist knowledge), staffing levels and staff organization, and rewards.
- The user interface will be a unifying Graphical User Interface (GUI) facade so that all the applications are presented to the users as a single integrated application, rather than as a set of stand-alone applications. A set of stand-alone mainframe-based systems is migrated to a client-server environment employing object-oriented technologies or a client-server front end is developed leaving the legacy systems intact at the back end.

- Frequently there is at least one piece of so-called commercial-off-the-shelf (COTS) software, i.e., a commercial software package that addresses part of the required functionality. By implication, the COTS software has its own idiosyncratic user interface, and the design challenge is to fit the additional software (frequently labeled "COTS extensions" though the extensions are often more substantial than the COTS core) with the COTS software. The degree of COTS integration may vary considerably, from no integration at all to modifying the COTS user interface architecture and code so that the user is unaware of the separate pieces of software.
- Frequently the software is developed in part or in whole by an outside software development company, i.e., a systems integration or consulting firm adding the complexities of a customer/supplier relationship to the project.
- There are 30 to 100 software developers and a total project staff of 100 to 300 people (including business representatives, technical writers, trainers, roll-out planners, etc.).
- The duration of the project, including roll-out, may be 2 to 4 years.
- The organization is at the lowest of the five levels of the Software Capability Maturity Model (Paulk, Curtis, Chrissis and Weber, 1993), Level 1(Initial) and occasionally at Level 2 (Repeatable) .
- The nature of the assignment may be firefighting or fire prevention.
- One or two usabililty engineers are available for firefighting, three to six are available for fire-prevention (the number of usability engineers is more often dictated by the project budget rather than project size or type).
- In a fire prevention assignment, usability engineers are involved during systems analysis and design full time for 6 to 12 months, part time during coding for ongoing feedback to developers and quality assurance, and again full time during field trials and acceptance testing.
- Real users are available, though in very limited numbers only. Typically, three to six users are seconded to the project full time or part time, with additional users being available part time for testing to represent the diversity of users. While a larger number of users is desirable to ensure representation of a large and often diverse user population, three to six users full time or part time is usually all that is possible (and it may take weeks to secure their participation because of management concerns).

1.2. OVERVIEW

Section 2 describes the necessary usability planning and infrastructure in terms of user involvement, skill sets, tool kits, specially equipped rooms, and the project plan. Section 3 describes the necessary work/task analysis process and results from which to begin user interface design, i.e., the foundation for the bridge. In a usability engineering project plan, this is usually called the usability analysis phase. Section 4 describes the actual design process, i.e., the building of the bridge. In a usability engineering project plan, this is usually called the usability design phase. It includes iterative design, prototyping, and testing. Formal usability evaluations with the coded application are conducted in the usability evaluation phase, which is not addressed here. Table 8.1 provides an overview of usability project phases and tasks and their corresponding sections.

In each section, the heuristics for the choice of methods and approaches will be provided for fire prevention and firefighting assignments. In fire prevention

Table 8.1 Overview of Usability Project Phases and Tasks and Their Corresponding Sections

Usability Project Phase	Section Number	Usability Project Task
Usability project planning — planning the construction of the bridge	2.1	Structure for user involvement
	2.2	Required usability engineering skill set
	2.3	Usability engineering tool kit
	2.4	Usability engineering room
	2.5	Usability engineering project plan
Usability analysis — laying the foundation of the bridge	3.1	Business objectives for the application
	3.2	Definition of current and new user classes
	3.3	Current task definitions
	3.4	Malfunction analysis of current system
	3.5	System requirements, functional require ments and functional specifications
	3.6	Training and documentation strategy
	3.7	Hardware/software environment
Usability design — building the bridge	4.1	New task definitions
	4.2	Usability performance objectives
	4.3.1	Design and use of metaphors
	4.3.2	Task vs. subject orientation in the user interface
	4.3.3	Designing the user interface horizontally first: opening screen and navigation principles
	4.3.4	Vertical user interface design second: design for each task
	4.4	Detailed design
Usability evaluation — testing the bridge	Not covered here	Field trials and usability acceptance testing

assignments, usability is integrated into the overall project plan right from the start, allowing for a reasonably polished user interface design in an orderly fashion. By contrast, the usability work done in firefighting assignments is aimed at quickly addressing the most glaring usability problems within the confines of project schedule, resources, and budget. Usually there is not much opportunity for exploring user interface design alternatives. It is by no means a comprehensive usability effort, and many shortcuts are taken — often discounting even discount usability (Nielsen, 1989). Extra effort put into the same project task in fire prevention means higher-quality information for decision making and more exploration of design alternatives. In fire prevention assignments, there is a higher level of quality and a higher level of confidence in the resulting user interface design. Some remarks on critical success factors for building a solid bridge (Section 6) conclude the discussion.

Throughout the chapter, a fictitious project for redesigning a complex legacy system will be used to illustrate some of the issues, though these illustrations are not intended as a comprehensive case study. The project takes place at the XYZ Finance & Insurance Company, a fictitious company that offers a wide range of financial and insurance services to its customers through a network of branch offices and sales representatives, who visit customers in their homes.

2. USABILITY PROJECT PLANNING — PLANNING THE CONSTRUCTION OF THE BRIDGE

This section describes five components necessary for sound usability engineering planning and infrastructure:

- A structure for user involvement (Section 2.1).
- A required usability engineering skill set (Section 2.2).
- A usability engineering tool kit (Section 2.3).
- A usability engineering room (Section 2.4).
- A usability engineering project plan (Section 2.5).

2.1. STRUCTURE FOR USER INVOLVEMENT

At the beginning of a firefighting or fire-prevention usability engineering effort for the redevelopment of a set of legacy systems, it is essential to secure user involvement to the degree that the corporate culture, the project plan, and the budget permit. A two-tiered structure for user involvement has worked well on a number of in-house application development projects. A User Committee represents the users of the application, while a Usability Steering Committee represents senior user management and other senior management involved in the project.

A User Committee consists of three to six representative users who are seconded to the committee full time or part time for the duration of the project. The mandate of the User Committee is to

- Provide detailed information during the usability analysis phase and review the results of the analysis.
- Provide feedback on all aspects of the user interface design (particularly during the usability design phase) and review results from prototyping sessions and recommend priorities for improvement.
- Review results from field trials and acceptance tests during the usability evaluation phase and recommend priorities for improvement.
- Review and approve all project usability work and deliverables before they are submitted to the Usability Steering Committee for review and approval.

It is important that the User Committee is staffed with users who possess the following qualifications:

- Users should be experienced staff members, because experience is essential to describe current user tasks and malfunctions (see Section 3.4).
- Users should be representative of a diverse user population to the degree possible.
- Users should be generalists with a wide range of task experience so that they can contribute their knowledge to a larger number of tasks (specialists are consulted if necessary).
- Users should be part of a network of colleagues from whom they can obtain specialist knowledge or reviews.
- Users should be outspoken.
- Some users should have had supervisory experience in order to address supervisory issues, e.g., review and approve issues.
- Some users should be experienced in training new employees on the job, because such users know the most frequent sources of errors and those parts of the job and the application that are the most difficult for a new employee to learn. These areas will require special attention during the user interface design phase of the project.

The role of the User Committee is to work jointly with the usability engineers on all aspects of the usability work. The users are effectively co-designers. Even though such a small number of users is a rather narrow representation of a large user community, a small number of users is important for the group work throughout the usability engineering effort (user interface design by large committee is not effective). A small number of users is usually all that managers are willing and able to provide (when the users are co-designing instead of doing their regular job, someone has to fill in for them). The intensity of work on a User Committee tends to cycle from several days or weeks of continuous effort to periods of little or no activity. Typically, staff members serving on a User Committee are seconded to the project for 2 to 5 days every week, depending on the amount and the nature of the work to be done.

In addition, real or surrogate users are involved in iterative prototyping and usability testing. These users must represent the larger user community in terms of regional differences, specialist knowledge and requirements, and new employees or transfer employees.

A Usability Steering Committee consists of the usability engineering project manager (usually without decision-making and voting power), three to five senior managers from the business area affected by the project, as well as senior managers from the training, policies and procedures, and information technology departments. The Steering Committee meets as required, approximately every 2 weeks. The mandate of the Steering Committee is to:

- Review and approve all usability deliverables.
- Review and approve designs before they become part of a deliverable. In particular, the Steering Committee chooses one of the proposed user interface design alternatives in situations where a business issue masquerades as a user interface issue (see Section 4.3.2).
- Resolve issues requiring senior management approval. Typical examples are policy issues, modifications to business processes, and changes in organizational responsibility and accountability.

- Make decisions on project direction. These are directly associated with the project and business objectives. Typical examples are decisions on usability and usefulness of system functions, determining appropriate levels of involvement of participants in decision making beyond the Usability Steering Committee, and assessing the cost and benefit of alternative designs.

It is possible that the views and recommendations of the User Committee do not agree with the views and recommendations of the Usability Steering Committee. In that case, the views and recommendations of the Usability Steering Committee prevail. The usability project manager may sometimes find him- or herself in the role of a mediator between the two committees, but must respect the authority of the Steering Committee at all times. This often requires considerable diplomatic skill.

The usability project manager must be a member of the overall Project Management Committee, which consists of the managers of the teams involved, e.g., the software development team, the database team, the network team, etc. Both the Usability Steering Committee and the Project Management Committee report to the Project Steering Committee, which is comprised of senior executives from the business area affected by or involved in the project.

The User Committee and the Usability Steering Committee are required for both fire prevention and firefighting assignments. However, in a firefighting assignment, it may not be possible to establish the committees formally. In this case, the usability project manager must secure the full time or at least part time involvement of two to three subject matter experts (i.e., users with a wide range of task experience and some supervisory experience) to function as a User Committee. The usability project manager must also identify key senior managers who, as a group, function as a Usability Steering Committee. Without this kind of minimal user and management support, a firefighting usability assignment is unlikely to succeed.

2.2. REQUIRED USABILITY ENGINEERING SKILL SET

The usability engineering skill set includes:

- User interface analysis, design and evaluation skills.
- People and facilitation skills, especially for Joint Application Design (JAD) and focus group sessions.
- Project management experience.
- Background in software analysis, design, programming, and testing, in order to understand how much effort a user interface change might require.
- Ability to read any data, object, or process model.
- Ability to learn to use any prototyping tool.
- Ability to become a subject matter expert very quickly.

- Ability to set aside one's own preferred mental models, interaction styles, and software/hardware platform details.
- Courage and persistence to pursue an effective user interface design, grace to accept user interface design flaws that cannot be changed, and the wisdom to distinguish one from the other.

Not all members of the usability engineering team need to possess all of these skills, but all skills should be represented on the team.

2.3. USABILITY ENGINEERING TOOL KIT

The usability engineering tool kit to produce rough drafts contains flip charts, white boards, string, colored stickies, colored markers, colored dots, tape, scissors, and a big cookie jar. The author's experience has been that low-cost prototyping with such a tool kit is the most effective, efficient, and cheapest prototyping method up to and including the first pass of detailed design for the development of most applications or products. Only after this stage is it worthwhile to build computer-based prototypes for polishing the user interface design. A wise choice of the computer-based prototyping tool will allow the polished prototype to be carried over into development.

2.4. USABILITY ENGINEERING ROOM

A usability engineering room is essential to aid in the construction and maintenance of subject matter knowledge and user interface design ideas. Sometimes called a "war room" (see Chapter 10 by Simpson), it is used to post flip charts with specific usability principles, designs, unresolved and resolved issues, to conduct focus group meetings and JAD sessions, and to hold free and open discussions of design alternatives. There is no specific allocation of wall space to particular types of postings; rather, the wall space is used and reused for postings as needed.

2.5. USABILITY ENGINEERING PROJECT PLAN

Understanding the overall project plan and budget allows the usability engineering project manager to position usability activities from the usability project plan within the overall project plan. It is essential to identify clearly the scope and content of each usability engineering deliverable. Provisions must be made for including design rationale in each deliverable so that there is a record of user interface design trade-offs and decisions. Each level two subsection in sections 3 and 4 below corresponds to a deliverable in the usability engineering project plan. If the project employs a traditional "waterfall" development approach, scheduling iterative user interface design work is often difficult.

3. USABILITY ANALYSIS — LAYING THE FOUNDATION OF THE BRIDGE

The bridge from user/system requirements to a reasonably polished user interface design for a complex legacy system must have a solid foundation, the results of the usability analysis phase. The following information should be available or constructed as part of the usability engineering effort, and then documented, reviewed, and approved by the Steering Committee:

- Business objectives for the application (Section 3.1).
- Definition and description of current and new user classes (Section 3.2).
- Current task definitions (Section 3.3).
- Malfunction analysis of the current system (Section 3.4).
- System requirements, functional requirements, and functional specifications (Section 3.5).
- Training and documentation strategy (Section 3.6).
- Hardware/software environment (Section 3.7).

3.1. BUSINESS OBJECTIVES FOR THE APPLICATION

Business objectives must be expressed as specific measures of success such as cutting the turnaround for loan applications down to one business day, reducing the error rate from 30% to less than 5% when filling in a form for a specific product, or reducing training for the application from 5 days to 1 day. These business objectives state the measures of success from a business perspective; they drive the usability performance objectives and the usability project plan and budget. For example, if one of the business objectives is to reduce training time required, then the usability plan and budget will allocate effort and money specifically to designing the user interface for learnability. Business objectives are often found in business case descriptions for a project, in a Request for Proposal, or in a requirements definition document.

The usability engineers must "translate" the business objectives into general usability design principles for the application. For example, to reduce the error rate, the usability principle of preventing errors (Molich and Nielsen, 1990) must be applied, specifically, by guiding the user through the steps of a task, by checking for errors immediately rather than at task completion, and by providing graceful error recovery mechanisms. The last is especially important when a customer and a user look at a screen together. These application-specific guidelines are the foundation for the later definition of usability performance objectives.

The application-specific guidelines are documented in a memorandum and posted on flip charts in the usability engineering room. The guidelines are required for both fire prevention and firefighting assignments; the difference is in the effort expended to identify them and have them approved. For fire prevention assignments they are identified by thorough analysis based on brief interviews with all stake holders. This obtains buy-in from the stake holders, and it is a good opportunity to sell usability within the organization. For firefighting assignments, principles are identified in a JAD session with the Steering Committee.

3.2. DEFINITION AND DESCRIPTION OF CURRENT AND NEW USER CLASSES

The description of current and new user classes includes the users' experience with the existing application or similar products/applications and their familiarity with the task at hand (familiar vs. undergoing major changes in terms of business process re-engineering vs. completely new tasks). For example, at the XYZ Finance & Insurance Company a new user class consisted of users who would be conducting a limited range of transactions with customers over the phone. These users were familiar with conducting the transactions face-to-face with a customer, but they were not familiar with conducting them over the phone. The definition of new user classes also includes patterns of staff turnover. This will yield the ratio of experienced to novice users throughout the lifetime of the application. Usability effort and money can then be allocated to learnability vs. efficient use.

The number of users per class with a 1-3-5 year projection and the characteristics of each class are documented in a report and posted on flip charts in the usability engineering room. For fire prevention assignments, a more thorough analysis is conducted to include actual numbers and input from the User Departments, Human Resources, and Training Departments. The user class descriptions are more comprehensive and are matched to employee classifications. For firefighting assignments, user classes are identified in a JAD session with the User and Steering Committees, including estimates for the total number of users in different classes. User class descriptions are in point form, approximately half a page per user class.

3.3. CURRENT TASK DEFINITIONS

Current task definitions describe how users currently perform the tasks, both for manual and computerized systems. The definitions include others participating in the interaction. For example, if the user is a sales representative, others participating in the interaction could be customers or the supervisor. At the XYZ Finance & Insurance Company, the current task definitions included a task to explain financial and insurance instruments to a customer. This task was not supported by computer-based applications. Users relied on brochures for general information and calculated individual rates with a pocket calculator. Sometimes users sketched graphs on paper to illustrate concepts, such as compound interest for a customer. Users expected this task to be supported by appropriate computer-based applications in the redesigned legacy system.

The author's experience has been that a point form narrative is usually sufficient. Each step in a task is described by one or several lines of text, e.g., "ask customer about assets and the value of each" or "print agreement". The level of detail required is at the object/function level from the user's perspective, but not at the keystroke level. The point form narrative identifies branches in the task flow and alternate sequences of steps.

Sometimes the value of describing current user tasks is questioned because the new user tasks will be different. Understanding how tasks are currently performed provides an important part of the foundation for the design process: it allows the user interface designers to:

- Understand the user's current work environment and the idiosyncrasies of the business processes and policies that are often overlooked in high-level work redesign.
- Maintain those aspects of the current tasks that work well and are, therefore, not changed in the revised application (the "if it ain't broke, don't fix it" principle).
- Understand the user's (mental) model of the current application, i.e., the available objects and actions, the metaphor(s) through which they are expressed, and the sequence in which to use them to accomplish a task (see Section 4.3). This model should be preserved in the revised application to the degree possible in order to minimize learning when migrating to the re-designed version.
- Appreciate how big the leap will be for the users from the old to the new application. This information is very useful for making decisions on the training and documentation strategy (see Section 3.6).

In fire prevention assignments, the current task definitions are documented in a report. In firefighting assignments, the current task definitions are not developed; rather, the User Committee provides this information (with prompting) during the new task definition effort (see Section 4.1).

3.4. MALFUNCTION ANALYSIS OF CURRENT SYSTEM

A malfunction analysis of the current system identifies usability problems with the existing system (including manual and/or computerized tasks), as well as gaps in functionality and problems in the business process as it is currently carried out. If a business process re-engineering exercise has been conducted, much of the process- and task-related malfunctions will already have been identified, and the usability analysis can be limited to usability problems at the user model, and at the dialogue and detailed level of the user interface. If no business process re-engineering has been done, the usability engineers frequently identify the opportunities for process and task improvements. Often this implies significant changes to functional requirements/specifications and business policies and procedures, and hence, rework and project delays.

For example, at the XYZ Finance & Insurance Company, the malfunction analysis revealed a fair amount of duplicate data entry: if a customer bought more than one financial or insurance instrument, basic customer information had to be entered for each instrument. Access to the existing legacy system functionality was through a large number of transaction codes. Experienced users knew the most frequently used codes from memory and used them efficiently for quick customer service. Novice users required the use of a reference booklet for several weeks, until they memorized the frequently used codes. Users felt that having to use a reference booklet in the presence of a customer did not project a professional image.

Malfunction analysis is essential for application redesign so that usability problems will not be repeated. When carrying out a malfunction analysis, it is also very useful to identify those parts or features of the application that users deem particularly useful so that they can be preserved where appropriate.

Malfunctions are rated according to their severity and classified as critical, serious, or minor. The severity of a usability problem is a combination of three factors:

- Frequency: how common is the problem?
- Impact: how easy or difficult will it be for the users to overcome the problem?
- Persistence: is it a one-time problem that users can overcome once they know about it or will users repeatedly be bothered by the problem?

These three components are combined into a single severity rating as an overall assessment of each malfunction. The ratings (described below) are provided to assist in prioritizing improvements and decision making:

- *Critical* problems make successful task completion impossible, unacceptably long, or are fraught with significant (costly or embarrassing) errors or they have a detrimental effect on how an organization conducts its business.
- *Serious* problems have a major impact on the user's performance and/or the operation of the system overall, but do not prevent users from eventually performing the task.
- *Minor* problems do not greatly affect the user's job performance, but when taken as a group, negatively affect the user's perceptions.

In many cases, it is difficult to separate the causes of malfunctions and to rate them only on an individual basis, as submalfunctions often also contribute to, or are part of the cause of, these malfunctions. Therefore, ratings are given to malfunctions which may also include less severe sub-malfunctions, though these submalfunctions are not rated individually. For example, malfunctions with navigation may be rated as Critical. However, these also include related submalfunctions, such as problems with the wording of menu choices which, taken on their own, may have been rated as only Minor. Critical malfunctions must be addressed in the redesign; serious malfunctions should be addressed in the redesign.

Usability performance objectives can often be derived from malfunctions. When evaluating user interface designs during iterative prototyping and testing in the usability design phase, user interface designs are assessed in terms of how well they address the malfunctions and the derived usability performance objectives (see Section 4.2). The process of understanding and rating malfunctions forms an important part of the foundation of the bridge.

If the project involves commercial-off-the-shelf software (COTS) software, it is essential that a quick malfunction analysis be conducted, at a minimum as a heuristic evaluation and preferably as a quick co-operative evaluation (Nielsen, 1992; Monk et al., 1993). The purpose is to assess which aspects of the COTS user interface should or should not be replicated in the extensions and other applications in the set. The objective is to determine whether, or to what extent, to adopt the user's model, navigation style, and widget operation into the extensions and other applications in the set. Frequently, COTS software is chosen early on in a project for its functionality and price, with little or no regard for its usability (which frequently leaves a lot to be desired).

Malfunctions are documented in a report and posted in the usability engineering room. In the case of a fire prevention assignment, the malfunction analysis is typically carried out as a co-operative evaluation augmented by the analysis of data from user surveys, hot line support services and comments collected by, for example, the user departments. In the case of a fire fighting assignment, the malfunction analysis is carried out in two JAD sessions with the User Committee and the Steering Committee.

3.5. SYSTEM REQUIREMENTS, FUNCTIONAL REQUIREMENTS, AND FUNCTIONAL SPECIFICATIONS

The usability engineer must be able to read and understand the models of the business and the system/application developed by business systems analysts or systems engineers (see Sowa and Zachman, 1992). The usability engineer must also be able to read or interpret the results of whatever object-oriented software engineering tool or computer-assisted software engineering tool is employed in the project. Frequently, the user interface designer has to map these detailed models onto objects from a user's perspective (these are usually higher level objects) and then track the mapping throughout the user interface design process.

Designing the user interface objects and actions first and then mapping them onto the system/application model would seem a more logical approach to designing the user interface. However, it carries a significant risk. Without an understanding of the system/application model, the user interface design of objects and actions may include functionality that is out of project scope (the scope is defined through the system/application model). Inadvertently exceeding project scope by designing the user interface without an understanding of the system/application model may create user expectations that cannot be satisfied, leaving the users disappointed.

It has been the author's experience that managing user expectations is one of the key concerns of senior management and a main obstacle to securing user involvement. Demonstrating an understanding of and respect for the project scope by understanding the system/application model is an effective way of addressing these concerns. If the usability engineers base the user interface design on the system/application model that is used by all other teams on the project, the usability engineers will significantly enhance their credibility with the software developers.

There are also projects where development is fast tracked, going from high level system requirements directly to abbreviated requirements analysis/software design and coding, skipping the detailed definition of functional requirements and business processes. In such situations, the usability engineer has to take on the role of the systems analyst in order to define the functional requirements and business processes to a level of detail from which new user work flow and task design can begin.

3.6. TRAINING AND DOCUMENTATION STRATEGY

The user interface design, as well as the user interface project and budget allocation, will be heavily influenced by the training and documentation strategy. For example, if the training strategy is self-teaching on the job, then designing for guessability and learnability will require more effort, and the usability performance objectives (see Section 4.2) will likely have to be defined very stringently. Conversely, if intense training is planned for, then the training can address user interface design shortcomings and the usability performance objectives can be lowered. While the latter strategy may not be desirable from a quality user interface design point of view, it may nevertheless be a more cost-effective strategy from a business point of view. However, the reality of the train-around-the-usability-problem approach is frequently that users are well trained at roll-out, but users joining the organization later or changing jobs only get on-the-job training from co-workers. This may lead to inefficient system use and co-workers training their colleagues, instead of doing their actual work — a hidden cost. These trade-offs have to be brought to the attention of the Usability Steering Committee. The strategies and their implications for the user interface design must be documented, usually in a memorandum.

3.7. HARDWARE/SOFTWARE ENVIRONMENT

The hardware/software environment has usually been chosen by the time user interface work begins. At best, there is some flexibility in the choice of development tools. Understanding the hardware/software environment and the opportunities and constraints it offers will allow for implementable user interface designs. For example, if an application is to run on both large workstation screens and on laptop screens with half the capacity of the workstation screen, then decisions will have to be made about two software versions or one software version but with two different sets of usability performance objectives. If there is only one software version, then the user interface design has to address, for example, the scrolling problem created by the two different screen sizes.

In firefighting assessments, the usability engineer conducts a brief (one-day) assessment and documents it in a memorandum, indicating the trade-offs. In a fire prevention assignment, a more thorough assessment of the options and trade-offs can be conducted.

4. USABILITY DESIGN — BUILDING THE BRIDGE

The design process consists of four distinct project tasks:

- Defining the new user tasks (Section 4.1).
- Defining usability performance objectives (Section 4.2).
- Designing the system's model for the user (Section 4.3).
- Designing detailed screens (Section 4.4).

Except for the definition of usability performance objectives, there are several tightly coupled design/prototype/evaluate iterations within each task, and there are also some iterations between these tasks. For example, discoveries in detailed design may lead to modifications of the user's model or the new user task definitions, causing some rework in these earlier project tasks and possibly causing a revision of the usability performance objectives for these tasks. A frequent source of such causes for partial rework are idiosyncrasies of business process exception and error handling conditions. Another frequent source for rework is a change in project scope. For example, development of a part of the functionality may be moved into later releases of an application in order to meet the original roll-out deadline. If the usability design process addresses only the reduced functionality, then moving to full functionality may involve extensive user interface design rework to accommodate the full functionality in the user interface. This, in turn, increases the software development cost for later releases.

In most legacy system redesigns, users will quickly migrate from being novice users to becoming efficient users for many years to come (see Section 3.2). Therefore, it is recommended that designs first reflect efficiency of use and then address learning issues.

4.1. NEW TASK DEFINITIONS

The process of building the bridge from the information described thus far to a reasonably polished design in the redesign of a legacy application is a rather systematic process. The first step in the design process is a quick storyboarding of the new user tasks with input from:

- Business process re-engineering.
- Functional requirements/specifications.
- Current task definitions.
- Malfunction analysis of the existing application(s).
- Opportunities and constraints of the proposed technologies.

When storyboarding, it is recommended that emphasis be placed on the task flow, i.e., the steps with loops for repetitions, interrupts, and input/reviews/ approvals. It is essential to identify common subtasks and key variations, e.g., regional differences and user preferences. In an object-oriented environment, the new user tasks typically correspond to use cases (Jacobson et al., 1994).

For each step, the following information needs to be identified, independent of any partitioning into screens:

- Information that must be displayed for this step or that must be quickly available (e.g., look-up type information) and special attention should be paid to information that has to be available "at a glance".
- Information required from the user, i.e., information that has to be entered, or choices and decisions that have to be made.
- The information supplied by the system or calculated/reasoned by the system.
- Any mandatory sequencing of user and system actions.

To ensure scope control of the user interface design, it is useful to map the new user tasks onto the functional decomposition, if one exists. A functional decomposition, also called a process hierarchy diagram or a leveled data flow diagram, is a hierarchical breakdown of system functions. This ensures that there are no orphaned new user tasks (i.e., there is no functionality to support the task) and no orphaned functions (i.e., each function is used in at least one new user task). In conjunction with the database of user classes/new tasks/frequency (see Section 4.3.3), this information also allows the software engineers and capacity planners to fine tune their load planning. Providing this information to the project team is a good example of how usability engineering can contribute to software development.

If the redesigned legacy system provides a new front-end to the existing transaction-oriented back end, then the transaction codes must be mapped onto the new task definitions. This will ensure that every new task is supported by one or more transactions at the back end, and conversely, that every transaction is used in at least one new task. For example, at the XYZ Finance & Insurance Company, the new task definition for filling in application forms required some legacy transaction behind the scenes to retrieve customer data automatically for prefilling the forms. This addressed one malfunction of the existing legacy system, namely the duplicate data entry for existing customers.

The new task definitions are documented in a report. A complete list and a few detailed samples are posted in the usability engineering room. In the case of a fire prevention assignment, all the new tasks can be defined. In the case of a firefighting assignment, it is recommended that focus be placed on key tasks for key user classes and that they be developed as examples to be followed.

4.2. USABILITY PERFORMANCE OBJECTIVES

Usability performance objectives are modeled after system performance objectives, e.g., database throughput or acceptable levels of system availability. The key characteristics of usability performance objectives are that they make the quality of the user interface design measurable in a way that is meaningful for users and their organization. They are derived from the organization's business objectives (see Section 3.1) and the malfunctions of the current system (see Section 3.4). Usability performance objectives define the user interface design targets and the level of acceptable designs (Preece et al., 1994). They are posted in the usability engineering room. The most common usability performance objectives are targets for:

- Task-specific error rates, e.g., no more than 5% errors in an insurance application after 3 days of use.
- Task-specific use of on-line help, e.g., invoking on-line help no more than once for a specific task after 1 day of use.
- Task-specific and/or overall satisfaction with ease of use or efficiency of use, e.g., at least 5 out of 7 on a scale: "overall, the task/system is ..." "very difficult to perform/use (1)" to "very easy to perform/use (7)".
- Overall guessability, e.g. 80% of the icons guessed correctly the first time.
- Overall satisfaction with ease of use or efficiency of use, e.g., at least 5 out of 7 on a scale: "overall, the system is ..." "very difficult to use (1)" to "very easy to use (7)".

Typically, usability performance objectives are established for key tasks only (i.e., tasks that are performed frequently or are key to achieving business objectives) or for those tasks where errors have serious consequences. In addition, some overall ratings are usually included. For example, if staff turnover is high, then overall ratings will focus on guessability and learnability. By contrast, if fast customer service is essential and staff turnover is low, then overall ratings will focus on efficiency of use.

4.3. BUILDING A MODEL FOR THE USER

Any interactive computer system expresses an underlying model on the screen through words and/or graphics. The model consists of the objects and actions available, any sequencing of object use, and the navigation mechanisms available. This model will be called the system model here. The system model represents the designer's understanding of the application and the user's work.

When working with an interactive computer system, users form a (mental) model of the objects and actions available to them including how the system works, i.e., which objects and actions to use, and in what sequence, in order to accomplish a task (Norman, 1986; Preece et al., 1994). This (mental) model will be referred to here as the user's model.

When users begin to work with a system for the first time, they try to match the objects and actions they know from their work/tasks to the objects and actions they see on the screen, i.e., they try to match their (mental) model with the system's model. As part of their model, users determine how to navigate within the system: where to find objects and actions and how to activate them. If there is a good match between the system's and the user's models, then the system is intuitive and users will be able to complete a task on the first attempt with little help, and they will quickly progress to mastering the use of the system. If, on the other hand, the system's and user's models do not match well, users will have difficulty completing a task on the first attempt and will require frequent help.

The user's model of the current application should be preserved in the system model of the revised application to the greatest degree possible in order to minimize learning when migrating to the redesigned version. The user's model of the current application is discovered as part of the current task definitions (see Section 3.3), and the malfunction analysis of the current application identifies problems with the user's current model. Measuring against usability performance objectives provides reliable data about the quality of the new system's model.

This section describes the four project tasks involved in building a system model appropriate for the users:

- Design and use of metaphors (Section 4.3.1).
- Design decisions on task vs. object orientation in the system's model (Section 4.3.2).
- Horizontal user interface design first: design of the opening screen, navigation principles, and principles for displaying objects (Section 4.3.3).
- Vertical user interface design second: design for each task (Section 4.3.4).

Some tips for managing design iterations are provided in Section 4.5, and some suggestions for documenting the design are contained in Section 5.

Within each of these four project tasks, there are several tightly coupled design/prototype/evaluate iterations, and there are also some iterations between them. For example, discoveries in individual task design may lead to modifications of the opening screen or the navigation techniques, causing some rework in these earlier project tasks. A frequent source of such causes for partial rework are ommissions of objects and functions that allow users to manage all their tasks in an efficient manner, e.g., to look up the status of an application, or to mark the progress of certain aspects of their work.

4.3.1. Design and Use of Metaphors

Frequently, an object in a system's model or even the entire system's model is described by a metaphor (i.e., an analogy to the real world) such as a desktop, a receipt, a list, or a shop floor (Carroll et al., 1988; Preece et al., 1994). The metaphor may be represented through words on the screen, e.g., appropriate screen/field/widget titles, or the metaphor may be represented pictorially, e.g., through icons or graphics. For example, an alphabetical list of customer names can be represented through words by a drop-down list box or pictorially by the graphical representation of a rolodex or a box of index cards. In each case, the underlying object is an alphabetical list of customer names, but the metaphor chosen to represent the object is different (note that a "list" is also a metaphor...). When designing metaphors, it is important to separate the metaphor from its verbal or pictorial representation on the screen. The method used to represent the metaphor on the screen (i.e., through words or pictures or a combination of both) is influenced by the underlying technology and the time available for development.

The author's experience has been that, for the redesign of legacy systems, the detailed graphic representation of metaphors (folders with tabs, rolodexes, index cards, etc.) is less important than identifying the appropriate objects themselves and the grouping of objects according to steps in a task. In usability evaluations, it was found that users rarely noticed the detailed graphical representations, i.e., the graphical representations did not help the users find the correct object for a step in a task. When the objects were poorly structured, the detailed graphical representations actually interfered with task performance, and when they were brought to the users' attention, the representations did not improve users' understanding. Users thought of groups and sequences of screens as representing a task and its associated objects and actions.

Compared to detailed object representations, the information presented on the screens and its organization was far more crucial to learning and efficient use; users formed a (mental) model of the system based on the screen titles, layout, and content of fields and widgets. Furthermore, users commented that the graphics for such objects occupied precious screen space that could be better used for displaying important information. An efficient and effective organization of and access to user tasks is critical, i.e., the effort expended is focused on efficient task organization, and within a task, on efficient object organization. Essentially, this is an issue of navigation and screen organization, which depends to some degree on the technologies and tools employed.

It is also helpful to identify where and how the metaphor will be used, irrespective of how it is represented on the screen (by words or pictures). For example, a metaphor may work well for novice users but may be perceived as superfluous by experienced users. A metaphor may be used explicitly in documentation and training material and implicitly on the screen itself. The presentation of the metaphor may also influence users. For example, for one application, the initial cartoon-style presentation of a metaphor suggested that this was not a "serious" application. When the presentation style was changed to elegant drawings, users found it acceptable and helpful.

For a metaphor to be successful, it must be consistent with existing metaphors used in the workplace (see Section 3.3), it should be sustainable throughout the user interface, it should be able to accommodate exception and error conditions, and it should be extendible as new tasks are learned or created (these are the criteria for evaluating metaphors during the design sessions described above). It is essential to understand the user's initial (mental) model of the current application (see Section 3.3) and then build on that understanding with the appropriate metaphor. If the functionality of the application is "new" (i.e., unfamiliar to the users) it is helpful to understand the analogies or models users employ to make sense of the "new" functionality. This happens in legacy system redesign when new functionality is introduced (as an extension) that users have not encountered before or where new functionality is provided to support or enforce the new way of doing business. Design of a metaphor is particularly challenging when the malfunctions analysis of the COTS software revealed critical or serious malfunctions in the COTS system model.

For example, the XYZ Finance & Insurance Company introduced functionality to explain and illustrate its financial and insurance instruments to the customer. The current user's model (discovered in the malfunction analysis) consisted of the application form metaphor for collecting and analysing customer data and the contract metaphor for the sales documentation. Users deemed the metaphor of a slide show appropriate for the explanations and illustrations. These could be customized with individual customer data, consistent with the concept of customizing slides, and they could be printed for the customer to keep.

The choice of appropriate metaphors for an application is the most challenging and most far-reaching user interface design decision on any project. It is also the most enjoyable part of any project. The author's experience has been that metaphors are best generated by a joint working group of user interface designers, users, and business and systems analysts. Brainstorming techniques, the usability engineering tool kit (see Section 2.3), the design room (see Section 2.4), and copious amounts of chocolate, cookies and coffee, and/or pizza and beer are helpful. There is no well-defined process for generating metaphors. It is best to start with the metaphor of the current application or the COTS software (see Sections 3.3 and 3.4) and to examine carefully how well it fits with the new task definitions (see Section 4.1).

An iterative design approach with user testing is essential to the design of the metaphor to ensure that the final metaphor matches the user's model. If users form a model different from that conveyed through the metaphor, then they will very likely not be able to use the functionality as intended.

The metaphor is documented as part of the User Interface Architecture (see Section 5) and posted in the usability engineering room. In fire prevention assignments, sufficient resources should be allocated to this project task. In firefighting assignments where time is of the essence, it is best to rely on the results of the malfunction analysis and adopt a metaphor based on the user's model of the current application rather than spending time exploring other metaphors.

4.3.2. Task vs. Object Orientation in the User Interface

At the beginning of dialogue design, it is necessary to determine whether the system should provide a task-oriented dialogue (i.e., the user is guided by the system through the tasks to be accomplished) or an object-oriented dialogue (i.e., the user knows which objects to work with and selects them in the appropriate order). Frequently, a hybrid will be required, with novice users often preferring task-oriented dialogues and more-experienced users preferring an object-oriented approach. There are a variety of design alternatives for providing the necessary guidance for tasks, e.g., use of wizards or task lists.

While users generally have some degree of flexibility in deciding in which order they want to do their day's work, there is generally less flexibility in the order in which steps in a task are carried out. For example, money for a loan cannot be advanced to a customer unless a number of steps have been taken, e.g., the credit bureau check is in the customer's favor, the loan application has been reviewed, the loan has been approved, and the necessary documents have been signed. The order of steps is important, e.g., the loan cannot be reviewed without the credit bureau check having been completed first. Experienced users know this, but less-experienced users may not. Organizations have policies and procedures that prescribe the sequence of steps, and these are enforced in an application to varying degrees. Policies and procedures are reflected in functional specifications and the current task definitions (see Section 3.3). Problems in this area are documented in the malfunction analysis of the current system (see Section 3.4).

A key issue in determining task vs. object orientation in a user interface is the amount of control given to users, especially with respect to variations in how to perform a task. For example, the business objective of the XYZ Finance & Insurance Company was to increase sales, and a means to do that was the sales approach taught in sales training. Therefore, corporate management at the XYZ Finance & Insurance Company wanted all users to use the sales approach taught in sales training courses. As a result, the sales presentations were predesigned for specific kinds of customers. The sales representatives, however, wanted to be able to create their own sales presentations for specific kinds of customers. For in-house business applications in particular, the issue of user control may raise differences of opinion between users and corporate management. While usability engineers may want to take a position on such an issue, it is the Usability Steering Committee that makes the decision. Such issues are no longer user interface issues; rather, they are business issues masquerading as user interface issues.

A frequent concern about task-oriented user interfaces is that users do not have easy access to the appropriate information at each step in a task. In the author's experience, this is a user interface design problem, not a problem inherent in task-oriented user interfaces. When designing a user interface with a stronger task orientation, it is essential to determine which objects are required for each step in the task and to ensure that these objects are indeed easily available at each step.

The degree of task vs. object orientation in the user interface is documented as part of the User Interface Architecture (see Section 5). A summary is posted in the usability engineering room, and the new task definitions are annotated to indicate where a sequence of steps must be adhered to. In fire prevention assignments, sufficient resources should be allocated to this project task. In firefighting assignments, only sample definitions for key tasks are annotated.

4.3.3. Designing the User Interface Horizontally First — Opening Screen and Navigation Principles

The foundation for designing the opening screen and navigation principles is a database, mapping relationships among user objects, functions, user classes, new task definitions, and frequency of task performance. The author's experience has been that such a database is invaluable for making user interface design decisions about foregrounding/backgrounding objects and functions at the interaction level, as well as detail design level of the user interface. Generally, information or cues to frequently performed tasks will be in the foreground, at higher levels of a menu hierarchy, or on special "hot keys/fast paths". On the other hand, information or cues to less frequently performed tasks will be placed in lower levels of a menu hierarchy or be presented in such a way that they are always accompanied by an explanation of when to invoke this task. Note that the foregrounding/backgrounding of tasks does not necessarily imply a task-oriented user interface.

The starting point for navigation design is the database of user objects, functions, user classes, new task definitions, and frequency of task performance. It is documented in the User Interface Architecture (see Section 5). Clusters in the user class and new task definition matrix suggest initial groupings for the navigation design, and the new task definitions themselves provide the initial flow. The first round of navigation design is aimed at ensuring that all tasks and user classes are covered by the high-level navigation design and that users are able to find and start key tasks.

The following example from the XYZ Finance & Insurance Company is intended to illustrate some of the points raised above. In the first round of navigation design, the clusters in the user class and new task definition/frequency matrix indicated that some user classes performed a fairly narrow range of advisory-type tasks several times during the day. Other user classes performed a wide range of tasks, with a core set of transaction-oriented tasks being performed many times during the day and a much wider range of advisory-type tasks being performed infrequently, i.e., once or twice a day.

A comparison of steps in all tasks revealed that both advisory- and transaction-type tasks had a common first step: the identification of a customer. As it was one of the client's business objectives to provide a more personal service to customers, it was decided at the very outset that the customer should be identified on the opening screen as quickly as possible. A number of alternative means would be provided so that key information about the customer could be displayed. This would allow the user to form a picture of the customer quickly and then choose the service to be provided in accordance with the customer's wishes. Displaying as much information about the customer as possible, as well as displaying sales suggestions generated by the program, had to be balanced with providing fast access to the large range of tasks.

With the XYZ Finance & Insurance Company project, in the next round of navigation design for each task, decisions had to be made regarding the use of chained windows vs. parent/child windows. Where task steps had to be carried out in strict sequence, chained windows were employed. Each window in the chain was considered a parent window. Child windows would pop up or be invoked by the user to handle exceptions. To move between tasks, including moving between suspended tasks, users requested a kind of task list, which included all the tasks touched upon in a session with a customer, and which, if any financial or insurance instruments the customer had purchased during the session. While moving back and forth between multiple windows/tasks is common in any windowing environment, the users had identified the requirement for displaying only one window at a time at full screen size. They were also concerned that the customers, who would also be looking at the screen, would be distracted by partially visible windows.

The matrix of user classes/tasks/task frequency, the opening screen, and the navigation principles are documented in the User Interface Architecture (see Section 5) and posted in the usability engineering room. In a fire prevention assignment, the matrix can be constructed in a computerized database, which can then be printed for display in the usability engineering room. In a firefighting assignment, the database is frequently constructed on flip charts that are posted in the usability engineering room or on a spreadsheet.

4.3.4. Vertical User Interface Design Second — Design for Each Task

The design for each task is accomplished through a combination of storyboarding scenarios and initial, rough screen layouts. These should not include the actual screen details. For example, "customer information" may be used, but not the actual fields such as first name, last name, etc. The focus is on identifying information that must be available at a glance and on the sequencing in which the information is generated (either by user input or system calculation/reasoning). Typically, a user interface designer provides a rough draft that is iteratively tested and refined with users and reviewed in JAD sessions, attended by the user interface designers, users, business analysts, and developers. The rough designs form the basis for the next usability project task, the detailed design. The rough designs agreed upon in the JAD sessions are also useful to the software development and quality assurance teams for the preparation of test cases.

The rough designs are documented in the User Interface Architecture (see Section 5) and posted in the usability engineering room. In a fire prevention assignment, rough designs are prepared for each task. In a firefighting assignment, rough designs are prepared only for key tasks.

4.4. DETAILED DESIGN

Detailed design requires the detailed data models and functional specifications developed by the systems analysts and designers. It follows established design principles (e.g., the appropriate widget to choose for making a selection) and design guidelines (Preece, Rogers, Sharp, Benyon, Holland, and Carey 1994). The author's experience has been that using vendor guidelines such as MS Windows or Motif lead to diverse (i.e., inconsistent) designs across a team of developers because there is often wide latitude given for making choices.

For example, several teams of developers at the XYZ Finance & Insurance Company were working on the design of independent modules, each representing both a set of related user tasks and a functional area. Users would be using the modules in various sequences as the need arose. Common data were exchanged automatically in the background to avoid duplication of data entry. One of the vendor guidelines was used to ensure consistent user interface design. During the user interface design phase for the modules, there was very little contact between the different development teams. They assumed that it was not required because all teams were using the same guidelines. The first usability tests requiring users to use several of the modules revealed that different developer teams had used "Cancel" in three different ways: to cancel all data entry on the current window, to cancel all data entry on screens in a chain of windows, and to cancel all data entry in a module. While all three ways of employing Cancel are permitted under the guidelines, the effect of the Cancel is no longer predictable for users. An alternative design was developed that indicated clearly to the users which data entry and actions were canceled (different words were chosen for the three types of Cancel).

An application-specific style guide (see Section 5) with a computerized prototype example that considers user classes, tasks, and implementation tool capabilities and constraints is required to obtain consistency. It must be coupled with tight quality assurance for conformance to ensure usable designs. The prototype represents the concrete user interface design. The scope of such a prototype usually includes the opening screen and the detailed design for one or several key tasks. If the dialogue design is well thought out and tested, no more than two iterations should be required for detailed user interface design and testing. Additional detailed design is required for learning use and error prevention.

In fire prevention assignments, the application-specific style guide and proper user interface specification can be developed (see Section 5). In firefighting assignments, it is recommended that effort be placed on producing the application-specific style guide with one or two computerized prototyped tasks. Often developers will require training to use a style guide effectively, with additional, ongoing coaching during the development process. The prototypes become "sample" user interface specifications.

4.5. TIPS FOR MANAGING DESIGN ITERATIONS

It is best to time-box user interface design effort according to the overall project plan and budget. On a fire-prevention type user interface project, three to five iterations are usually required to reach a satisfactory design, i.e., a design which meets or approaches the usability performance objectives. On a firefighting type user interface project the number of iterations is severely limited. Typically, one or two iterations have to focus on the most glaring usability problems at the navigation level.

For both kinds of projects, tight user interface project management is essential to control the number and duration of iterations. At the end of each iteration, the design approach and rationale must be documented, including rejected ideas and the reasons why. Results from tests against usability performance objectives must be documented in order to show design progress. Each usability problem uncovered in a test must be rated like a malfunction (see Section 3.4). Last, but not least, there must be agreement on the usability problems that will be addressed in the next iteration (because it is usually impossible to address them all) and why (i.e., based on the criticality of the problem).

5. USABILITY DELIVERABLES — DOCUMENTING THE USER INTERFACE DESIGN

In the author's experience, the user interface design should be documented in three distinct deliverables:

- User interface architecture (Section 5.1).
- Application style guide (Section 5.2).
- User interface specifications (Section 5.3).

5.1. USER INTERFACE ARCHITECTURE

The reason for preparing the User Interface Architecture is to provide high-level user interface design information. In the framework for information systems architecture (Sowa and Zachman, 1992), the user interface architecture (called a Human Interface Architecture in Sowa and Zachman, 1992) expresses the model of the information system from the users' view. By comparison, a data model expresses the data view, and a distributed systems architecture expresses the network view of the application. The user interface architecture document should contain:

- Key information from the usability analysis phase and its implications for the user interface design:
    - Business objectives for the application.
    - A brief definition of new user classes and the implications from the comparison to existing user classes.
    - Salient points from the current task definitions.
    - A summary of the malfunction analysis of the current system.
    - A summary of training and documentation strategies and their implications for user interface design.
    - A brief description of the hardware/software environment and its implications for user interface design.
- New task definitions.
- Usability performance objectives.
- A system model, including metaphors.
- The degree of task vs. object orientation.
- Implications from the analysis of the database of user objects, functions, user classes, new task definitions, and frequency of task performance.

- The opening screen (rough sketch) and navigation principles.
- The rough designs for each task.

Each section of the user interface architecture document should contain the design rationale (i.e., a brief description of which alternatives were examined and accepted or rejected) and a rationale (e.g., based on test results from sessions with users or because of technology constraints or opportunities). Just like a distributed systems architecture, a user interface architecture is written over a period of time as the tasks during the user interface design phase are being completed.

The audiences of the user interface architecture include the software engineers who will be building the application and those who will work on fixing usability problems or extending the functionality of the redesigned application after initial roll-out. Usually, these are software engineers who were not part of the initial redesign effort and therefore are not familiar with the history and rationale of the user interface design.

In fire prevention assignments, the user interface architecture is part of the set of architecture documents prepared during the application design phase. In firefighting assignments, no such document usually exists, and there usually is no time to prepare one. However, where time and budget permit, the findings from a firefighting assignment should be documented in point form in a reduced user interface architecture document or they should be included in the application style guide.

5.2. APPLICATION STYLE GUIDE

The point of the application style guide is to document the guidelines and prescriptions for detailed user interface design. In the framework for information systems architecture (Sowa and Zachman, 1992), the application style guide would be part of the technology model expressing this model from the user's view (called the Human/Technology Interface in Sowa and Zachman, 1992).

An application style guide is usually based on a vendor style guide, but considers user classes, tasks, and implementation tool capabilities and constraints. For example, application style guides specify the subset of widgets appropriate for the users and tasks at hand, screen layouts for specific types of objects, use of common functions, use of the corporate logo, or use of business-specific terminology (and translations of this terminology if the application is multilingual). Each section of the application style guide should contain the supporting design rationale. The construction of a prototype representing the concrete user interface design is recommended as a living illustration of the application style guide. The scope of such a prototype usually includes the opening screen and the detailed design for one or several key tasks.

The audiences of the application style guide include the software engineers who will be building the application and those who will work on fixing usability problems or extending the functionality of the redesigned application after initial roll-out. The application style guide is also relevant for the quality assurance specialists who will be checking the software for conformance to the application style guide.

In fire prevention assignments, the application style guide and prototype are prepared during the detailed user interface design phase. In firefighting assignments, the application style guide may have to be reduced and sections of a vendor guide may have to be referred to or substituted. The prototype is essential but can be reduced in scope to a few sample screens.

5.3. USER INTERFACE SPECIFICATION

The user interface specification provides the details of the user interface for the software developers to implement. In the framework for information systems architecture (Sowa and Zachman, 1992), the user interface specification would be part of the technology model. The user interface specification expresses the technology model from the user's view (called the Human/Technology Interface in Sowa and Zachman, 1992). A user interface specification contains all the screens for all the tasks except for error conditions and help, which are standardized in the application style guide.

The user interface specification is geared toward the software engineers who will be building the application and those who will work on fixing usability problems or extending the functionality of the redesigned application after initial roll-out. The user interface specification is also important for the quality assurance specialists who will be checking the software for conformance to the user interface specifications. Software engineers working in testing often find the user interface specification useful for developing test cases.

In fire prevention assignments, the user interface specification is prepared during the detailed user interface design phase. In firefighting assignments, there is usually no time to prepare the user interface specification or it must be reduced to a sample specification. It has been the author's experience that, when usability resources are scarce in a firefighting assignment, time is best spent working with the software developers to review screens they have developed and coach and advise them on good user interface design rather than write user interface specifications.

6. CONCLUSIONS

It is appropriate to recognize that, regardless of the methods and techniques employed, the success of a usability engineering program depends to a large extent on the willingness of developers and senior management to accept and implement usability recommendations. Usability engineering is more often than not about making or recommending trade-off decisions between development, usability, and project issues. These decisions are business decisions (though they at first appear to be usability decisions). Usability engineers are not usually the final decision makers for high-profile issues, but can provide the information necessary for making informed choices. The recommended approach is to build a business case which supports the argument in favor of usability. A solid business case will often demonstrate the value of usability efforts to project managers and senior management, opening the door for the effective employment of usability engineering methods and techniques.

7. ACKNOWLEDGMENTS

The author would like to thank Diane McKerlie of DMA Consulting Inc. for her excellent contribution to this chapter both as a reviewer and fellow firefighter. Many of the ideas and methods presented in this chapter have been fine tuned in consulting assignments we worked on together. Her support, her sense of humor and the chocolate cookies she brings when the going gets tough are much appreciated. The author would like to thank the reviewers — Tom Graefe, Kevin Simpson, Ron Zeno, and Tom Dayton — for their detailed comments and thoughtful observations. They contributed much to clarifying the descriptions of methods and heuristics. The author would like to thank Marie-Louise Liebe-Harkort for her careful editing and encouragement. Finally, the author would like to thank Larry Wood, Ron Zeno, and the workshop participants for the opportunity to compare ideas and experiences and learn from each other at the workshop.

8. REFERENCES

Carroll, J. M. , Mack, R. L., and Kellogg, W. A., Interface metaphors and user interface design, in *Handbook of Human-Computer Interaction,* Helander, M., Ed., North Holland, Amsterdam,1988.

Jacobson, I., Ericsson, M., and Jacobson, A., *The Object Advantage*, Addison-Wesley, New York, 1994.

Molich, R. and Nielsen, J., Improving a human-computer dialogue, *Communications of the ACM*, 33(3), 338-348, 1990.

Monk, A., Wright, P., Haber, J., and Davenport, L., *Improving Your Human-Computer Interface: A Practical Technique,* Prentice Hall, New York, 1993.

Nielsen, J., Usability engineering at a discount, in *Designing and Using Human-Computer Interfaces and Knowledge Based Systems*, Salvendy, G. and Smith, M. J., Eds., Elsevier, Amsterdam, 1989.

Nielsen, J., Finding usability problems through heuristic evaluation, in *Human Factors in Computing Systems, Proceedings CHI, 1992*, Baversfield, P., Bennett, J., and Lynch, G., Eds., ACM Press, New York, 1992.

Norman, D. A., Cognitive engineering, in *User-Centered System Design*, Norman, D. A. and Draper, S., Eds., Lawrence Erlbaum Associates, Hillsdale, NJ, 1986.

Paulk, M. C., Curtis, B., Chrissis, M. B., and Weber, C. V., Capability maturity model version 1.1, in *IEEE Software, July 1993*, 18-27, 1993.

Preece, J., Rogers, Y., Sharp, H., Benyon, D., Holland, S., and Carey, T,. *Human-Computer Interaction*, Addison-Wesley, Reading, MA, 1994.

Sowa, J. F. and Zachman, J. A., Extending and formalizing the framework for information systems architecture, *IBM Systems Journal*, 31(3), 1992.

CHAPTER 9

Systematic Creativity: A Bridge for the Gaps in the Software Development Process

Jean Scholtz
National Institute of Standards and Technology, Gaithersburg, Maryland
email: Jean.Scholtz@nist.gov

Tony Salvador
Intel Corporation, Hillsboro, Oregon
email: tony_salvador@ccm.jf.intel.com

TABLE OF CONTENTS

ABSTRACT

This chapter describes a method that was developed and used by the authors while they were co-managers of the Human Factors Services group within the Personal Conferencing Division at Intel Corporation. The method described here was developed to help bridge several gaps we saw occurring in the process of incorporating user information into the definition, design, implementation, and evaluation of new software products. The method was targeted for use in developing new products based on new technology and therefore, not currently available. Our primary goal was to ensure that early adopters of these new products could see immediate, as well as potential, benefits of this new technology. Achieving this goal would facilitate the acceptance of this technology in the market place. The largest gap we saw was transforming user information into product design, both in terms of required functionality and in providing the necessary support for this functionality via the user interface. Additionally, we saw smaller gaps during the definition and development process that also needed to be bridged. In essence, what we wanted to create was a framework that could be used at every step during design, development, and testing to make decisions based on the original user information. In this chapter, we'll describe the framework we created and we'll describe how we use the methodology in theory, along with examples from one of the systems we worked on. This product was a second version of an earlier product, but with some radically different functionality added.

1. THE PROBLEMS

One goal at Intel is to make the personal computer the communication device of choice. Intel's software development efforts focus on producing technology and products to enhance the home and professional lives of the general public. As human factors engineers, we were faced with the usual problems, as well as having to produce user requirements for products that users did not currently have and, possibly, did not even foresee.

1.1. PRODUCING REQUIREMENTS FOR NOVEL PRODUCTS

Human factors engineers at Intel are faced with the challenge of producing user requirements and user interface designs for products not currently on the market. Moreover, these products have to be such that they can be readily adopted by many people — not just the early adopters of technology. This is difficult as market niches continue to decrease, making the search for a truly useful and usable product more and more difficult (Moore, 1991). Our biggest problem is communicating with users about nonexistent products based on nonexistent technology. It is difficult for users to quickly grasp a concept and then to imagine how this could possibly fit into their daily home life or their business environment. While a prototype system is often useful in explaining *what* could be offered, it can also make it difficult for users to envision a very different use the technology. For this reason, we suspected that methods such as PICTIVE (Mueller, 1993) and other participatory design methods would not be sufficient to obtain the user information we needed. Contextual Inquiry (Holtzblatt and Jones, 1993) is more closely related to what we wanted to do. Contextual Inquiry pairs observation with questions about what the user is doing in order to produce several types of models about the users' work, including work flow and objects. As our products are new to the market, we are interested more in identifying problems in users' current work practices than in exactly how they perform their work presently. We need information about how goals that users desired to accomplish fit with respect to their other job responsibilities. Moreover, we need to collect that information quickly and organize it in a way that the rest of the product team can easily understand the information.

1.2. MINIMIZING TIME TO MARKET

Once a product is identified, the time to market has to be minimized to launch the product before another company does. This places an additional constraint on our work, as up front requirements work has to be done very quickly. In addition, it is important that development occurs as quickly as possible. This type of environment is more suited to decisions and changes that are made early during product definition and design, rather than during usability testing. The decisions concerning functionality of the product, metaphor selection for the product, and overall user interface design are critical to achieving our goal. We need to be able to produce good designs in a short amount of time. We also want to be able to evaluate usability problems within the context of the original user requirements. We need a way to quickly identify the most critical usability problems to fix, thereby helping to achieve a shorter time to market.

1.3. CUSTOMERS AND USERS

Developing software for use in medium-large companies differs in many respects to developing software products for general or home use. One difference we viewed as critical was that we needed to uncover two types of requirements. Users must certainly be considered. However, users, in medium-to-large companies, are *not* the customers. Customers are the managers in the Information Technology groups. Their concerns are the network requirements and demands for these new products and technologies. Feature requests from the customer are necessary but don't give us any insight into how these features will be used by the end users. Marketing research focuses on obtaining the requirements from these customers which is used in to establish the boundaries for the product. Our work, as human factors engineers, was to produce the user requirements. These two sets of requirements must be merged, along with some general requirements from marketing, to produce the final product requirements. The situation in the home products market is also different. As the practice of "bundling" software onto a new computer increases, the customers become the producers of the computer systems and the users are the people buying the system for their use. In this case, marketing collects the requirements from the retailer while human factors specialists work with potential end users.

1.4. COMMUNICATING WITH TEAM MEMBERS

Because our products tend to be leading edge, communication and agreement among team members is often difficult. We suspect that this is due in part to the different goals that team members hold. The technical team tends to view a product as successful if the technology can be successfully implemented. The marketing members tend to view a product as successful if customers buy a sufficient quantity. The human factors members tend to view a product as successful if the end users actually use it. We needed a way to discuss functionality and brainstorm on designs. First, we needed team agreement on the requirements needed to produce a product that will be viewed as "successful" by all members.

We needed to clearly identify and agree upon the functionality the product should have. Once we have found a process for obtaining user input for these type of products, we need to find a way to communicate this input to the rest of the team. Developers, in this type of environment, have little time to accompany human factors engineers in the information gathering process. We need a way to organize our information so that they can easily form a picture of how users would use such a product. Moreover, communication is a problem throughout the development cycle. Even after a global design is produced, new products often encounter technology snags during implementation. Solutions to these problems need to be produced within the context of the integrated set of requirements. We needed a way to capture and structure the input from marketing, engineering, and human factors to make it accessible and useful to the team on a daily basis.

1.5. INTEGRATING REQUIREMENTS WITH USABILITY TESTING

We already mentioned the need to evaluate usability problems based on product requirements. It's not feasible to fix everything when problems do arise. We need to have a way of assessing the seriousness of the problem and to design a solution that is compatible with the original design. What to test for usability is also a problem, especially for very large applications. It's not always feasible to test everything, so we must make some judgment about what to test. We wanted a systematic way of identifying the most important tasks for usability testing.

1.6. A METHOD THAT CAN BE STARTED AT ANY STAGE OF PRODUCT DEVELOPMENT

Our final problem is that of timing. Unfortunately, we are not always present for the early requirements work, due to other commitments or just not being invited. We then face the problem of trying to do interface design or evaluation based on incomplete information. We need a method that can be used to show missing requirements or requirements that are contradictory to user needs.

1.7. SUMMARY OF OUR NEEDS

Our needs can be summarized as follows:

- A method to obtain user requirements for nonexistent technology, quickly.
- A method to integrate customer requirements, user requirements, and technological requirements.
- A method to communicate these requirements clearly to other team members.
- A method to facilitate user-centered decision making at all stages of definition, design, implementation, and evaluation.
- A method that can be used, regardless of the product stage at which it is started.
- A method that works with short time to market constraints (e.g., 6 months to a year).

2. THE GAPS

Early human factors work was relatively new to researchers and developers at Intel at the time we developed our methodology. In assessing our needs, we identified gaps between user input and decision making in the following stages of product development:

1. Creating and evaluating product definitions and user interface designs.
2. Evaluating alternative implementations.
3. Evaluating usability input.

While the first gap was of major importance to us, we realized that smaller gaps existed at other points in the current process. We had no way to make sure that smaller decisions made (with or without our input) during development were not negatively effecting decisions we had made during product definition and design. We had no way to tie the usability decisions we made back to the original definition and design criteria. We decided that a more comprehensive solution was needed. We needed to develop a vehicle that could be used as the basis for communication and decision making throughout the entire software lifecycle.

3. SYSTEMATIC CREATIVITY

The Systematic Creativity process was developed by Dr. Anthony Salvador and Dr. Jean Scholtz (Salvador and Scholtz, 1996). The name, Systematic Creativity, stems from the fact that design is creative. It *should* be creative. It *must* be creative in order to achieve a competitive lead. However, that creativity needs to have a systematic basis. The process used in product definition, design, and implementation needs to be systematic to achieve a time to market advantage. Additionally, all decisions made during the software process need to be made in the context of the integrated requirements.

3.1. THE FRAMEWORK

We developed two techniques: a method for collecting requirements from end users in an efficient manner and a framework for collecting, storing, and using this information during product definition, design, and evaluation. Our method is based on the underlying assumption that the work users do changes less frequently than how the work is done.

We'll discuss the framework first, as our requirements gathering technique is based on collecting the information types discussed in the framework. The framework separates product definition (what the product will do) from product design (how the product will do it.) Figure 9.1 identifies the data classes that comprise the framework. The data classes in the framework display one of three types of

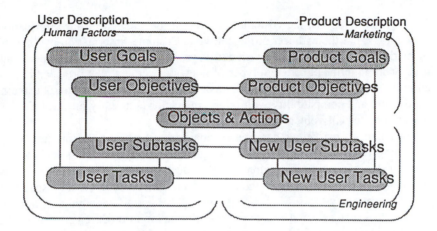

Figure 9.1 Systematic creativity framework.

relationships to the data class above or below them in the hierarchy: one-to-one, one-to-many, or many-to-one. For example, several goals may be related to one objective. Likewise, one goal can support several objectives.

Although the framework is statically represented here, the information in it is generated at different times. Think of the process as proceeding from the outer corners inward, starting from the upper right corner and moving counter clockwise. Information from marketing is combined with human factors input and engineering input. The culmination of this process results in the definition of the goals that must be supported in the product, along with the necessary actions and objects.

In this section we will define the data classes and discuss the reason we collect each one. The definitions are in the order that the various data classes would ideally be collected. The use of the various data classes is discussed in the section on "Using Systematic Creativity" and demonstrated using examples from a product where we employed this method.

3.1.1. Product Goals and Objectives

Goals are what users or customers want to do. Objectives are the reasons they want to accomplish given goals. Objectives may be personal: the customer or user wants to get promoted. Customer and user objectives also support the company objectives, for example, helping the company to increase revenue. A consultant in advertising might have goals of obtaining and distributing the most up-to-date information to her clients. Objectives for this could include obtaining more work from current clients or from their recommendations to others.

Product goals and objectives come from marketing research as well as from the marketing team itself. Remember, if the software being produced is intended for large corporations, the customer is likely to be someone from Information Technology, not the end user of the software. Customer information is obtained by marketing through customer visits, surveys, focus groups, etc. Customer goals usually are in terms of different types of networks, servers, platforms, and operating systems that the product should run on. Other goals are related to robustness, bandwidth, and compatibility with other applications currently in place. Objectives are not usually obtained from customers.

In addition, marketing contributes goals they have for the product from marketing research. Examples of these goals are that they must include the functionality of a previous version of the product, must include the functionality of another product currently on the market, must be compatible with a specified list of operating systems. Marketing also produces certain requirements of their own. A goal such as being able to collect information through registration of the software is an example of this type of input. An objective for this could be to collect information as to which users would be interested in other products being developed.

3.1.2. User Goals, Objectives, and Tasks

User goals, objectives, and tasks are now acquired by the human factors team, using an interview process (described in the next section). We are primarily interested in the goals and objectives for use in product definition. We use this input, along with the marketing input on product goals and objectives, as the basis for product definition and design. We also collect the tasks that the users carry out to achieve their goals. Depending on the scope of an envisioned product, we may do one set of interviews or two. If we are envisioning a large product or one that supports many different types of users, we may do an initial set of interviews to collect goals, objectives, and prioritization of goals. However, integrating our user input with marketing input, we can agree on the functionality essential for the product. We would then do another set of interviews to collect task information before we start the design phase.

Human factors engineers may also collect information about customer tasks. If customers express goals of installing, monitoring, or regulating use of the envisioned product, it may be necessary to provide another interface to access such functionality. In this case, the human factors staff interviews system administrators about tasks they currently do in other systems to support such goals.

3.1.3. Facilitators and Obstacles for Tasks and Goals

There are two more data classes not shown on the diagram in Figure 9.1 that are also collected: facilitators and obstacles. Facilitators and obstacles are associated with tasks, that is, what makes it easy or difficult for users in their current work environment to achieve their goals and objectives. Figure 9.2 shows a one-to-one relationship between tasks and facilitators and obstacles. As with goals, objec-

User Task Data Structure

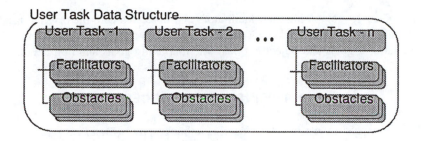

Figure 9.2 User task data structure.

tives, and tasks, facilitators and obstacles may also have many-to-one and one-to-many relationships. The obstacles and facilitators are constraints which help us evaluate alternative designs and implementations. Can we reduce the current obstacles and maintain or enhance the current facilitators in defining new user tasks in our software?

3.1.4. Actions and Objects Derived from Marketing Input and Human Factors Input

Once the team has agreed upon the set of goals that the product will support, the necessary actions and objects need to be identified. We start by extracting the current set of actions and objects identified in our interviews about tasks with users. These objects are used as the beginning of the objects that need to be "visible" in the user interface. The design also needs to support the actions (collected to date) that will have to be performed on the various objects. We add to the framework the objects and actions needed to support marketing goals as the task for those goals are defined. For example, to register a product a user needs a registration form that can be filled in, modified, and sent to the company. The goals that will be supported and the actions and objects that are needed for those goals provide us with a starting point for considering possible metaphors and designs that can be used to present the functionality to users.

3.1.5. New User Tasks and Subtasks

Engineering input to the framework occurs continually through product definition, design, and implementation. Initially there may be some engineering input based on known technology constraints. As we work with design possibilities the "new" user tasks are produced. This refers to automating a currently manual task or streamlining an already automated task. The "new" user tasks can introduce new objects and actions into the existing framework. Technology constraints discovered as design and implementation continues can add new user tasks, along with new actions and objects, to the framework. The basic framework allows evaluation of these new user tasks and subtasks along with any associated actions and objects by comparing their facilitators and obstacles with the original task's facilitators and obstacles. We also evaluate the new tasks in relationship to the original user goals and objectives or to the marketing goals and objectives.

4. THE INTERVIEW PROCESS

We use a process we call "engineering ethnography" (Mateas et al.,1996) to collect the user data. We need a way to collect and analysis data very quickly. Our time frame can be anywhere from a week or two to several months (several months is *very* rare). Our method depends on a skilled interviewing process, using a very unstructured interview. Because we are collecting a broad type of data, we may collect the data in several phases: a first pass to collect goals and objectives and a later set of interviews to collect the actual task information. Thus the first pass collects data used in product definition and the second pass is used to collect data for product design. If the scope of the project is sufficiently small, we may elect to collect both types of information in one pass.

In order to collect data about user goals and objectives, we start with a direction obtained from the marketing team. An example might be to investigate the types of communication that executives might prefer to do through a PC. Then we conduct interviews with six to eight people who fit our target market segment. Depending on how broad the target market is, we may conduct a series of vertical market interviews to determine if there is any commonality between goals and objectives for the different vertical markets and if the new technology adequately addresses the facilitators and obstacles of the different groups.

4.1. HOW THE INTERVIEW IS CONDUCTED

A team of two interviewers visits the users. One member of the team conducts the interview while the second team member structures what the user says into the data classes described in the framework section. We start by asking the user to tell us about his/her job. After we get an overview of the user's job, we encourage the user to discuss in more depth the goals and objectives which are in line with our broad direction. This first part of the interview gives us a good idea as to the importance of this smaller piece within the total responsibilities of our user. We organize the goals and objectives into our data classes as the interview proceeds. At times we'll pause to review these goals with the user to make sure that we've captured them correctly. After all the goals have been collected, we ask the user to prioritize them with respect to success in their job.

We then query the user, in depth, about goals and objectives that are in line with the direction we want to investigate for product definition. We capture the tasks, actions, objects as well as the associated facilitators and obstacles. As we conduct the interview, the interview team needs to interact with each other. The person conducting the interview will, at times, ask the person structuring the data if there are points that need elaboration. If any are identified, the interviewer then pursues this direction until the necessary information is obtained.

We do not have a list of questions that we ask the user. The team member doing the interview must listen very carefully to what the user says and construct each successive question based on previous input. However, we do "learn" from previous interviews we conduct. Therefore, if a previous interview has uncovered some surprising information, we will probe in that direction with future users to see if that information is validated. If, during an interview, we uncover some information that we haven't heard previously, we'll probe in depth in that direction.

Facilitators and obstacles are often volunteered by the users. When they describe how they do something, they often include phrases such as "we try to do this but it's not always easy because....". If facilitators and obstacles are not volunteered, we do ask "is that easy to do?" or "is that difficult to do?".

We use the same two people do conduct all the interviews if possible. This is just to minimize "mind sharing" between interviewers during analysis. If the time or number of interviews prohibit this, we use several teams and switch around so that all possible pairs are formed to do interviews. Frequent discussions are then encouraged among the interviewers. Ongoing analysis is encouraged, as is frequent viewing of the structured data, while teams are in the interview phase.

In the best situation the interview team is able to analyze one interview before conducting the next. If a complete analysis is not possible, the team has a short discussion after each interview to summarize any new information, to identify any conflicts with previous information, and to note any information that verifies what they have already collected. This produces several possible areas to probe in succeeding interviews. However, this has to be evaluated with respect to the overview information supplied by the next user. If any of these areas appear to be within that user's job description, then probing is possible. However, the interviewer needs to determine whether other information supplied by the user is more interesting.

We also switch the roles for the interview team members. We usually try to switch every other interview. We feel that this helps us to maintain better balance. The team member structuring the data gets a better sense of the user's tasks than does the team member conducting the interview. The interviewer has to listen for and recognize new information and probe in that direction if anything new is identified.

It is important to note that all our interviews are conducted at the user's workplace. In addition to conducting the interview, we do a careful observation of the user's office. Often we find items there that we ask about. For example, a user may have a large whiteboard schedule on his wall. We would ask (if the user doesn't mention it) what role this object plays in his daily tasks. Users sometimes open up file cabinets and explain how they store information or take us on short tours to explain how a certain process flows within their organization.

We take audio tape recorders along if companies will permit us to tape our interviews. This allows us to listen to prior interviews to obtain or clarify information we may have missed. We also ask for permission to take a still photo of the people we interview. Taking a photo back to incorporate with the structured data helps to make the information more "real" to the product team.

The interviewing process is not an easy one. Both members of the team must be skilled interviewers. They need to know how to listen and quickly interpret what the user says and how to probe for information rather than just asking a set of predetermined questions. Structuring the data is also difficult as it needs to be done quickly. We take breaks at times and assess how we're doing with the data. The interviewer cannot keep track of all the information and needs feedback from the team member, structuring the data, about points that were not adequately covered.

4.2. ANALYZING THE DATA

It is best to conduct an interview, analyze that data, and incorporate it into the accumulated data, then do the next interview. When we analyze the data collected during an interview, we normalize it. That is, we try to use the same terminology to describe the goals, objectives, and tasks for all our users. As the interview phase continues, we are able to structure the data using normalized terms instead of specific terms. Each interview builds on the one before it. Once we find the same type of goals and supporting tasks in successive interviews, we probe lightly only to ensure that there are no differences. We probe more deeply in areas where we have little or no data.

When do we stop interviewing users? We continually incorporate the data from each interview into what we have accumulated. When we find that we are getting little new data, we discontinue our interviews and go onto the next phase of our work. An easy way to identify the amount of new information added to the framework is to simply color code the information. Only new contributions are added for each interview conducted. When the new contributions appear in a different color, it is easy to see the amount of new information being added. When the new information is relatively small, it is safe to assume that sufficient information has been collected for product definition. The number of users will depend on the homogeneity of the target market.

As we collect the data, we structure it, using an outline form of a word processor. We use the different levels in the outline to represent the different data classes we collect. The first level is the objective. The next level lists goals that support this objective. At the next level, goals are expanded to show the tasks needed to support the goal, followed by subtasks. Facilitators and obstacles are expanded under the tasks. The next level contains actions and objects needed for the task or subtask. At this point, we move the data to spreadsheets. We sort the data in different ways, producing a sheet for each view. We have a sheet sorted by objectives, another sheet sorted by goals, etc. We use a numbering system to tie each data class back to the original objective and goal. We also note where the objective and goals came from — human factors input or marketing input. Using this method we can easily ask questions during design. For example, we can see which actions are performed on the same objects, or we can view all the goals that a task supports.

5. USING SYSTEMATIC CREATIVITY

We developed our method iteratively. We used parts of it on various portions of products we were working on at the time. This gave us the opportunity to refine and augment the method as needed. We used the method in five products during the time we were developing and evolving it. As we describe our methodology, we will illustrate the use of that particular technique by describing its use in one particular product we worked on. First, we'll describe the basic product. Then for each phase of our work we'll describe how the Systematic Creativity method was used. Please note that the screens used throughout the chapter as examples are from a simulation we built for evaluation purposes. The screens are similar to those in the final design, but not identical.

5.1. THE BASIC PRODUCT

In this instance we were producing a second version of a product. Intel had already produced CNN@Work [1] in conjunction with the people at CNN. Functionality included in the first product was limited to viewing CNN on your PC, recording portions of the broadcast, obtaining stock information, and tracking a portfolio of stocks. Very little human factors work had been done on the original product. When the time came to revise the product, human factors engineers were included in the team from the very beginning. The direction that was taken was actually worked out in cooperation with CNN. The ability to send additional text information along with the satellite video feed was now possible so users could view text stories as well as video stories.

5.2. PRODUCT DEFINITION

We begin by having marketing explain the proposed market direction. At this point in time, many questions and few answers exist. Each team then goes off to do the necessary investigation, with frequent meetings to synchronize what we are uncovering. After we collect sufficient user information, we meet with the other groups to collect the marketing goals and engineering constraints and incorporate them into our structured data. We start by looking at the user goals that we have collected along with the customer goals collected by marketing. We need to

[1] "Third-party brands and names are the property of their respective owners."

identify any that conflict. If we find such conflicts, we need to do further investigation to ensure that we understand what is needed and desired in our product. We also look at the priorities that we have collected from our users to identify the primary focus for our product. The framework gives all team members easy access to the data needed during this discussion. Engineering input is also vital at this point as we need estimations of how expensive supporting the different goals will be. Additionally, we need to be confident that we can reduce the obstacles and maintain the same level of facilitators users currently encounter in their tasks. There are several different scenarios here. It may be necessary for marketing or for the human factors team to do more research. We may decide that we don't have a product we can produce within the time or cost limits that will support the necessary user goals. If this is true, we iterate through collecting marketing goals and user goals in some modified direction. If we feel that we can develop a product that will support what users want to do, we proceed to the design phase.

5.2.1. Product Definition for CNN@Work

In this example, the basic product had already been developed. The added functionality being considered was (1) viewing text stories, (2) automatic capture of news based on user defined "filters" or descriptions of news that was of interest, (3) saving captured news, (4) filing captured news for long term storage, and (5) alerting users when news had been captured. We decided (due to time pressures) to only concentrate on collecting user information pertaining to the new functionality under consideration.

We identified possible users as being those who needed daily news information to do their jobs. We wanted to find out how people found the news they used, how they saved the news they found, how and if they distributed the news they found, what formats of information they collected (text, photos, videos, audio), and in what time frame they needed this type of information. We went to the workplace of the potential users, except in two instances. In one instance we were not allowed in because of security restrictions. In another instance it was impossible to conduct an uninterrupted interview in this particular environment.

As always, we asked users to tell us about their jobs. After collecting the overview information, we started probing for the different responsibilities that might include using information from the general news.

We found that most people spent little time sitting at their desks and, therefore, capturing news was a higher priority than watching news live. In fact, one obstacle that people described was not being able to watch broadcast news at a certain time due to other commitments. Our interviewees also mentioned the difficulty involved in catching up on the news after a business trip. They often gave up on this task as there simply wasn't time to review past news. We discovered that general news was not, in most cases, time critical. Time critical information was supplied by more specialized sources. People did not need to know about general news the minute it was captured.

We found that the type of news that people watched for their jobs did not change frequently. For example, people in advertising typically had several fields of expertise that did not change. They wouldn't suddenly switch from working in the food division to working in the automobile division. This implied to us that people would be more likely to spend a little more time constructing and refining filters for capturing the news they needed as these filters would be used for a long period of time.

The biggest obstacle for users was having to go to many different sources to look for news and finding the time to do so. Finding the news, given a source and time to look, was a relatively easy task. Users either scanned for particular sections in magazines or newspapers, listened or watched news broadcasts at a certain time, or just scanned for particular words in news publications that were signals of possible articles they should read. Users were pretty certain that they didn't miss any news of interest, assuming they had the time to look.

We had considered putting together a filing system within the program to allow people to categorize the captured news in ways that facilitated retrieval. However, we found that people used unique filing systems. Some were based on categories — storing everything about a certain category together. Some used dates to organize their files. The majority of users wanted to integrate information from many sources and many also wanted to use hard copy for filing. We found that people wanted to share portions of the news they captured with others in and outside of their company. This led us to prioritize exporting news stories to existing file managers, rather than developing a complex filing mechanism within the product.

In summary, our initial work allowed the product team to prioritize the needed functionality. We knew that we could eliminate developing an elaborate filing system and that users were more interesting in capturing information than in watching it live. We knew that users were not particularly interested in being alerted when news was captured but that they wanted to immediately see how much had been captured whenever they went to look. We also knew that we had to make the process of defining filters to capture the news easy and give users enough feedback to refine these filters. As the type of information people looked for did not change frequently, we were encouraged that they could see the benefits of taking time to explicitly define filters that could be used for an extended period of time.

Requirements work produced these user goals (among others):

- Selectively filter text and video stories on keywords and text.
- Refine filters based on feedback.
- Obtain feedback on the number of stories captured (to get information useful in refining filters).
- View captured news and save stories in any filing system (the ability to export data).
- Share news with others in organization.
- Capture news that occurs at a particular time.

- Produce basic filters easily and quickly.
- View news in the background while doing other PC work.

5.3. PRODUCT DESIGN

Once the team has agreed upon the goals that the product will support, it is time to begin product design. We use two portions of the data for the beginning of product design: goals that the product will support and the actions and objects needed to support those goals. Our framework allows designers to construct design possibilities based on the goals, actions, and objects that have been collected. This information helps us decide what type of metaphor, if any, would be useful in conveying the supported functionality to our users. We use the user and customer goals and the actions and objects currently identified to help in the evaluation of metaphors or design ideas. How well does a suggested design indicate support of the required goals? How well can we represent the actions and objects needed within a particular design? While Systematic Creativity doesn't give an easy answer for what the design should be, the framework facilitates brainstorming and decision making with all the collected information laid out. We think this allows better first cuts at design. Once we have come up with some viable alternatives, we can solicit user input via low-fidelity prototypes. This is merely a task of bringing in users and asking them to speculate on what a product will do given the opening screen (our low-fidelity prototype). We keep track of what functionality they correctly identify as well as any functionality they identify that we don't plan to support.

Once we've decided upon a particular design direction or metaphor, we need to work on the precise representation for the actions and objects (note that we've already factored in feasibility about these representations when selecting design possibilities) and we need to design the new user tasks and subtasks. We use the prioritization of goals to determine the amount of visibility and access for tasks and subtasks. We use the facilitators and obstacles in the users' current environments to evaluate the new possibilities for tasks and subtasks. At times, automating tasks results in adding more obstacles than in the current user tasks. We must, therefore, make sure that users can see reduced obstacles in later tasks and that these reduced obstacles will produce a sufficient reason to use the product. As we're designing these tasks and subtasks, we continually bring in users to test out our designs. We use a combination of high- and low-fidelity prototypes depending on the type of information we need to get from a user. If we're only interested in whether they can find the path needed for doing a task, we will probably use paper screens with paper pull-down menus. If we need to evaluate task details, we will produce a high-fidelity prototype of at least that portion of the product.

We use general design guidelines and platform-style guidelines as design work progresses. We do not have corporate style guides for new products as most of these products have very novel interfaces. We do keep track of other products being developed and try to be consistent with designs already used for similar functionality. In some cases, we use this opportunity to learn from any earlier design mistakes.

As our design progresses, new tasks and hence, new actions and objects, are added. These must all be evaluated with respect to the goodness of the fit within the proposed design and with respect to the goals that they support. When tradeoffs need to be made, we use goal prioritization to help our user-centered decision making. The most important user goals must be streamlined at the cost of lesser goals. The Systematic Creativity framework allows us to easily check on prioritization of goals.

At the more detailed levels of design, actions are given initiators and feedback is defined to show the results of an action on an object. An initiator defines how users will perform an action. For example, a user could select a menu item, select an icon in a toolbar, or the action could be automatic. Does the same initiator work for all objects on which this action is performed? Feedback is needed to indicate to the user the results of the action. Is the same feedback appropriate for that action on all objects? Our framework is continually updated as new actions and objects are added. We can then look to see which actions are used on each object by simply sorting spreadsheets as needed. This helps us make decisions about initiators and feedback at a global level. That is, will changing an initiator for one action on one object work for all other objects on which this action is performed? We can ensure that the design takes into consideration sets of actions and sets of objects. This helps us design both terminology and visual feedback by taking sets of objects and actions into consideration.

5.3.1. Product Design for CNN@Work

The user goals included:

- Selectively filter text and video stories on keywords and text.
- Refine filters based on feedback.
- Obtain feedback on the number of stories captured (to get information useful in refining filters).
- View captured news and save stories in any filing system (the ability to export data).
- Share news with others in organization.
- Capture news that occurs at a particular time.
- Produce basic filters easily and quickly.
- View news in the background while doing other PC work.

Marketing goals included:

- Display that text stories are available.
- Give customers (not users) the ability to monitor the system.
- Customers have the ability to create an internal channel used for distribution of company talks, news, and training.

Figure 9.3 A window similar to this was used for the opening window in CNN@Work, Version 1.

- Give users information about what types of information (text, audio, video) are available on each channel.

Engineering informed us that not all channels from CNN would have video, text, and audio information. Also, customers defining their own channels could choose which types of information would be broadcast. Therefore, we identified a new goal: users should be able to quickly determine what type of information would be broadcast on each channel.

We had identified actions and objects that needed to be represented in our interface. The objects identified, along with a subset of actions on them, included:

- Text stories — view, save, export, delete.
- Video stories — view, save, export, delete.
- Filters — view, create, modify, delete, activate, deactivate — but save.
- Channels — switch, view types of information available.

As we were working on a second version of the product, we started with an interface and had to decide if the new goals we supported and the new actions and objects we needed could be represented using the original metaphor. The first version of CNN@Work used a TV metaphor and allowed the user to change channels, change volume, adjust the picture, record information, and bring up the stock view. Figure 9.3 illustrates the original interface.

The thought among the product team was that we should use the same metaphor for the main window of the new version of CNN@Work and display the availability of text stories. We brought in users to try out versions of this using paper prototypes, as well as very simple prototypes built on top of the original product. We were not successful in portraying this functionality to users. Users were certain that they could watch video using this application, but they were completely unaware that text stories were also available. Users had no idea they could set up any sort of individualized capture mechanism to save video stories that came across while they were away from their desk. They knew that they could do timed recording in the first version but had no idea that they could do recording based on the content of video stories. Most of the efforts to try to get this information across concentrated on menu items and on icons in the toolbar. Due to the limited space we had for the interface, this was a necessity. One goal supported by the original product was to watch the news live in the background while working on another task. This meant that the interface had to be reduced to a small size that still allowed users to see the video.

Given that capturing news stories and viewing text stories were high priority goals for the users, we felt that a drastic redesign was needed. We decided to abandon the TV metaphor and make text stories and capturing news the focus of the interface. As viewers had prioritized capturing news above watching TV we felt we needed to make sure they could easily find this type of functionality in the interface. Figure 9.4 shows a design for the main window which is similar to the final design.

We used several different ways in the final design to display that text stories were available and that news could be captured. We displayed the active channel and noted what type of information was available on that channel. Recall that corporations using CNN@Work could choose to have their own channels, and that CNN had several channels: HeadLine News, CNN, and CNN FN (the financial news channel). Of these, only HeadLine News would currently carry text stories. Local corporate channels might only have text announcements on them and occasionally might broadcast a speech by one of the corporate officers. We didn't want users to be confused about which services were available on each channel. This also gave us the opportunity to display the different types of information available. We discovered during design testing that users were confused about what channel or channels filters would monitor. We needed to convey that filters only applied to the currently selected channel. We used the label "active channel" to convey this message to users.

We gave the users a window displaying story titles that were currently available. We could cache stories for a certain period of time before they would be replaced by new stories coming in. We presented the story names in a scrolling list, including the present video story and the next video story to play. Recall that since many of the actions for text stories were the same as those for video stories, we wanted to treat those objects in the same fashion. From the main window, users could view either kind of story (by double clicking or by selecting a story title and

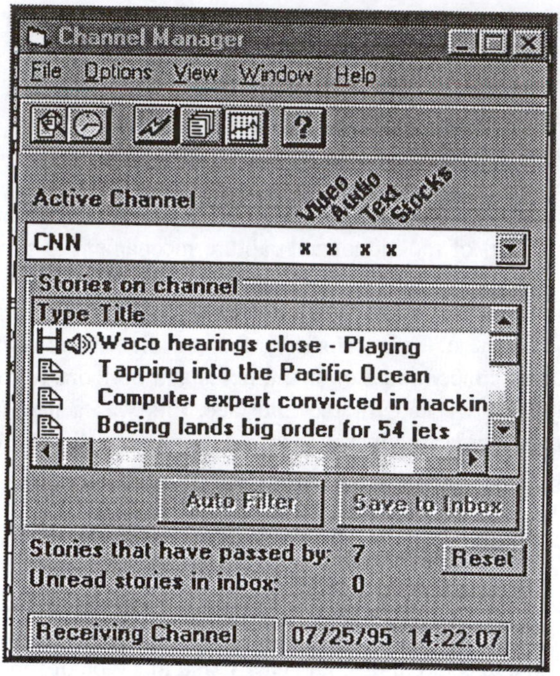

Figure 9.4 Opening window for CNN@Work, Version 2 showing text story and capture capability.

pressing a view button that was added to the final window design), set a filter based on a story title for either video or text, and save the story directly to the inbox. The one exception was the "upcoming video story". We used the method of appending "next to play" and "playing" next to these story titles to alert the user to this exception, while still portraying that this list was a list of stories that were available for a limited amount of time.

We wanted to assist users in defining filters for capturing news stories as we found this was a high-priority goal. We found that finding news was easy for users to do currently. They scanned newspapers searching for keywords or for company names. They listened to news for the same types of keywords. They looked in certain sections of the paper or tuned into certain broadcasts that they knew would provide the information they needed. During initial design testing, we experimented with different ways of having users describe filters to capture the news and found (not surprisingly) that using Boolean expressions was a difficult task. In our case, the problem was more severe as the news stories were available for viewing and capturing only temporarily. News that is not captured is replaced by new stories, thus making it impossible for the user to tell what, if anything, he or she has missed. We needed to provide feedback on the number of stories transmitted during a given time. We put in a count of the number of stories that had appeared in the story window since the user had been logged in. Users could also view

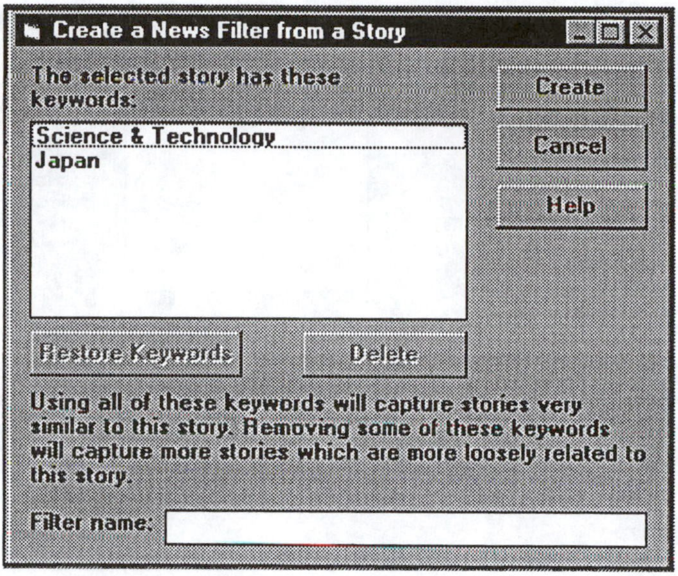

Figure 9.5 The autofilter windows that appears when a story is selected and the autofilter command is given.

captured stories by the name of the filter that had captured this story. Thus, if a user found that several hundred stories had appeared and that his/her filter had failed to capture any stories, he/she might suspect that the filter needed to be revised.

We put an "autofilter" button on the opening window. Not only did this serve to alert users to the filtering functionality, it provided easy access to an example of a filter. All a user had to do was to select a story displayed in the story window and press "autofilter". The auto filter window (shown in Figure 9.5) then opened to display a filter which would capture a story just like the one the user had selected. This filter could be saved as is or it could be modified by the user slightly to capture more or fewer stories about this particular topic.

The filter creation window (shown in Figure 9.6) provided several aids to users. Keywords were provided and were divided into different categories. We worked with CNN to ensure that these same keywords would be used for classifying and capturing stories. As users entered keywords and supplied the proper AND or OR connectors, a summary window gave feedback in natural language about what the filter would capture. For example, a response might say "this filter will find stories with the industry classification of government and the subject classification of aviation and the key words of jet propulsion". In addition, we predefined some filters that could be used as is or could be refined slightly according to users' requirements. For example, "high tech", "defense", and "environmental regulations" could serve as predefined filters.

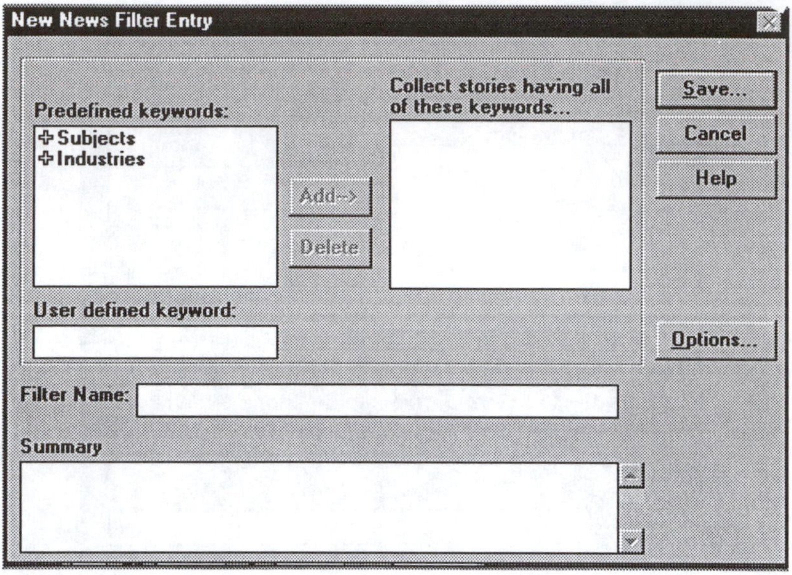

Figure 9.6 The window for filter creation.

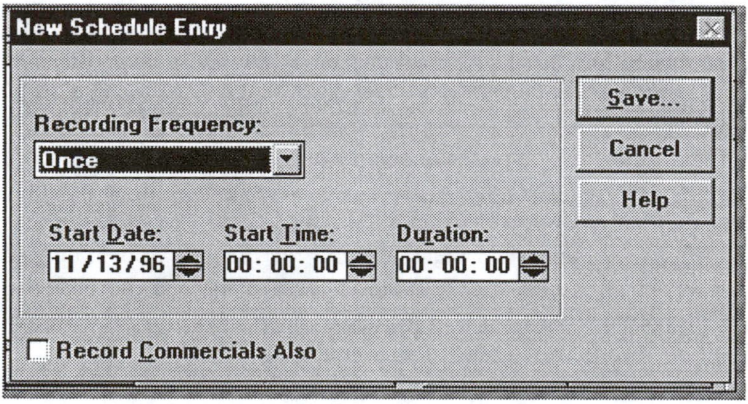

Figure 9.7 The window used to setup a time based filter.

We knew that users went to certain sections of the newspaper or certain television channels to find pertinent news. We needed to support this functionality as well. In addition to allowing users to define filters based on keywords, we provided a way to define time-based filters. We also predefined filters for various segments of CNN to use as is or to modify. The window for creating time-based filters was similar to the dialog window for creating keyword filters. Figure 9.7 shows the dialog window for creating time-based filters.

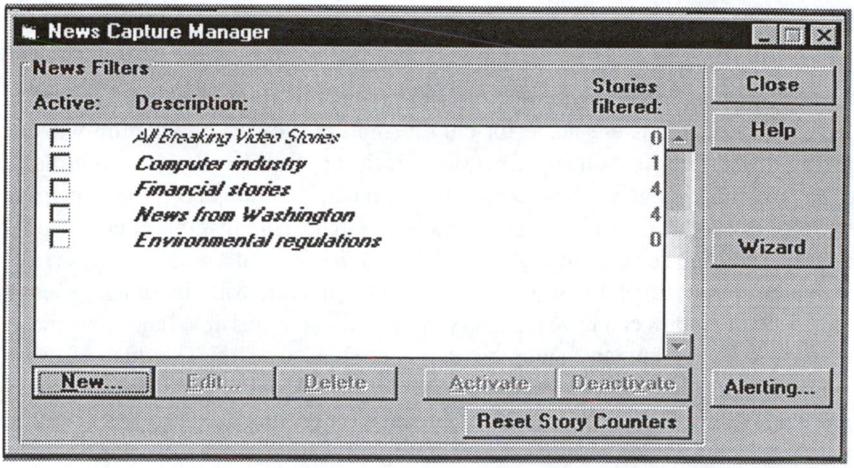

Figure 9.8 Filter manager.

We provided users with a way to manage the filters they had created. This is an example of new user tasks being created as a result of automating other user tasks. The filter manager dialog allowed users to activate and deactivate filters and to save or delete deactivated filters. The filter manager (see Figure 9.8) provided an easy way for users to view the status of any filters. The filter manager also provided users with the ability to select a given filter and modify it to create a new filter.

Another problem encountered during design testing was how to convey to the users where the captured stories were saved. We wanted to create our own storage area so that stories could be saved by their title, rather than automatically creating one or requiring the user to create a title for each story. We created a "Save to Inbox" button on the main window to accomplish two things. First, users could see where the captured news items could be found. Second, users had a method for capturing a story "on the fly". We had wanted to develop a wizard to walk users through the filter setup process, providing advice if users attempted to define filters that would not capture any stories. We were not able to implement this feature due to time constraints. However, we did design the user interface for a wizard that could be incorporated into subsequent versions.

It is important to note that we started with an original set of goals and used them to evaluate different design alternatives. The goals were readily available to use as scenarios for design testing with users. As we proceeded with design testing, we also verified our original set of goals with participants in the design testing. After the actual testing, we asked them about different functionality and how important this was to their particular job.

5.4. PRODUCT IMPLEMENTATION

Designs often get modified during product implementation with only a local view. That is, modifications are made for only a small part of the application without looking to see the affect on any other parts of the application. Perhaps an initiator for an action is changed to be more useful for a particular object. If the developer were looking at the global level, he or she would make sure that this change would be a positive one for all objects on which this action is defined. While several small less-than-optimal decisions rarely affect the overall usability of the product, many such decisions can have a negative impact. It is impossible (and most likely not even safe) for human factors engineers to stand over the shoulder of every developer and check every decision made or to do usability testing on every decision. We needed a way to convey information to developers so that they can make implementation decisions within the global framework. We feel that the Systematic Creativity framework facilitates this communication. Developers can use the framework to see the effect that a decision will have on the entire product. If this decision affects a high priority goal or many goals, then a human factors expert should definitely be called in. If the decision is at a lower level and affects very low-priority goals, the developer can use the framework to help evaluate his decision.

5.4.1. Product Implementation for CNN@Work

At this point in the development of our process of Systematic Creativity, we were still working on the best way to format information in the spreadsheets and, given the time restrictions we were under, we decided that we needed to share the information quickly with the product team. We did this by having the team as a whole do a walkthrough of several of the critical tasks, step by step. We used overheads of the interface as it currently existed. We put up the main window and asked the team members to write down what they would do to achieve a particular task. We asked, after each choice in the process, how many had selected the correct choice and which, if any, other choices had been selected. Then we went on to the next step. We continued this process for the subset of tasks we had selected. Team members quickly got a different view of the interface when they looked at the tasks users were expected to do in order to accomplish the ultimate goal. This process succeeded in convincing team members of the value added by viewing the system from the users' perspective. In fact, we would recommend that product revision teams start by doing a walkthrough of the previous product to quickly understand the extent of the changes that should be made and to start off with the users' view in mind.

We were working closely with the developers during product implementation. This was a relatively small project and the head developers had been convinced of our added value during our design work. Therefore, major decisions during implementation were not made without consulting one of the human factors staff on the team.

5.5. USABILITY TESTING

There are two aspects to usability testing: what to test and how to evaluate the results. The Systematic Creativity framework helps with both of these issues. We use the prioritized goals to address what to test. It is also worth noting that the goals form the basis for the user scenarios needed for the test plan. While some elaboration is needed, the framework contains the basic information needed for constructing user scenarios. If tapes have been made of the user interviews, usability people can refer to these if help is needed in refining the test plans. Looking at the facilitators and obstacles in the new user tasks also help us construct questionnaires to be used in testing. We want to know if we have sufficiently reduced the obstacles so that users perceive our product as beneficial in achieving a goal.

The framework is vital to evaluating the results of usability testing. From the framework we can classify failures in the following manner:

1. Failure to support a desired goal.
2. Failure to sufficiently reduce obstacles.
3. Failure to make visible the support for a desired goal.
4. Failure to provide a necessary action or object.
5. Failure to provide meaningful feedback on task progress.
6. Failure to provide initiators that are visible or meaningful to the user.

The first failure is catastrophic but should not happen if we have done sufficient design testing. Questions of supporting goals should be identified during our design iterations and incorporated into the product. However, if our involvement with the product occurs late in the cycle, this may be a possibility. The development team will need to decide if the lack of support for certain goals still results in a viable product.

Failure to sufficiently reduce the obstacles associated with the tasks is also a very serious error. Again, this should have been identified during design testing. Producing a more efficient user task can be a large redesign problem that can seriously affect the product schedule. The Systematic Creativity framework can be used to identify the importance of this task which can help the team members decide if the time for redesign needs to be taken.

Failures 3 and 4 are major failures and again should have been detected earlier in the design iteration. If little up-front work has been done, these failures will be detected at this time. Using the framework we can see what goals and tasks need the particular action or object. We can then evaluate the seriousness of this failure based on the priority of the affected goals and the difficulty of adding the visibility or the action or object needed.

Failures 5 and 6 are the least severe — at least from the standpoint of how much redesign needs to be done to correct them. Having the Systematic Creativity framework in place, the team can locate an individual action or object and see how changes made in the context of that particular task will affect other tasks using that particular action or object. The tasks in which the action or object is used can be traced back to user goals, thus allowing the team to make the corrections in a more global fashion, rather than making a change and subsequently discovering effects in other portions of the interface.

5.5.1. Usability Testing of CNN@Work

It is always difficult to determine when design testing stops and usability testing begins. We tend to think of usability testing as more formal testing later in product implementation. In usability testing we concentrate on testing that our usability goals have been verified. In defining the usability goals for this product, we specified percentages of users that should be able to accomplish basic tasks during their first encounter with the system. We also specified what percentage of users should rate each task within a specified range we had defined to represent "perceived ease of use". Specifying these usability goals is an extremely difficult task, especially when the product or the functionality is new. We were able to use some information from usability tests on the first version to produce specifications for previously supported functionality. We based the specifications for new functionality on the priorities of user goals in relationship to priorities of previously supported goals. More important than having "exact" specifications in the requirements document, we now had agreement from the team that these requirements were as real as functionality requirements.

Basic tasks for this product included:

- Changing channels.
- Setting up a simple filter from scratch.
- Identifying where a story was captured and retrieving that story.
- Viewing a story currently available.
- Viewing a story currently available and storing it.
- Viewing a story currently available and creating a filter based on this story.

A usability test determined if our product met the specified usability goals we had established. The usability test focused on the same tasks that we concentrated on during design, those that were of the highest priority to users.

6. HOW DOES SYSTEMATIC CREATIVITY BRIDGE THE GAP(S)?

In this product we concentrated on using our methodology for product definition and design. Did Systematic Creativity help in defining a product and why? Our process facilitated communication between marketing, engineering, and human factors as the information was gathered in one place and laid out in a prioritized fashion and showed where the different goals came from. This allowed us to make the necessary tradeoffs in a knowledgeable fashion. We were able to identify the goals that we must support in addition to those that it would be nice to support.

As the data was in text form, we were all focused at the same level. All we could discuss was the priority of the functionality to users' goals and to the marketing goals.

Systematic Creativity was very useful in deciding on the look of the interface. Changing the main window from the television metaphor to a story window/ channel changing design could not have happened without having the integrated product goals systematically laid out. This helped the team agree that conveying the functionality of viewing and capturing text stories was essential to the success of the new product. Taking the extra time to produce the autofilter capability and to produce the sample filters was also an essential part of the product, again convincingly argued from looking at the facilitators in the Systematic Creativity framework, along with the results of design testing. The decision about where stories were to be filed was also guided by the Systematic Creativity data. Knowing that users wanted flexibility in their filing systems and that many wanted to integrate the captured stories with data from many sources helped us decide to prioritize development of an export facility over development of a more elaborate filing system within the application itself.

We made some use of Systematic Creativity during product implementation and usability testing, but our major contribution to this product was during product definition and design. Systematic Creativity was useful as a framework that allowed decision making at each phase of the definition and development process to be made based on the same information.

7. OTHER WAYS TO USE SYSTEMATIC CREATIVITY

7.1. GETTING OFF TO A LATE START

What if the human factors team is not involved at the very beginning of the product definition process? Can the Systematic Creativity method still be used? The answer is yes, and we see this as a particular strength of the process. While not being involved in the up-front work is less than ideal, we feel that this process gives us a way to deal more effectively than most with the situation.

Suppose we are involved at the design phase, but not early enough to do any interviewing and requirements work with a user population. We still have the customer goals from marketing to use. In this situation, we produce, along with marketing and the development team, what we believe to be valid user goals. Then our early low fidelity prototypes reflect these goals. As we bring in users to assess the prototypes, we collect two types of information: what functionality they think the prototypes reflect and how this functionality fits with their work goals. We collect information about the validity of our goal assumptions along with information about the proposed design. This may result in more iterations than normal if we discover that our goal assumptions are incorrect.

Suppose that we aren't consulted until the implementation is being done. Producing a usability test plan essentially constitutes putting together assumptions about user goals and goal priorities. It is essential that the development team be consulted and agree upon the test plan. Are these the goals that they think this product supports? Again, as testing is done, questions need to be asked about the appropriateness of the goals, as well as measuring the problems users have in completing certain tasks. The problem with finding this information out at this time is that it is often too late in the production cycle to do add more functionality. We have a sound basis for recommending a starting place for a revision or even slipping the release schedule for the current product if the problem is serious enough. If work starts during implementation, we would probably expand the framework beyond goals which would be the basis for our testing scenarios. If we find particular problems in a given task, then we might do some probing with usability test participants to determine how they currently do these tasks.

7.2. NEW AND REVISED PRODUCTS

We find this method to be most useful for new products — products where the goals and objectives that must be supported aren't clearly known. This was in fact the reason that we developed the method — we found other methods insufficient to support this type of product development. However, we still find Systematic Creativity to be useful for making revisions to existing products. In these cases, only the direction considered for the revision needs to be probed for in the interview process. Existing goals and supporting tasks currently in the interface can be documented from the interface itself. This might also be an ideal time to examine facilitators and obstacles that exist in the current product and see if there are some candidates here to consider in the revision process. Candidates for the new revision can be evaluated by going through the Systematic Creativity process, but only the new directions need to be evaluated. However, such issues as redesign of metaphors and the visibility of functionality should be considered globally. Including goals supported in the existing product into the Systematic Creativity framework is helpful in evaluating overall definition and design.

7.3. BUILDING MODELS

We have used the framework at a higher level, addressing only goals and objectives, to produce models of user populations. We believe these models can be used to evaluate new proposals for products, assuming we keep the models up to date. It would also be advantageous to include a way to construct different views of the data in any tool we design, to allow us to look across different sections of the populations. As we probe in depth in areas suggested by the models, we need a way of incorporating the old and new data, into a new product definition framework. We have yet to update a model but this ability suggests that we need a way to view the data from different perspectives in time and also a way to document changes that may have occurred during that time period (cheaper technology, new technology, wider adoption of technology by certain industries, etc.).

8. DIRECTIONS FOR SYSTEMATIC CREATIVITY

Currently we have been using time-consuming tools for putting together the framework. We use outline versions of word processing systems tied with spreadsheets that can be sorted in multiple views. This requires much effort on the part of the human factors team. This work must be done to construct the original framework and to update it during product development. Having a tool that could automatically provide links and allow us to assemble different views coupled with the ability to trace objects and actions back to the original user goals would definitely speed up the tedious work. As we work with the framework, we are evolving our requirements for an automated system to help in maintaining the data and the relationships between them.

The framework could also be the starting point for design rationale. Consider for example, making a decision not to include a particular feature that is very beneficial to users because of the present cost of the needed technology. This decision may result in the inclusion of other features to partially provide the omitted feature. We need a way to document these design decisions so that later revisions can be made knowing why a particular decision was made and the ramifications of that decision.

Currently the data for the framework needs to be collected by people trained in interviewing techniques. This makes it difficult to take along developers or other team members as they have no time for training in this area. On one hand, this wasn't a limitation for us, as we have considerable difficulty finding team members who are able to take the time to accompany us on these interviews. It would, however, be nice to give product team members more of a firsthand look at the users rather than seeing impersonal text. One way of doing this would be to incorporate audio or video clips attached to different data classes that illustrate issues users told us about during data collection. Rather than bringing the team to the users, we would like to use intranet technologies to bring the users to the team by providing a multimedia framework. Use of an intranet site could also be used to generate and collect discussion about particular points. A framework diagram containing hot spots that team members could use to view current discussions or to contribute ideas would facilitate input from the team and would promote more of a shared view of the product.

9. SUMMARY

Systematic Creativity facilitates team communication and decision making. Providing a way to lay out all the issues and see conflicts of goals and priorities of goals is a great facilitator in product definition. It gives all team members the same basis of information to start from and enables user-centered decision making. The same is true of the design process. Creativity is not stifled but it is evaluated by assessing all the information and noting how all the needed goals are supported.

Having such a framework produces better product design as all goals are taken into account when the initial brainstorming is done. Having the information in text form, rather than visual form, has proven to be a good idea. Too often we find ourselves arguing about the form of the visual rather than the basic ideas of what functionality it supports. Having only text there for the beginning of product definition allows us to concentrate on the real issues — what functionality do we have to support and what can we support well.

We feel that this method has great promise in creating new products as well as revising existing products. The ability to generate and view data about user requirements systematically allows us to do a more complete product definition and design. Decisions about what to include in the product and how to include particular features can be made knowing what it is that users really want to do.

10. ACKNOWLEDGMENTS

This work was done by the authors along with other human factors engineers at Intel Corporation. We thank Doug Sorensen and James Newbery for their work in information gathering, information displaying, and their devotion to using this method for design and design testing. Michael Mateas worked on the development of the CNN@Work product and the screen shots in this chapter are from a simulation written by Michael. Thanks also to the user interface developers on the CNN@Work team for their support of our work.

11. REFERENCES

Holtzblatt, K. and Jones, S., Contextual inquiry: a participatory technique for system design, in *Participatory Design, Principles and Practices*, Schuler, D. and Namioka, A., Eds., Lawrence Erlbaum Associates, Hillsdale, New Jersey, 1993, 177-210.

Mateas, M., Salvador, T., Scholtz, J., and Sorenson, D., Engineering ethnography in the home, in *Common Ground, CHI'96 Conference Companion*, Tauber, M., Ed., ACM Press, New York, 283-284, 1996.

Moore, G.A., *Crossing the Chasm*, Harper Collins, New South Wales, 1991.

Mueller, M., PICTIVE: democratizing the dynamics of the design session, in *Participatory Design, Principles and Practices*, Schuler, D. and Namioka, A., Eds., Lawrence Erlbaum Associates, Hillsdale, New Jersey, 1993, 211-238.

Salvador, A.C. and Scholtz, J. C., (1996). Systematic creativity: a methodology for integrating user, market and engineering requirements for product definition, design and usability testing, in *Engineering for Human-Computer Interaction*, Bass, L. J. and Unger, C., Eds., Chapman & Hall, London, 1996, 307-329.

CHAPTER 10

The UI War Room and Design Prism: A User Interface Design Approach from Multiple Perspectives

Kevin T. Simpson
Financial Models Company, Mississauga, Canada
email: kevin.simpson@hwcn.org

TABLE OF CONTENTS

ABSTRACT

This chapter focuses on two practical design approaches to bridging the gap: the User Interface War Room method and the Design Prism method. The walls of the "user interface war room" served as a metaphor used in redesigning the interface of a computer-aided software engineering (CASE) tool for telecommunications research. To begin, user requests (derived from task analysis interviews with software developers) were posted on the first wall of the war room. The English text describing these requests was grammatically parsed to yield user objects (and the functions which acted on them). These user objects were organized into hierarchical relationships and posted on the second wall. Design ideas were then generated in a creative process that drew ideas from team members, users, existing software, and scenario data. This led to the development of several mutually exclusive prototype systems, which could then be verified against the original user requests to make sure that concrete designs matched user requirements.

In the Design Prism work, which involved redesigning the interface for a power plant, the user objects and functions of the war room were subdivided into four categories of user elements: Information, Objects, Goals, and Actions. Relationships between these user elements were captured in a "table of relations." Prototype ideas were then sketched from the perspective of each category (e.g., from a user Goals perspective first). These idea sketches were fleshed out into actual screen designs, with the help of plant-specific design guides for coding information and for displaying graphical objects. Finally, the alternative designs from each of the four perspectives were consolidated to yield either a single "best-of" prototype or several distinct alternatives that could then be evaluated with users.

1. INTRODUCTION

1.1. WHY THIS CHAPTER

I began my career in Human-Computer Interaction both thinking and writing about the topic of this book. One of the first documents I wrote at work was entitled "Techniques for Translating User Task Analysis Information into User Interface Prototypes". It was written as an attempt to fill a hole that I had perceived in the existing literature on the topic. I had just recently entered the field at this point, and I think my very naiveté gave me a valuable perspective for the writing. I knew what I needed to know, and I knew what wasn't there. There was a lot of "magic" — a skill that I hadn't yet developed — in this thing called interface design.

My first position was an apprenticeship-type position with a user interface specialist at a telecommunications company. We were working on the design of the interface for a computer-aided software engineering (CASE) tool. We had just completed the first formal user task analysis this tool had ever seen. As a result of delayed software releases, our UI specialist's vacation time happened to fall right when we were about to take all of our carefully gathered user information and turn it somehow... magically... into concrete design.

I'd seen designs before, of course — they're all around you when you turn on your computer. There were even some good rules-of-thumb to help me assess whether the design I created was halfway decent or not. But now that I had some good, solid user data on which to base a design... I didn't know quite what to do with it.

I had discovered "the gap", and I hadn't the magic necessary to get me across.

I searched the literature, and it was then that I become aware of the surprising scarcity of guidance that deals directly and practically with this crucial aspect of the design cycle. I began to pay close attention and to document the techniques my colleagues and I were using. Since that time, I have continued to evolve these techniques on my own and to monitor their successes and their limitations.

1.2. DESIGN CONTEXT

For the sake of clarity, I will make a distinction between the two different work environments in which my user-interface design techniques evolved:

- Telecommunications research — high-level redesign of the interface for a computer-aided software engineering tool.
- Power plant design — computerization of existing plant procedures, characterized by a strong emphasis on the replication of existing functionality.

The User Interface (UI) War Room method discussed in this chapter is based on my telecommunications research. The Design Prism approach was originated during interface design and analysis for the power plant. In the sections that describe each of these methods, I will further define the design context in which the work was done and on which the method is based.

The design context presented in these sections is meant to situate the design recommendations presented in this chapter and give the reader a sense of the conditions in which an approach has been effectively used. The techniques presented may be more suitable for some design environments than for others. I do not believe that we should be looking for a single method of design as much as for a set of tools that can be used under particular circumstances. I encourage the reader to try out the methods used in this chapter and to try combining them with other methods from this book and from personal experience. Each interface design project is unique and different circumstances call for different measures.

One of the ideas which has taken form in my methods is the exploration of multiple perspectives... multiple ways of looking at and approaching design. In this spirit, I present two different techniques that I have found to be useful in practice — the User Interface War Room and the Design Prism. I would ask you to consider these two methods separately to begin with, since they were developed under different circumstances. After I've introduced and explained each of them, I will give some suggestions on how they might be used in conjunction, based on my own future intentions to explore.

2. THE "USER INTERFACE WAR ROOM" AS A METAPHOR FOR INTERFACE DESIGN

A "user interface war room" is an affectionate way of describing a room dedicated to the purpose of getting ideas to flow freely, putting them up on paper, discussing them, and ending up with paper prototypes of a system. When our design team acquired just such a room, I began to use it as a metaphor for the interface design process I originally documented in my telecommunications work.[1]

Figure 10.1 shows a picture of the room, to give an idea of its layout. As you can see, this is your standard four-walled room, with floor and door. Each of the walls in the room was designated for a particular step in the design process.[2] At this stage of the cycle, we had already extracted key user requests from our task analysis interviews and documented them in an overall user task analysis report. These *user requests* were prioritized and placed — one user request per sheet — on the left-hand wall of our UI war room. On the back wall we pasted *user objects*.

---

[1]   Though we were fortunate enough to have the use of a dedicated UI war room, the methods described in this section could also be used in the absence of such a room.

[2]   The reader might find it interesting to compare the war room we set up here to the room described by Karat and Bennett (1991) in their "four-walls design environment", which I have since come across. The walls of their room were designated for Scenarios, Design Constraints, Open Questions, and Design Sketches.

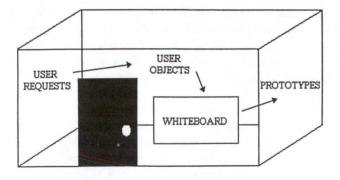

Figure 10.1 The user interface war room.

These came directly from the interviews. They were things like "module", "architecture diagram", "key element", "layer of software" — words that represented some sort of concrete conceptual item to users, in their language (our users were software developers). We took these objects and arranged them on the wall to show hierarchies and interrelations. Then we would flesh out some creative ideas on *the whiteboard* (usually working with a partner) and post the more refined ideas on the right-hand wall. We constructed and refined higher-level, top-down views of the system, while at the same time developing the sketches that came from bottom-up styles of idea generation. In the end, we could check the resultant paper *prototypes* against the user requests and user objects, to make sure that the prototypes reflected the user needs and information we had gathered.

2.1. DESIGN CONTEXT — THE UI WAR ROOM

As a basis for the UI war room design, we used task analysis information in the form of interview write-ups. An overall user task analysis report described key commonalities and general information extracted from the individual interviews. This was a purposefully informal document, consisting of an introduction, a description of the subjects interviewed, "what they are trying to do", "how they are trying to do it", and "what they would like" (i.e., key user requests). The user task analysis report, in combination with the individual interview write-ups and our own understanding from talking to users, provided a foundation for design.

Our user population consisted of software developers working on telecommunications code in a proprietary programming language. The following characteristics are descriptive of this population:

- Expert computer users.
- Fairly homogeneous, consisting of two main types: those troubleshooting existing code (less experienced) and those designing new code (more experienced).
- Internal company employees.

Our design team consisted of eight software developers, a team leader, a documentation specialist, a senior user interface specialist and myself, a junior UI designer. Most of my design work in the war room was conducted alongside one of the team's software developers who had an interest in user interface design. Other team members played a role by contributing design ideas and making decisions that surrounded and contextualized the design occurring in the war room.

The team, as a whole, had relative freedom to pursue desired directions in both design and implementation. This meant that we had the luxury of working on high-level design for the interface as we wanted it to look some 2 years down the road, to give us a well-thought-out migration path. The product design can be characterized by:

- Fire-preventing, rather than fire-fighting.
- Providing a graphical view of an existing software system — where existing code, the basis of design, was structured hierarchically.
- Lots of physical space available (a roomful).

2.2. USER REQUESTS

User requests had been parsed from the individual task analysis interview write-ups, as part of the user task analysis report. On each user request, we noted the rough number of developers who desired a particular capability (e.g., "several developers asked for...", "all developers agreed...").

Examples of user requests are as follows:

- Graphical representation of data structures

    Several developers indicated that they would like to see graphical representation of data structures, for both global and local data. They want to see tables, fields, pointers to other tables (type resolution), where those are initialized, and to what. They also want to see initial values of parameters and identifiers, and where/when they are assigned. For any given data store, they also want to be able to determine who reads it, who writes it, and where it's allocated.

- Print for inclusion in design documents

    The majority of developers interviewed wanted to be able to print chunks of windows containing pertinent information. This hard copy could be used both in the design/development/debug process, but more importantly, in the design and development documentation, and eventually in training documentation.

We prioritized the user requests, using team consensus, and stuck them up on the left-hand wall of the war room. This was an informal process. We made the assumption that all of the key user requests summarized in the task analysis report

Table 10.1   **Assessing the Validity of User Objects in the Interface**

Where the Object came from...	Validity	Comments
Overall User Task Analysis report (e.g., "UTA)	Highest	Object has meaning and is of importance to most users
Specific user task analysis interview (e.g., "UTA — Cindy Lee")	High	Object is in the language of users and is of importance to at least a subset of users
Previous release of software (e.g., "3.0")	Medium	Caution required Replication from previous releases is generally desirable if there have been no customer complaints
Team member (e.g., "Kevin")	Low	No direct link to users; a team member felt it was a required object
Other software (e.g., "CodeBrowser 6.1")		Object derived (stolen?, liberated?) from other software Be sure to test these objects and parts of the interface with users

were of equal value to users, and allowed the team to prioritize the items through discussion and voting. A more formal method may have ensured a closer match between user priorities and our priorities, but this method helped provide team focus and commitment, which are not to be taken lightly in a real-world context.

2.3. USER OBJECTS

On the back wall we taped user objects — once again, one per sheet. These were objects that represented something concrete to a user — though an object may or may not have had a real-world counterpart. Each user object was labeled according to users' terminology (e.g., "buddy", "procedure variable", "the switch"). We tried to capture our knowledge about each user object on its sheet — writing down comments, definitions, and functions that acted on the object. We would expand on the definition of objects by referring to individual interview write-ups, which would in turn identify new objects to be defined.

2.3.1. Recording the Origins of Objects

Next to each user object, we would write down where the object came from (e.g., from the user task analysis report, an individual interviewee, a previous release of software, or a design-team member). This was a successful way of capturing the relative validity of each object's existence in the interface, and the need for usability-testing of the concept with users (see Table 10.1). However, just because a user object had low validity didn't necessarily mean that it belonged any less in the interface. It meant only that the object would have to be more rigorously investigated with users, to make certain that it was significant, unambiguous, and comprehensible.

We followed a rule that no object should end up in the user interface that was not among the user objects defined. If an object did appear in the interface that was not on the User Object Wall, then we would review the situation: Either the object would have to be added to the wall or else it would be removed from the interface. This helped us to ensure that we recognized where an object came from and why it was in our interface. If an object was added to the User Object Wall during prototyping, it was to be accompanied by the name of the team member who added it, and/or the name and version of the software product from which the idea came.

While it is necessary that all objects used in a prototype appear on the User Object Wall, it is not necessary, nor expected, that all user objects from the back wall will be used in the prototyped system. Some user objects (and user requests) will simply fall outside the scope of the application being designed. It is possible that we could be producing excellent, user-approved prototypes based on even a small portion of the assembled user objects. However, if it seems that too many user objects are not being used (particularly if they are objects of high validity), it might be a cause to rethink the interface.[3]

2.3.2. Organizing the Objects

We took advantage of the space available to us by organizing user objects on the wall, representing hierarchies and interrelations between the objects. This organization helped us to recognize some major categorical divisions and to structure the interface accordingly.

The following piece of text shows an example of raw user task analysis interview data and the user objects (italicized) that were parsed from it. Figure 10.2 shows one potential organization of these objects on the wall.

> Rebecca Mahony is now working to understand 6 new *modules* of code. She relies heavily on her "*buddy*" as a *resource,* since he originally developed some of this *code*. But the code has evolved and now the original few modules interact with many others. Rebecca often has to contact the *group heads* who "own" these modules, because the *module and procedure headers* (which are supposed to describe them) are so out of date. Otherwise, she is stuck reading *sections* upon sections of code. The *code library* lists the names of group heads. Rebecca would really like to see *parameters* into and out of a procedure, as well as the *structure* and *flow* of *data* that is accessed by procedures. Neither of these is provided in the text-based *cross-reference tool* she currently uses.

---

[3]   It could also just mean that the scope of your task analysis was particularly broad.

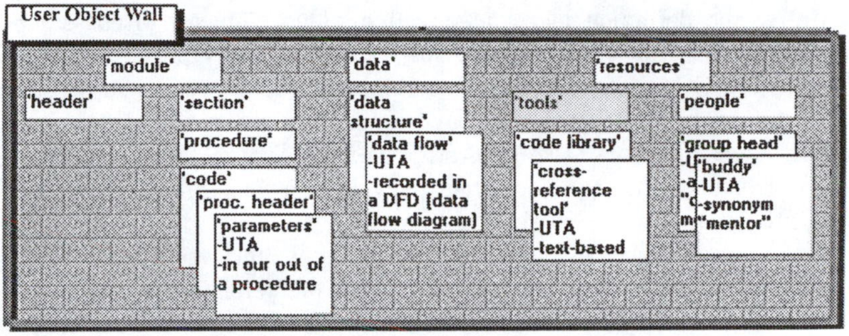

Figure 10.2 Organization of objects on the user object wall.

Categorization of user objects was largely a process of trial-and-error. An object might start off in one position and be moved to another position as more objects were put up on the wall and new categories emerged. This was a bottom-up process. We would organize objects to represent hierarchical relationships between them, only to begin to see some lateral/horizontal relationships across the subhierarchies. We would rearrange branches of the tree, so that these related items would be closer, but this would often have the effect of moving other relationships further apart. In the end, we just aimed for the best fit possible. Eventually, all the objects were organized in a hierarchical fashion, capturing relationships both vertically and horizontally. The techniques we used are not far removed from the Affinity Diagram method described by Cohen (1988) and taught by Holtzblatt and Jones (1992).

Let's take the objects "module" and "procedure" (both objects represented in our users' software code) from Figure 10.2 as an example. On the User Object Wall, we would place the word "module" *above* the word "procedure" to represent the relationship between them (i.e., "module" encompasses "procedure"). This is an example of what I call a vertical affinity (or vertical hierarchy, to be more specific). This is not a deterministic process. For instance, the word "code library", instead of showing up underneath "tools" (as it did in Figure 10.2), could as easily have appeared above "module" in the hierarchy.

Once vertical affinities had been mapped out, we tried to add horizontal affinities. In Figure 10.2, for example, I have intentionally placed the word "data" next to "procedure". I could have instead put the "data" branch on the other side of the "resources" branch. However, the "data" branch seems more closely related to the "module" branch than "resources" would. For this reason, I chose the horizontal position I did — to capture the horizontal affinity.

2.4. THE WHITEBOARD

On the third wall we hung a whiteboard. The whiteboard, in my mind, is a tangible symbol of the creative aspects of design. In this section, then, I will discuss some of the techniques I have used to generate design ideas.

Unlike the definition and categorization of user objects discussed in the previous section, the creative processes the whiteboard represents are not so firmly rooted in the physical location and timing of the war room itself. The ideas that go up on the whiteboard may have come from other sources than the task analysis alone. They may also have originated a long while ago, coming to life from a shelved product, a previous release cycle, or a walk through the park some sunny afternoon.

There are a number of methods we used within the war room to maintain creativity. The tools we used — yellow stickies, markers, big pieces of paper — are all conducive to a playful and creative way of thinking. The room itself, with ideas on the walls and plenty of space, helped further in maintaining a creative mindset. We also tried using common objects (e.g., pipes, conveyor belts, baskets) as temporary metaphors for users' conceptual models. Most importantly, we tried to get ideas from as many people and places as possible (e.g., team members, users, other software, the user's physical work environment).

We generally prototyped ideas first that had been given high priority on the User Request Wall. This, however, held more closely for detailed design. In the earlier stages, we followed an unwritten rule of pursuing any idea, right then and there, when it came to mind.

2.4.1 Too Few Cooks'll Spoil the Broth

I am of the opinion that the more people whose ideas we can get flowing, the better. If only one or two people are generating ideas, the ideas can all too quickly dry up. Even if the ideas keep coming, they are likely to become stagnant, and begin to follow a particular pattern. It is important to get fresh perspective on prototyping ideas — whether this is in the form of criticism, an entirely new direction, or an unexpected new suggestion. Respecting and valuing the ideas cultivated from users and from other team members also helps in gaining support for the final product and in increasing feelings of team cohesion.

One day in the UI war room a fellow team member was looking over the prototypes we had developed and began to ask me some questions about them. The conversation gradually turned to the current implementation of a piece of our tool. He was not fond of the way it worked and had some ideas about how it might function more effectively. He was, however, having some trouble getting the ideas across to me in words. As this was the case, I quickly persuaded him to draw them. He ended up — after some poking and prodding — illustrating what he meant on a piece of paper, which was then placed on the wall for general discussion... and to trigger our memories when the time came to further develop that feature. This "poking and prodding" I have playfully labeled the Spanish Inquisition Method and it becomes another tool for gathering ideas from people-sources.

2.4.2. User Involvement in Design

Some interface components that are developed in the war room may have come directly from suggestions or drawings made by users. These may include graphical, navigation, and layout ideas. It should come as no surprise that some of the most lucid design solutions are offered by users.

One strategy we used to elicit design ideas from users, during the task analysis interviews, was to ask them for drawings that they had made in the course of their work (or we copied down what was currently drawn on their own whiteboards). In many ways, these drawings give a good picture of how users visualize and understand information.

We also involved users throughout the task analysis process itself (of course), and in usability evaluations of prototypes at various stages. We did not, however, explore any truly participatory design work with users.

2.4.3. Existing Interfaces as a Source of Ideas

Existing interfaces are a valuable source of information and ideas that should not be overlooked. Interface solutions may come from other tools within your product, from tools outside (related or unrelated), from old ideas "on the shelf", and from past designs ("don't fix it if it ain't broke").

Studying other applications that users currently employ in their day-to-day work is also important in ensuring that your own tool will fit within their work environment.

2.4.4. Flirting with Scenario-Based Design

During our task analysis, we had the good fortune of working very closely with one user, with whom we conducted an observational interview. We watched and listened as he reviewed in the space of an hour how he had solved a software problem report over 2 weeks' time. The task information we recorded from this interview was heavily detailed.

I took the scenario for this one user problem and used it to drive the design directly. I designed a depth-first prototype (using very rough sketches) of an interface, based on the information we had gathered in the observational interview. I followed his process exactly, and simply mocked up part of a screen at each step that would fulfill what I perceived to be his needs during that step. I didn't worry about how full a screen was, because I was only intent on prototyping the part that our user was concerned with at that moment. I wasn't worried about originality at this point either, so I often took my drawings from other interfaces I had seen or from my own previous prototypes. This method kept me in a very creative, fast-flowing frame of mind. Every part-of-a-screen I designed would be labeled with an arrow pointing to the part-of-a-screen that came next in our user's task. Sometimes I would just label a screen with a title and leave it at that. Other times I might have an option box here and a few lines of code there or maybe just a link to another tool (or a picture of a telephone so that he could call his "buddy" for help). Not everything I drew was going to end up on a computer, let alone in our software.

I ended up constructing a series of fairly illegible and incohesive diagrams...but this did not matter. The main significance of the effort lay in evoking the frame of mind of an individual user at his task and in helping me to generate creative new ideas that could be expanded upon later, during the more slow-and-steady periods of prototyping. The development of these screens also helped to give me a stronger sense of the order and sequencing necessary for our interface. It gave me a very definite method of approach — that of translating our subject's verbal information into a prototype intended to capture *all* of the information he had given me. This forced me to be thorough in a new way: depth-first rather than breadth-first.

I was later able to transform some of the parts-of-screens I had created into more concrete prototyping ideas. In Figure 10.3, I provide an abstract view of the interface pieces I constructed (on the left) and how I might put these into an actual prototoype (on the right). In this example, the piece numbered "2" was used more than once in the user's task. This meant that he was doing roughly the same thing at two different stages (though there might have been small variations in context), and needed the same sort of information or control in both spots. To support him in this, I decided to place sketch number "2" at the top of his screen — as a static section of the interface — while the other pieces of the task were arranged beneath, on two separate screens. The intent was to make his most-used task available from any screen. In ways such as this, I experimented with synthesizing the scenario sketches I had created into meaningful prototypes.

We would have required scenario information from many more users if we had wanted to take the scenario-based design further and come up with representative user interface designs on this basis. Instead, the scenario mostly just helped me to generate new ideas, to step out of my current perspective, and to verify that our existing design attempts were on the right track.

2.5. PROTOTYPES

Most ideas would go through at least one iteration before they were tangible enough that we would feel comfortable posting them, autographed, on the Prototype Wall. We later found it possible to separate out mutually exclusive prototyping ideas that could not exist in the same interface. We developed these separate alternatives further — in turn or in parallel — as desired. If you consider the Whiteboard as the brainstorming stage, then the Prototype Wall represents the

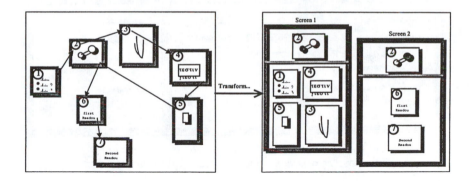

Figure 10.3 Abstract representation of a scenario-based design strategy.

stage where as-yet-uncriticized ideas from brainstorming are evaluated and synthesized and are organized into a cohesive whole to meet strategic needs.

2.5.1. Choosing between Idea Sketches

Earlier, on the User Object Wall, I had placed the word "module" above "procedure" to represent the relationship between these two concepts (Figure 10.2). The
next part involved mapping these relationships to the interface prototypes themselves (using the whiteboard). A number of representations of the relationship
could have resulted. We could have indented procedures in a list directly beneath
each module name (Design 1, in Figure 10.4), or, we could have used a box
(labeled with the module name) to encompass all of the procedures within a
module (Design 2). There was no deterministic process for choosing which idea
sketch would make it into a prototype. For the most part, we used informal criteria
to help us decide which of the proposed methods to use. Screen real estate was of
concern, for instance, so one of the more convincing strategies was to list procedures beneath a module name and to make the module names collapsible (Design
3; similar to Macintosh file directories). The user could then decide whether or not
they needed to see the procedures within that module.

In retrospect, a better-defined decision method such as the Questions, Options,
and Criteria (QOC) method (MacLean, Young, Bellotti, and Moran, 1991) could
have helped us, at this stage, to formalize and record our decision-making process.
A QOC-type method would have forced us to standardize and document the issues
(Questions) we considered in deciding which alternatives (Options) to keep. It
could have made clear the link between these options, the Criteria we used to
evaluate the issues, and the choices we made. A formal decision-making method
— most likely recorded *after*, rather than during a design session (so as not to stifle
creativity) — would help with maintainability of the interface design over time.

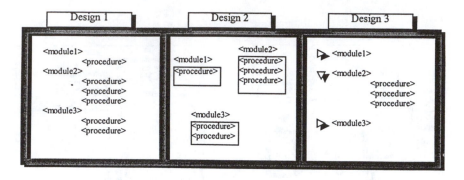

Figure 10.4 Three possible designs for "module" encompasses "procedure".

Where possible, the choice of designs could be left up to the user — by placing design alternatives into separate prototype systems or by performing formal usability testing on the different options.

2.5.2. Concurrent Top-Down Iteration

So far, most of the discussion has centered around bottom-up processes of design. At the same time as we were sketching ideas for features, we were also designing (and iterating) the high-level structure of the system's interface. We worked with the user requests, early on, to determine high-level categories within which we might best classify our user objects. To illustrate: at first we tried classifying our user objects into eight categories which covered all of the high-priority user requests: Data, Definition, Calls, User Interface, Control, Structure, Runtime, and External Information. We tried placing each of our objects into one of these categories. We stopped after less than half of the objects had been classified, feeling that the number of categories was increasing out of control and that the user objects were not fitting as well as we had hoped.

We began to feel blocked from our goal and looked for some other way in which to determine the key features of our prototype, and reduce the number of categories. Eventually, we ended up taking a hard look at our list of categories, and waded in with both feet to do some pruning. We decided that User Interface objects were not really major features of the tool, but that they would form its structure instead. We removed Control as a feature, because control flow and the order of procedure calls could be shown within the Calls section of our interface. We then decided to remove the External Information category, since it contained objects to which we would connect our tool, rather than features of the tool itself. Finally, by combining the Data and Definition pieces, we had cut the number of categories in half. We were left with Calls, Data/Definition, Runtime, and Structure as our major, structural features (see Figure 10.5).

Later, as we did some more bottom-up prototyping, we found that it made sense to reorganize the high-level structure we had created. We now combined the

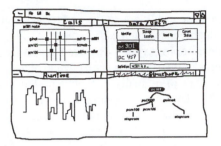

Figure 10.5 High-level prototype idea sketch.

Calls and Data pieces, instead of the Data and Definition pieces which were combined earlier. This changed the high-level categories to Cross-reference, Definition, Runtime, and Structure. Iterate and iterate again.

It was important to keep re-defining our interface at the top as well as at the bottom. For instance, if we had prototyped a Cross-reference part of the tool, without explicitly defining at the top-level that we were combining the Data and Calls, then the front end of our prototype would no longer have been in synch with the individual prototypes for each feature.

2.5.3. Separating out Mutually-Exclusive Prototype Systems

It is important that alternatives be explored in prototyping, for at least a couple of reasons. First, more than one prototype should be tested with users: It is too easy for a user to quickly say, given a single prototype, "Sure that looks good", leaving the designer with little valuable feedback. Second, many good ideas will come up during prototyping sessions, from a variety of sources. Not all of these ideas can possibly fit together into a cohesive whole. Some ideas will conflict with others.

We had a number of team members working on the interface. Most of the work in the early stages of the war room was being done by myself and by one of the software developers on the team: myself, because it was my responsibility as user interface designer, and the software developer because he had the time and the interest. To this point, the two of us had spent most of our time working together on a single prototype system (the one in Figure 10.5), with our view narrowed to the completion of this one framework.[4]

Other members of the team were also encouraged to use the war room and to post their ideas there. Some had been working in parallel on their own high-level views of the system. Feature ideas had been stewing throughout the previous release cycle, to the point where team members had even coded fairly sophisticated computer prototypes of potential features. These prototoypes were consid-

---

[4]   It should be noted, though, that many of our spur-of-the-moment, right-then-and-there ideas didn't fit within our main framework and were left sitting around like leftovers waiting for the right high-level prototype to pick them up.

ered valid and valuable contributions to the war room — but they were given no more weight than rough paper sketches.

Once a fair number of prototyping ideas were up on the wall, we were able to pick through the pieces of interfaces, organizing and rearranging them to come up with the smallest number of mutually exclusive systems possible. Some of the pieces represented different (or overlapping) ideas for one feature and, therefore, were unlikely to appear in the same prototype system. Other sketches could fit in any of the alternative systems, so the distribution of these pieces became an executive decision based on best fit. Still other pieces might end up in all of the alternative systems, if no other ideas were generated for that particular feature.

We ended up with six different prototype systems — where each alternative system could not be fully meshed with any of the others. Even so, pieces of systems could still be moved around, from one system to the other. As each of the systems was developed in more detail, the number of alternative systems could grow or contract as appropriate.

2.5.4. Matching User Requests to Developed Features

Once we had identified and developed a paper prototype of a system (however rough), we could then take individual user-request and user-object sheets and paste them on the prototype. In this way, we verified that important features were being covered and that the interface was built on user information, rather than on intuition alone. Simple as this may sound, pasting the sheets on the prototypes represented the completion of this part of our journey, for all we meant to do was to make our way across the room. Later, of course, user evaluation and iteration would occur. However, for the time being, the UI War Room process had given us some large and practical stepping stones to get from user information to first-draft concrete designs.

3. DESIGNING FROM MULTIPLE PERSPECTIVES — THE DESIGN PRISM

The literature on Human-Computer Interface design has historically maintained a focus on presenting alternatives to users. Let's look for a moment at what this asks of UI designers. It asks designers to develop more than one option in parallel. It asks them to do so while preferably still maintaining creativity and uniqueness between options. As individual designers, are we capable of meeting this demand?

To some extent, of course, designers are capable of pursuing multiple alternatives. However, it is my contention that we are restricted by a human tendency to reduce designs to single "solutions". This process of funneling information can be indispensable as a human problem-solving technique, but it can also interfere with our ability to pursue more than one solution at any given time. As we adopt (both consciously and unconsciously) what appear to be the best choices at the time, we are simultaneously losing a myriad of other possibilities. The problem isn't simply that we forget that other options existed, but that our "best" solution begins to block out other alternatives — so that we fail to even think of them in the first instance. We suffer from tunnel vision. Just as we have trouble dividing our attention in short-term cognitive tasks (e.g., Anderson, p. 52), I believe it is also difficult for the human mind to maintain a number of creative and distinct alternatives over long periods of time.

It is for the above reasons that I suggest an approach which looks at user data from several different perspectives and maintains these perspectives through the idea generation and initial prototyping stages.[5] This imposes a structured methodology which forces designers into thinking about and creating distinct alternatives, without imposing restrictions on the creativity within each perspective. When funneling occurs, ideas are now channeled in four different directions (instead of just one. Alternatives are pursued in parallel, up until the point where concrete designs can be reviewed by users.

I use the analogy of a prism to illustrate the design approach I have taken. Just as a prism splits light into a visible spectrum of color, so similarly I take raw user data and split it into distinct elements. The types of elements (or *design perspectives*) are user Information, Objects, Goals, and Actions. I create a table showing which elements in each perspective are related to which others. I then draw up rough sketches from each perspective (e.g., from the perspective of user Goals first). Finally, I consolidate these different views of the same problem. Depending on the nature of the task, this may result in a single "best-of" prototype or it may result in several distinct alternatives. These activities are illustrated in Figure 10.6.

3.1. DESIGN CONTEXT — THE DESIGN PRISM

In the Design Prism work, where replication of existing plant functions was the focus, user requirements were represented by (1) a hierarchical breakdown of operating procedures for the plant, which provided the grounding for (2) a task analysis. We called the hierarchical breakdown a function analysis. It presented goal statements for operator activity. At the top of this hierarchy was a single, highest-level operator function: "Operate the Plant to Setpoints, to Achieve Safety and Production Objectives". This top-level function was divided into six subfunctions. These sub-functions were each in turn divided and redivided, eventually creating a hierarchy intended to cover all operator functions that related to plant operation. At the bottom level, then, were individual, reasonably low-level goal statements. An example might be: "Control Liquid Level in Boric Acid

---

5 Another approach to preventing the loss of design alternatives is to carefully record unpursued alternatives and design decisions. While this is an important process (and I recommend it), it doesn't help with the actual generation of design alternatives themselves. In this respect, another alternate strategy would be to simply have more team focus in design. This might only succeed, however, if team members were to work in isolation, since the same problem of losing alternatives is likely to occur for teams, as well as for individuals (i.e., "groupthink").

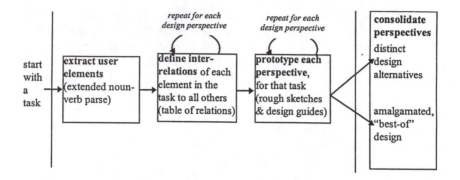

Figure 10.6 Design prism activities.

Storage Tank". These bottom-level functions became our individual user tasks for the task analysis.

The task analysis itself, then, needed only capture the timing and sequence of steps necessary to accomplish each of the bottom-level operator functions (individual tasks). The task analysis was also intended to cover branching and exception scenarios, where these were not already captured in the function analysis. The highly structured nature of the function analysis, with its clearly-defined individual user tasks, leant itself well to interface design on a piece-by-piece level.

Our user population consisted of operators of nuclear power plants. The following characteristics are descriptive of this population:

- Extensively trained on the software we create.
- Can be considered very homogeneous, as a result of training and educational background.
- Interval company employees, or employees of a client company.

The Design Prism techniques described in this section were developed by me mainly as an individual designer, working on my own. Other members of a team of four to six Human Factors specialists were available for review and criticism of the work I produced.

A few of the individuals on the team were working on design from the bottom up, while the most senior designers were working on the overall design of the control room. The bottom-up designers, myself included, would work on design one task at a time. The product design can be characterized by:

- Fire-preventing, rather than firefighting.
- Emphasis on replicating existing design — providing computerized access to existing physical procedures in the plant.
- Design conducted mostly at a desk, with limited physical space.
- The interface, for critical safety reasons, cannot be too "open" (i.e., user choice is strictly limited, so that the interface presents discrete and known possibilities to the user; windows cannot overlap one another)

Table 10.2   Example Elements within each Design Perspective

Design Perspective	Example User Element
Information	"Tank level" "Pressure is dangerously high"
Objects	"Tank" "Pneumatic valve"
Goals	"Control tank level"
Actions	"Start agitator"

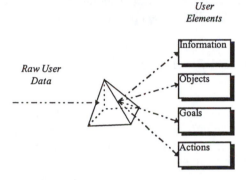

Figure 10.7 Extracting user elements.

3.2. EXTRACT USER ELEMENTS

I found it useful, in designing for the power plant, to subdivide the user objects and functions I had used in the UI war room into four categories: Information, Objects, Goals, and Actions [borrowed very loosely from the GOMS model (Kieras, 1988) and from object-oriented design]. Examples of the different types of user elements are shown in Table 10.2.

To extract the different user elements from the task analysis, I perform a variation of the noun-verb parse used in object-oriented design (Pressman, 1991, pp. 404-408). Given an English description, the "nouns" in the sentence fall into either the Information or Objects category, and the "verbs" fall into the Goals or Actions category. Then, it is a relatively intuitive process of dividing concrete "objects" from "information" and user "goals" from "actions". (In keeping with the prism analogy, I happen to use different colored highlighters to classify each of these element types, by color, as I read through the text). The process is illustrated in Figure 10.7.

I have found not only that these particular categories can be used in a mutually exclusive way, but that they also tend to be exhaustive (covering all of the important pieces of information from the task analysis). I find, also, that this categorization forces me to think about user elements that have not been explicitly defined in the task analysis (e.g., an Action is mentioned in the task analysis, but there is no mention of the Information needed for the user to confirm that it had the desired effect).

As the designer, you may find that Information, Objects, Goals, and Actions are not appropriate for the work you are doing. Though I have found these categorical distinctions to be helpful in my own work, the results may be different in another design context. I encourage you to try out your own user element classification and perspectives from which to design. The same principles of design should still apply, regardless of the categorization used.

Once having divided task analysis data into the four categories, I then take each category individually and approach design from the perspective of that category.

3.3. DEFINE INTERRELATIONS

First I want to define the relationship of each user element in a perspective to related elements in all of the other perspectives (including its own). For instance, if I decide to deal with Information first, then I will draw up a table (the *Table of Relations*) containing all of the Information elements for one task. For each Information element, I will list any Information, Object, Goal, or Action elements to which it is related. Then I will repeat this process from each of the three remaining perspectives.

I sometimes use brackets after an element in the Table of Relations to further define the nature of the relationship or the options available. For example, I added the options "open | closed | partially open", in brackets, after the "status of valve" Information element in Table 10.3.

In most cases, the related elements listed in Table 10.3 will already have been identified earlier in the process. For instance, "tank level" was already listed under the Information elements available, so when it came time to define relations for the Goal "control tank level", it was just a matter of noting that the two are related. In other cases, though, I identify new user elements while filling in the table. For instance, while completing the Information column, I realized that if the "pressure is dangerously high", then the user may want to know: "How long has it been dangerously high?" and "What is the cut-off level between dangerous and normal?".

Organizing the user elements in the table will sometimes also bring to light elements that were hidden or assumed. If, for instance, blank space is being used to convey information to the user, then this should be stated explicitly in the design model. Some information will inevitably be conveyed by location, whether this is a simple left-to-right hierarchy of importance, or some more complex form of coding. Reviewing one's prototypes from this point of view, to see what information *is* being conveyed by location, or color, or size, or shape, can be

Table 10.3   Sample Entries in the Table of Relations, for each Perspective

| User Element under Consideration | Information | Related Elements | | |
		Objects	Goals	Actions
Pressure is dangerously high (Iinformation)	Current pressure	Pressure release valve	Return pressure to normal level	Decrease pressure
	How long has it been dangerously high?	Tank	Maintain pressure at normal level	Open pressure release valve
	At what level did it become dangerous?			
Tank level	—	Tank	Control tank level	Increase Decrease
Pneumatic valve (object)	Status of valve (open I closed I partially open)	—	—	Open Close
Tank	Tank level	Tank1, Tank 2, Liquid 1, Liquid 2	Control tank level	
Control tank level (goal)	Tank level	Tank	Maintain tank level at current setpoint Change tank level	Set a new setpoint at <new volume> Increase (tank level) Decrease (tank level)
Start agitator (action)	Is agitator already started?	Agitator	Keep solute dissolved	—

instructive.[6] It may also highlight instances in which the information might better be conveyed in another manner.

The Table of Relations may appear to be a bit lengthy, but keep in mind that each table is completed for only one task at a time. It would, inarguably, be tedious to draw up a table for *all* user elements of an entire interface at one sitting. Instead, I draw up the table one task at time, then immediately move on to sketching ideas from each of the perspectives on that task. Only then do I start drawing up the Table of Relations for the next task. I find that this approach helps me to concentrate on one particular perspective at a time, and allows me to focus on and design separate alternatives in parallel.

3.4. PROTOTYPE EACH PERSPECTIVE

Next, I sketch preliminary design ideas from the perspective of each type of element. I might start, for instance, by designing a Goals-oriented interface based on the user elements in the Goals section of the Table of Relations. By following a similar process for each of the other three perspectives, I end up with a number of prototype ideas — from four different perspectives.

3.4.1. Idea Sketching from Each Perspective

Let us assume, for instance, that we are designing the controls for the liquid levels in two tanks found in the power plant (see Figure 10.8). By designing from the perspective of Objects, we end up with two objects (Tank1 and Tank2), on each of which we can apply the action "increase" or "decrease". However, when we design from the perspective of Actions, we find that we have instead designed a generic Increase/Decrease capability that works on either tank (depending which one is selected by the user). In the first case, the two tank objects became the key organizational features. In the second case, the actions were the key organizational features, and the two fluids (in the tanks) merely parameters upon which generic actions could be taken. This would be an excellent point at which to do an analysis of the trade-offs between the designs (whether via usability testing or an evaluation on the basis of some Human-Computer Interface design criteria).

I find that this method of design allows me to free myself from the constraints of a particular perspective (by forcing me to focus on four different perspectives), while I generate design ideas and solutions. Note, however, that some of the interface elements will be repeated across the sketches. Though I am designing from the perspective of one particular element at a time, I still put other element

---

6   A further example of this can be found in Collura et al. (1989). They specified in a design that what they referred to as "hot" information would appear at the bottom of the screen, while cold information (such as status information or summaries) would appear at the top. Making this distiction between types of information is important, but a distinction such as this comes only by stepping back and explicitly identifying user information, if not from past experience.

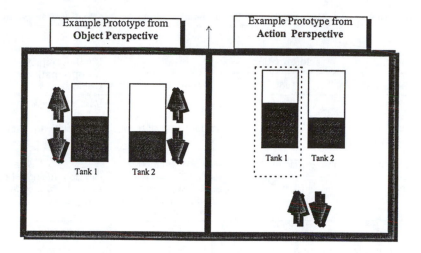

Figure 10.8 Example prototypes from different perspectives.

types into the interface as necessary, as long as they are within the focus of my perspective (e.g., in Figure 10.8 I use a tank object in the Action perspective because it falls within the focus of the design for that perspective). The user elements from other perspectives that do show up in the prototypes for the current perspective should be those elements that appeared in the "Related Elements" column of the Table of Relations (Table 10.3).

At this point, I tend to use only rough sketches of the design elements that are laid out as I would like them to appear in the interface. In the example, for instance (Figure 10.8), I presented a generic tank without measurement units or level markings. Similarly, if I needed to represent trend information in the interface, I might use a generic trend graph: in which axes would be labeled, but no scale given, and a generic line or curve would be drawn on the graph to represent the type of relationship.

3.4.2. Screen Design using Design Guides

Having drawn up some idea sketches from each perspective, I then want to resolve in detail how the objects will appear on the screen. I have again found it useful to draw up a table (such as the one shown in Table 10.4) for each task.

In Table 10.4, the Recommended Display Object for tank level ("vertical gauge") would be defined precisely (and pictured) in a Graphical Display Objects design guide. This design guide illustrates and specifies, in detail, the properties of graphical objects to be used in the interface. Its purpose is to maintain consistency across the system and to reduce the need to redefine and redraw objects that have already been created. If an object wasn't in the Graphical Display Objects

Table 10.4   **Detailed Design Documentation from an Information Perspective**

Information			Recommended Display Object (or Information Coding)
Required	**Type**	**Resolution**	
Tank level	Variable w/ precise value	0-400 cm	Vertical gauge
Pressure is dangerously high	Binary	"Is dangerously high", "is not dangerously high	Annunciation (Level 2)
Filter method being used	Discrete	Method1, method2, method3, <none>	Highlight (using a box)
Plant state	Discrete	Shutdown, normal operation, abnormal, emergency	Annunciation, state diagram

design guide, then the design guide would need to be updated to include the new object. For objects that are used only once or twice, however, it may not be worth the effort of including them in a design guide. In our power plant design, we drew up formal design guides for the use of all designers across the plant (who included both human factors specialists and software developers). In a smaller operation, something less formal would do.

You may notice that the Recommended Display Object for "filter method being used" is actually a type of Information Coding (rather than a graphical object). Guidelines on types of information coding to be used would be found in the Information Coding design guide. This design guide presents recommendations for the use of visual and auditory coding in an interface. Visual coding techniques include color, shape, magnitude, positioning, texture, flashing, and alphanumerics. Though I developed such a design guide specific to our power plant design environment, more general guidance is abundant in the Human-Computer Interaction literature (e.g., Banks and Weimer, 1992).

Using a table such as Table 10.4 encourages documentation of the design process. Others can now refer to the tables I've created (in coordination with the design guides) to find out why I chose a particular display object. In some cases, I would give a choice of two or more recommended display objects.

In the idea-sketching phase, I arranged the location of rough user elements on a prototype. Now I am able to fill in the details with specific graphical objects and information coding choices, to create what I could legitimately call a screen design. This could be done in the context of higher-fidelity computer prototyping, if desired.

3.5. CONSOLIDATE PERSPECTIVES

Think of the sketches that have been created as though they have been etched on thin sheets of glass, by the divergent bands of light from the prism. Now take these sheets of glass and place them one on top of the other, as though you were overlaying transparencies on an overhead projector. In places, the four different views will complement one another and the pieces will fit together as a whole. In other places, there will be incomplete overlap and the resulting image will be cluttered and obscured. It is in these sections that you must eventually erase one or the other of the images, if your interface is to appear as a single, clear image. These sections are the alternatives, and you would like to choose the best of these images for your design. You can do so by testing these with users to see which alternative would be clearest, or which fits best. In the end, you should find that there are fewer holes in your design than if you had simply shone light directly through a single sheet of glass, rather than through the prism and its etchings.

By this point, I will have created at least four design sketches (one from each perspective) for the particular task I am studying. I am now faced with several possibilities. The designs can be amalgamated, so that the best of each is represented in an overall, cohesive prototype, or it may be desirable to leave the sketches separate, to provide alternatives for usability testing. It is likely, however, that a middle road will be taken. Most often, there will be ideas and elements in one perspective that are not captured in any of the others. There will also be some ideas in one perspective that contradict the ideas in another, so that it is not possible for the two to coexist in a single interface. As a result of the choices I make in consolidating design perspectives, I might end up with one task that is represented by an Information perspective, while the next might be an amalgamation of the Goals and Action perspectives. Still a third task might be the synthesis of idea sketches from all four perspectives. The consolidation process is illustrated in Figure 10.9.

At the same time as I was designing for individual tasks, other members of our human factors group were working from the top-level, using their own methods to design the interface from above.[7] We were taking simultaneous top-down and bottom-up approaches. There is a danger in this — of having to redesign large parts of the interface if they don't mesh. However, an element of risk often accompanies design attempts, and this particular risk is accompanied by at least two positive features. First, this way of doing things can easily be more time and resource efficient. Two groups can work from different directions at the same time. Second, it again supports the multiple-perspectives approach. If we did come up with different solutions (from top and bottom) that did not mesh, then in the process we would have provided ourselves with a new set of alternatives to test with our users. For the sake of conservatism, communication between the two groups can help offset the risks.

---

[7]   I have not yet tried designing the overall, high-level structure of an interface using the Design Prism method, but there is no reason why the method couldn't be used for this purpose. For instance, the overall structure of a power plant control room could be designed from the perspective of the Information that an operator needs to run it. This might lead to an annunciation-centered control room. On the other hand, if the overview were designed again from the perspective of Actions, this might lead to an input-based control room. Consolidate the two and you get a typical modern control room.

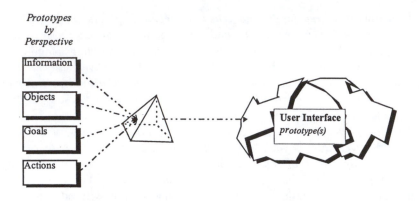

Figure 10.9 Consolidating perspectives

The consolidation stage is an important time to test alternatives with real users of your system. End users are the ones who can best tell you which design works for them. They can help you to decide which perspective, or combination of perspectives, your final design should take.

4. SOME SUGGESTIONS FOR MAKING SIMULTANEOUS USE OF THE WAR ROOM AND DESIGN PRISM METHODS

So far I have presented the Design Prism and the UI War Room as entirely separate entities. This form of presentation is as much for historical reasons as anything else, since these two approaches were grounded firmly in each of two separate design contexts. In the future, I plan to experiment with ideas for making simultaneous use of both methods. For now, I will just speculate on how I think this might be done. I leave the interpretation rather loose. It should be read in that spirit and in the spirit of maintaining multiple approaches/perspectives in design.

Let us start with user requests, as we did in the first stage of the original UI War Room. Paste these up on the wall. Prioritize the requests by team consensus or by another method if you prefer (e.g., you might want your priorities to reflect proportionately the number of users who requested an item, either explicitly or implicitly).

Instead of extracting and organizing user objects, as we did in the war room, this time parse the detailed task analysis data to yield Information, Objects, Goals, and Actions. This changes the "User Object Wall" into a "Perspectives Wall". Make up your own perspectives if you want (but don't use too many or they'll become difficult to manage). Assign a color to each perspective, and write out every user element (Information, Object, Goal, or Action) onto its appropriately colored piece of paper. Organize these user element sheets on the wall... creating four separate hierarchies.

Create a high-level overview of the system from each of the perspectives, taking the organization of user elements on the wall as the basis for your design. Rearrange the elements to see how a different high-level view might change things. The view (or views) you create will be continually refined as more ideas come in from bottom-up idea generation processes.

Meanwhile, proceed on the whiteboard. Start bottom-up prototyping. Take one of the most important user requests, or take an individual user task, and gather together the user elements for that task/request. Focus on one color at a time. Lay out all the elements of that color on a table or a wall. Map out everything you think the user needs to understand that group of elements, continually adding elements of other colors to make the picture clearer. Make up new elements if you find that there is something missing (but don't forget to make sure that these elements get posted back up on the Perspectives Wall, initialed with your name). Arrange the pieces of paper hierarchically or in sequence (or a bit of both) to show relationships between them. Write any additional information you need on or in-between these pieces of paper (use yellow stickies if it helps) to further define these relationships.

Get other people in the room with you. Use team members...bounce ideas off of each other. Get users to come in and help you out. If this isn't possible, then use ideas you gathered from them when you went to see them during the task analysis. You don't have to stick with their ideas if they don't work. Look at previous versions of your own software. What was good about them? What *didn't* users complain about? Have a peek at competitive products. Take ideas from software that has nothing to do with your own. If you're stuck, try out something you've seen in another chapter of this book to help get yourself unstuck. Ask a colleague for an idea. Put on a funny hat.

Take the sketches you have created and plug them into your high-level overviews. If they don't fit, then start a new high-level prototype. Keep iterating these top-down views to maintain the smallest (or most sensible) number of mutually exclusive prototype systems you can.

Once you have some of the main user requests covered, you are going to want to test out your ideas with users. However, at the moment you only have rough idea sketches, not concrete screen designs. Maybe you have the outline of a table, and possibly some of its headings, but nothing inside the table. You might want to test your crude sketches with a user or two (in fact, it's probably a good idea), but at some point you are going to want to refine them a little. Here's where the Design Guides come in.

Build up a Graphical Display Objects design guide. Start with a tentative guide early on in the process. Leave it rough, as sketches. Continue to iterate this design guide until the objects in it are well defined. Check it out with users, in isolation from the interface. What makes sense to them? Fill in your rough idea sketches with objects from this design guide, and continue to feed new objects back into the guide. Start to capture design rules that you are following, so that your colleagues can refer to them later on. Look up human factors research relevant to your users' environment and write up some Information Coding guidelines for your interface. Refer to the look-and-feel style guide for your interface platform. Apply your knowledge of Human-Computer Interaction. Record the decisions you make and why you are making them.

5. BENEFITS, LIMITATIONS, AND DIFFICULT QUESTIONS

In both of my interface design contexts, the intent was to redesign an existing system, based on some underlying structure (whether software or hardware). Are the structural techniques I have chosen only useful for incremental design then, or can they lead to innovation as well? Though I think that both of the design methods could provide a framework within which to pursue innovative design, they might need to be supplemented by other techniques, such as those presented by Colin Smith (Chapter 11). In both cases, my design context was fire-preventative, rather than fire fighting. We had the luxury of time available for creating design guides, filling in tables of relations, and designing from multiple perspectives. These techniques may not be well suited to a more fire fighting type of UI design context.

Perhaps more to the point, it is questionable whether any designer other than myself would be willing to go through the process of creating the tables I have created. It is easy enough to put together tables of one's own design, but when this becomes a step-by-step process dictated by somebody else, it loses some of its charm. Mind you, Table 10.4 (which I used in detailed design), was recommended by a supervisor, and still I found it to be a very useful structuring tool.

I think it is important to question whether my approach to display object design — through design guides and tables — can function outside of a power plant context. The technique is certainly adequate and well-suited to dealing with precisely-definable physical mimicry, but I am less sure whether it would be expedient to use outside of this context (except later in interface design or for maintainability). It may also be desirable — rather than opting for consistency — to maintain a variety of different graphical objects in early prototypes, so that these can be shown to users. In our case, the early definition of design guides was essential, because the graphical objects we defined were going to be used by many software designers (physically removed from each other and from the human factors professionals) in a safety-critical interface.

There is some question in my mind whether the perspectives of the Design Prism do indeed expand a designer's view, as I have claimed, or whether they just limit it in a new way. Could approaching design so intently from these four perspectives merely limit the sight of the designer from other ways of thinking? In addition, what does it mean to the consistency of an interface if one screen is developed from one perspective (e.g. user Goals) while the next is developed from another perspective (e.g., Information). Simply being aware of this issue may help to circumvent potential problems. At the same time, I continue to question whether the war room's User Object Wall wrongly predisposes the interface to being hierarchical in nature, by forcing the organization of objects into tree-like structures. How would the User Object Wall deal with a sequential task, like a software setup screen? How about a networking task? Need there be such an emphasis on hierarchical design, or is it just that hierarchical structures are consistent with human cognitive organization of information? How many other types of interfaces can we imagine? What is stopping us from imagining them?

I see a tension between structure and creativity in design. To maintain consistency, it is sometimes necessary to sacrifice originality and vice versa. Is there necessarily a trade-off between creativity and structure? What is the appropriate balance?

One particular strength of the Design Prism approach is that it provides a method for generating ideas from different perspectives, even when users are inaccessible or other team members are not available for creative input. This supports the designer in her difficult task of developing a number of creative ideas, in parallel, over a period of time. Perhaps the most promising aspect of the Design Prism is its unique approach of creating — simultaneously — a number of alternative designs. This may not entirely solve the problem we have of funneling alternatives into single solutions, but it certainly supports a designer's attempt to challenge some of the limitations of tunnel vision.

The main strength of the User Interface War Room is its use of space in structuring the design approach. The setup of the war room enables the designer to survey User Objects, User Requests, and various prototypes (completed or under construction) just by turning his head. The User Object Wall allows the designer the flexibility to quickly organize and view relationships between objects. The use of space helps in maintaining creativity in design. Some attempt is made, in the Whiteboard section of this chapter, to document the creative process of idea generation (though there is still a long way to go in this direction). Finally, it seems that the war room approach would be particularly amenable to participatory design with users. The structure is fun to work with, easy to use, and easy to learn (as is the Design Prism).

I think I have found some practical ways to bridge parts of the design gap... or to at least make the leap seem a bit more manageable. Despite my efforts, there is still a lot of magic to my methods. They have little to say about how to design the flow and navigation through an interface. They fall short on multimedia aspects of design. There is no suggestion in them as to how one might develop an interface that users find engaging or fun to use. There still remains a fairly sizable leap from the organization of user objects (or user elements) on the wall, to the idea sketches themselves.

In the introductory chapter of the book *Taking Software Design Seriously*, David Wroblewski considers the construction of human-computer interfaces as a craft. In keeping with this notion, perhaps then apprenticeship is one of the best methods for teaching this craft. I still firmly believe that we need to try to push ourselves to create well-defined and contextualized tools that can be used by beginners (and experts) as stepping stones toward the other side of the gap. However, I also consider myself fortunate to have started my own career in an apprenticeship-type position — where I could supplement the structure provided by a few walls and a handful of articles with somebody else's magic.

6. ACKNOWLEDGMENTS

I'd like to acknowledge the help of Tim Dudley, my "mentor" from Bell-Northern Research (now Nortel). As senior user interface designer on our team, he was responsible for procuring and directing the setup of our war room and originating the overall process. I'd also like to thank Tom Carey, at the University of Guelph, for reviewing drafts of this document and for suggesting new ways of approaching the topic that I had not previously seen. The idea for Table 10.4, Detailed Design Documentation from an Information Perspective came from Mark Feher, at Atomic Energy of Canada Limited.

7. REFERENCES

Anderson, J. R., *Cognitive Psychology and its Implications,* 3rd ed., W. H. Freeman and Company, New York, 1990.

Banks, W. W., Jr. and Weimer, J., *Effective Computer Display Design*, Prentice-Hall, Englewood Cliffs, New Jersey, 1992.

Cohen, L., Quality function deployment: an application perspective from Digital Equipment Corporation, *National Productivity Review,* 7(3), 197-208, 1988.

Collura, T. F., Jacobs, E. C., Burgess, R. C., and Klem, G. H., User-interface design for a clinical neurophysiological intensive monitoring system, in *Proceedings of the CHI'89 Conference on Human Factors in Computing Systems,* Bice, K. and Lewis, C., Eds., ACM Press, New York, 363-374, 1989.

Holtzblatt, K. and Jones, S., Contextual design: using contextual inquiry for system development, tutorial presented at the *CHI'92 Conference on Human Factors in Computing Systems*, Austin, Texas, 1992.

Karat, J. and Bennett, J. L., Using scenarios in design meetings — a case study example, in *Taking Software Design Seriously: Practical Techniques for Human-Computer Interface Design*, Karat, J., Ed., Academic Press, New York, 1991, ch.4.

Kieras, D. E., Towards a practical GOMS model methodology for user interface design, in *Handbook of Human-Computer Interaction*, Helander, M., Ed., Elsevier Science Publishers (North-Holland), New York, 1988, 135-157.

MacLean, A., Young, R., Bellotti, V., and Moran, T., Questions, options, and criteria: elements of design space analysis, *Human-Computer Interaction*, 6, 201-250, 1991.

Pressman, R. S., *Software Engineering: A Practitioner's Approach*, 3rd ed., McGraw-Hill, New York, 1991.

Wroblewski, D. A., The construction of human-computer interfaces considered as a craft, in *Taking Software Design Seriously: Practical Techniques for Human-Computer Interface Design,* Karat, J., Ed., Academic Press, New York, 1991, ch. 1.

CHAPTER 11

Transforming User-Centered Analysis into User Interface: The Design of New-Generation Products

Colin D. Smith
Nortel Technology (Northern Telecom), Ottawa, Ontario, Canada
email: cdsmith@nortel.ca

TABLE OF CONTENTS

ABSTRACT

The challenge of "Bridging the Design Gap" is examined in a case study of the design of a new wireless personal communication product. This chapter discusses applicable design methods, their relative strengths and weaknesses, how much information is needed before proceeding, and how to get that information.

A multidisciplinary team used an iterative design approach to (1) explore, (2) discover, (3) define, (4) design, and (5) evaluate new product opportunities. A three-stage design transformation process is recommended: Exploratory, Refinement and Analysis, and Formal Design. Scenarios are a key device used to bridge the stages. User feedback is solicited to guide the evolution of the design in all stages.

The purpose of the Exploratory Design Stage is to identify and conceptualize potential new high-value products and services that will satisfy key user needs not being met by today's solutions. The goal of the Refinement and Analysis Stage is to verify the key user values and define the attributes required of successful product. The Formal Design Stage is characterized by the design of the users' conceptual model, which is communicated in the interface through dialog design as well as the use of metaphors. At this stage, low- and high-fidelity prototypes are built and subjected to usability testing. High-fidelity prototypes are also used to capture the design intent and communicate it to product implementation partners.

1. INTRODUCTION

The methods described in this chapter apply to the design of exploratory new-generation products. The techniques used for the design of new-generation products are different from those used to upgrade an existing product, add a new product to an existing market (e.g., designing another spreadsheet application) or add a new product to extend an existing suite of products. The characteristics of new-generation projects include:

- No defined product direction given to the design team at the beginning of the project (the team both defines the problem space and the product requirements).
- No clear understanding of user requirements.
- No clear definition of who will use the product.
- Involves new or not-yet-existing hardware and software technology.
- Constantly evolving product features.
- No comparable existing product to benchmark against.

These characteristics have a number of consequences for the design process. The Gap between analysis of user requirements and the design of a new generation product is far too great to be bridged in a single transformation. With new-generation products, the target market, the user values and tasks, and the technologies are all typically unknown or poorly understood. Thus, the usual starting stage of understanding user requirements is preceded by an Exploratory Design Stage. The combined Exploratory and Refinement and Analysis Stages are much longer relative to the other types of projects, and the level of early user involvement is much higher.

In the design process described in this chapter, there is not a *single* large Gap to be bridged between analysis and design. Design occurs *before* analysis (in the Exploratory Design Stage), *during* analysis (in the Concept Refinement and Analysis Stage), and *after* analysis (in the Formal Design Stage). However, the three stages are not cleanly separated; rather there is a gradual shift of emphasis from one stage to another, with some overlap between the stages. Different techniques are used as iterative stepping stones, to move the design through the three stages (see Figure 11.1). This chapter discusses the techniques, when they are most useful, their relative strengths and weaknesses, how much information is needed before proceeding, and how to get that information.

1.1. EXAMPLE OF A NEW-GENERATION PRODUCT

Most UI design addresses the requirements of the mainstream business computer market and is dominated by the WIMP (windows, icon, menu, pointer) paradigm pioneered with the Star interface (developed at Xerox PARC over 25 years ago; Winograd, 1996). The interface design discussion is also limited to standard computer hardware, which includes a large visual display, a QWERTY keyboard, and a mouse. However, advances in communication and computing are bringing new devices onto the market that mark a "paradigm shift". The devices that embody this shift are small, mobile, and wireless, and users will interact with them through tactile, gestural, voice, and electronic pen input. Unlike the serial dialogue

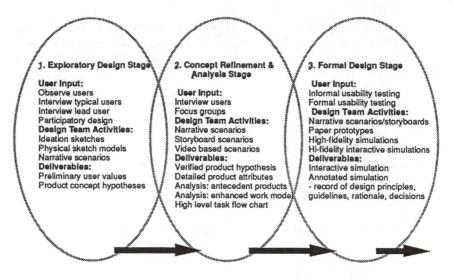

Figure 11.1 Stages of design for new-generation products.

that is typical of WIMP-based products, these new generation devices are characterized by several parallel streams of input and output. These new devices bear little resemblance to conventional computers, and therefore they offer both new opportunities and challenges to the user interface designer.

The development of the Orbitor Wireless Communicator project is a good case study of a new-generation product. The Orbitor combines and extends capabilities far beyond traditional cellular telephones, electronic organizers, PDA's (personal digital assistants), and two-way pagers.

The challenge for the Orbitor design team was to develop a pocket-able device that would offer voice-centric communication, as well as messaging, graphical notes capability, and other not-yet-defined services. The size constraint coupled with the extensive and expanding list of feature requirements necessitated a high degree of co-evolution between the graphical on-screen interface and the physical interface. The user interface design encompassed both the screen-based interface and the physical-product interface. The team had to adopt an exploratory, iterative approach to allow them to integrate newly emerging features and services while also supporting key customer values.

2. EXPLORATORY DESIGN STAGE

Exploratory Design is the first stage in the overall UI design process for new generation products. The purpose of the Exploratory Design Stage is to identify potential new high-value products and services that will satisfy key user needs not being met by today's solutions (Note: hereafter *product* will refer to the combined physical interface and software interface). More importantly, the Exploratory Stage is used to conceptualize the tasks users might want to perform with the new product (see Figure 11.2).

The Exploratory Design Stage is "characterized by confusion and unease within the design team. Nothing is settled. Although the design team has a set of constraints, many are often no more than accidents of circumstance. Typically, the design team will... have some indications of appropriate directions or application areas which may have been provided by upper management or distilled from the corporate zeitgeist..." (Erickson, 1995, p.43).

The Exploratory Stage may be pursued by a variety of groups or individuals, including a marketing group, a product manager, an executive, or an entire design team. In the design of the Orbitor, the Exploratory Stage was done by a multi-disciplinary design team which included User Interface Designers, User Needs Assessment Professionals (Cognitive Psychologists), Industrial Designers, and Mechanical Engineers in partnership with an Advanced Hardware/Software Technology Group and a Marketing Group.

2.1. VISUALIZATION AND IDEATION

In exploratory design, new product concepts are often first conceived through rough sketches and rudimentary physical models (constructed from paper, cardboard, or foam). One source of inspiration for these new concepts is the identification and exploration of awkward features associated with current related products: these suggest new opportunity areas. It can also be useful to informally observe users in their actual "work" and "play" environments (e.g., people use products such as telephones very differently in their car, in their home, and in their office).

The emphasis at this phase is on the creation of a large number of diverse sketches illustrating new product value and functionality without any attempt at critical analysis. The use of analysis techniques is avoided because they can overly constrain the creative thinking of the design team. Also, there is not any great importance attached to the *first* conceptual sketches of a design; the issue of importance is articulating and communicating ideas.

The exploratory UI design process is similar to the classic *ideation* techniques used by architects, industrial designers, and graphic designers. Many of the concept-generating techniques perfected in these professions are directly transferable to the design of new-generation user interfaces. For example, using the ideation process a designer will typically sketch many rough thumbnail concept drawings which reflect a wide variety of different ideas. The better thumbnail concept-sketches are redrawn at a larger scale, and then continuously refined using trace paper overlays. The act of sketching in itself is a design and learning tool (see also Hanks, 1977; Porter, 1979; Ching, 1979).

2.2. SCENARIOS

With new-generation products, *scenarios* are a key device used to bridge the Exploratory, Refinement and Analysis, and Formal Design Stages. Scenario techniques have been applied in many different ways, and indeed the term "scenario" itself has many interpretations (see Caroll, 1995). This chapter will focus on "user interaction scenarios", which are narrative descriptions of what people do and experience as they try to make use of a product and its applications.

One of the characteristics of new-generation products is that potential users can have difficulty understanding the proposed new product or articulating what they would want the new product to do. Unlike lists of features, scenarios provide potential users with a feel for how the product would perform in a specific situation or context. Scenarios include a concrete description of the users' activities, focusing on a particular instance of use. Scenarios are a user-centric perspective on task/application interaction: what happens, how it happens, and why it happens. Particularly with consumer products, the scenario should encompass and present a totally integrated package for evaluation by the user. This package can include the interface, the physical product, the context of use, and the various users.

The user-centric perspective is important in that the users' model and the designer's model are usually different. Spool (1996) uses the example of Walt Disney World"s Haunted House: "The designers decide what ghosts, lighting, screams and general spookiness the guests would experience... If the guests come out of the ride thinking that the 180 watt surround sound speaker system really added to the ride, then the ride itself has failed."

User interaction scenarios can be communicated in a variety of forms, for example, a narrated story (text-based narrative), a picture-based story (using story-boards), a scripted computer-based simulation, a simple scripted play with live "actors" (actors can be members of the design team), or a video with professional actors. Caroll (1995) provides a good overview of the advantages and disadvantages associated with the various scenario presentation techniques.

2.2.1. Role of Scenarios in the Exploratory Stage

In the Exploratory Stage, scenarios are used to clarify the use of a new-generation product, not only for the end user, but also for the design team. They are an effective method of brainstorming to create new product concepts and a shared vision in a multidisciplinary team. This is because team members from different technical backgrounds can all contribute to and understand the creation of a narrative scenario. Scenarios can also be used to motivate and direct a newly formed design team, and to facilitate external communication: ensuring consistency in the design vision and clearly communicating the state of a project to senior managers.

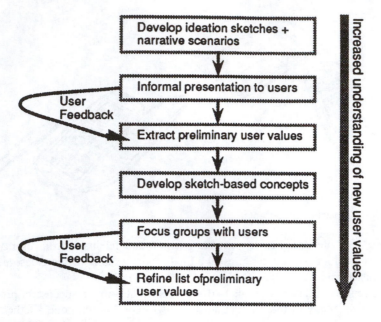

Figure 11.2 User feedback to concepts.

One of the limitations of a scenario is that it is intrinsically single-threaded: it does not immediately point out errors or better alternatives to either the design team or the user during testing. The way to overcome this disadvantage in the Exploratory Stage is to develop and test multiple, highly divergent scripted scenarios such that many alternative concepts are examined simultaneously.

In the Orbitor project, we developed a series of scenarios in combination with the ideation sketches discussed earlier. Brainstorming using an electronic whiteboard was an effective tool for this stage of design. We used the hard-copy capability of an electronic whiteboard to capture transient design ideas. As a graphical tool, the whiteboard was ideal for the rapid development of a graphics-based interface. With Orbitor, this method was used to optimize the interaction between the physical-product user interface and the screen-based user interface.

Early sketch-based scenarios are used as stimulus material in presentations and discussions with potential end users and senior management. From these sessions, the design team may then begin to define a list of the preliminary user values and user requirements for the product (see Figure 11.2). *User values* encompass the intended customer's *future* needs, desires, and goals.

2.3. PRODUCT CONCEPT HYPOTHESES

Using the list of preliminary user values as a guide, the team then develops several product concept hypotheses to meet those user values and requirements. The concepts are not finished designs or even what might be considered "good"

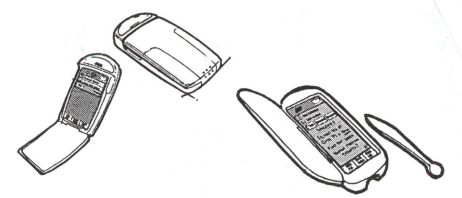

Figure 11.3 Typical early concepts.

designs; they are designed to provoke reaction and feedback from users. The concepts are not designed to represent a final product; rather they are designed to represent alternative design solutions (see Figure 11.3).

Concept hypotheses are tools to discover attributes that a successful product should have. Many of the product attributes will conflict with one another. For example the desire of customers to have an easy to use feature-packed cellular phone will conflict with their demand for small size and mobility. The best combination of attributes for a given group of users will be determined in the Refinement and Analysis Stage.

The number of initial UI design concepts is held at three to four, to allow users to give reasonable feedback. Four seems to be the optimum number of concept options that users can comprehend in a single session. Therefore, it is important to pick sketches that best articulate a diversity of possible user interface designs. With exploratory design it is important to present a clear and distinct range of contrasting concepts to stimulate responses from customers, and thus to better understand their values.

It is often insightful to explore concepts which might be "controversial", forcing users to make tradeoffs and clearly identify what they like and dislike. For example, some of the Orbitor concepts which were presented did not have traditional telephone dialpads. Prior studies had suggested that these nontraditional concepts were not popular, but we included these concepts to further explore this finding.

Concepts are explored in focus groups which are set up to maximize the design team's learning in the least number of trials. Users are asked to discuss what they like best and least, what changes they would like to see, and what ideas they have for combining various concept attributes to provide new solutions. The team's learning should minimally include:

- What are the attributes that contribute to user value?
- What are the critical user tasks?
- What are the bottlenecks in the usability of the new product concept?

Table 11.1   Example of Key User Values from the Orbitor Project

1. Mobility
   • People want to send and receive voice calls and messages anywhere/anytime

2. Ease of use
   • People seek simplicity despite underlying complexity

3. Controlled accessibility
   • People want control over who gets through to them, when they can be reached, and by what means (voice, voice message, note, etc.)

4. Personalization
   • People want to customize the interface to their unique requirements

5. Call closure through multitasking
   • People want to complete a communication task using either voice or note communication, or both simultaneously

The subjects should be chosen to represent a sample of the target market population. Lead users, "power users", or "early adopters" (e.g., real estate agents in the case of pagers and cellular telephones) should be included in the research. It can be very helpful to study less proficient potential users because they will give the UI designer insights into what design concepts are workable for a heterogeneous user group.

2.4. OUTPUT OF THE EXPLORATORY DESIGN STAGE

The first major output of the Exploratory Design Stage is the identification of high-level *user values* (see Table 11.1). The second output of the Exploratory Stage is a *set of new-generation product concepts*. Through these product design concepts, the team clearly defines:

• What the goals of the products are
• What the products are used for
• How the products are used

The design concepts and the list of preliminary user values represent the design team's hypothesis of what will make a successful product. This hypothesis is later tested in the Refinement and Analysis Stage.

3. CONCEPT REFINEMENT AND ANALYSIS STAGE

Concept refinement and analysis of users and tasks is the second stage in the overall UI design process for new generation products. The goal of the Refinement and Analysis Stage of development is to verify the user values and define the product attributes.

3.1. LIMITATIONS OF TASK ANALYSIS FOR NEW-GENERATION PRODUCT CONCEPTS

For new-generation products one of the limitations of the task analysis process is that there is a large gap between the *existing work model* (i.e., work carried out with current products) and the *enhanced work model* (i.e., work carried out with the new design concepts). New-generation products encompass features and services for tasks that do not yet exist, and detailed task analysis of the enhanced model would constrain the creativity of the design team without contributing useful information. In the analysis Stage of new-generation products, the focus is more on discovering and verifying *user values* and detailed product attributes required to deliver these values. The success of this strategy relies upon an iterative design process with substantial user input.

3.2. ANTECEDENT PRODUCTS — TASK ANALYSIS OF THE CURRENT WORK MODEL

While the emphasis with new generation products is on the discovery and analysis of user values associated with the enhanced work model, this is not to suggest that the current work model should be ignored. Conducting limited task analysis of the current work model can be useful for identifying new product opportunities. New products will often integrate or replace the features supported by several older products. Tasks in the past which might have been accomplished using a diverse array of products might be done with a single new product. For new generation product design, it is helpful to understand the typical tasks performed with several of the *antecedent* products. For example, the Orbitor team required an understanding of how people used current telephones (desktop and cellular), text pagers, electronic schedulers, answering machines, fax machines, and E-mail applications (see Table 11.2).

Task analysis of the current work model may include the following:

- List of user goals (i.e., what is the user trying to accomplish).
- List of the tasks to be performed.
- List and sequence of the steps within each task (subtasks).
- List of which features of a task are critically important.
- List of related information required by the user to accomplish a task.
- Relationship and interdependencies between various tasks.
- Relative frequency with which various tasks are performed.
- Priority of the task based upon on frequency of occurrence.
- Priority of the task based on perceived level of importance to the user.
- Identification and exploration of awkward features of tasks conducted with current products (breakdowns are a source of inspiration for new designs).

Studying antecedent products also allows the design team to do functional analysis, i.e., understanding the underlying functional reasons for the task, and not

Table 11.2 Partial Chart of Task Analysis from an Antecedent Product (Basic Cellular Telephone)

Task Analysis Function	Associated Element	Location of Use*	User Priority /Freq.	1 cs. 2 Hands	Video Ref. No.
Incoming call/message					
Call alert	Display: Calling Line identification and associated softkeys (Tone if call waiting)	H E S	High	—	2
Adjust ringer volume during alert	Mode switch OR Volume switch	H S	Med.	1	—
Answer call	Talk, flap, ANS softkey (or LINK softkey if call waiting)	H E S	High	1	2
Dispose of call (send to Voice Mail, forward to another number, ...)	Associated softkey (SEND, FWD, ...)	H S	Med.	2	2
Note alert	Display: message and associated softkeys	H E S	High	—	3
On a call					
Initiate network features (ex. 3-way Calling)	LINK softkey or feature-programmed softkey	H E S	Low	2	2
Terminate calls and exit the user from any task	End	H E S	High	1	2
Enter extra numbers (IVR systems)	Dialpad	H S	Med.	1	—
Switch to headset	Headset jack	H E S	Low	2	—
Switch to handsfree	Handsfree	H E S	Low	1	—
Adjust speaker volume	Volume switch	H E S	Med.	1	—
Mute the call	Mute	H E S	Med.	1	—
Dial out Directory items while offhook	TBD	H S	Med.	1	—
Using radio link (general)					
Out of range warning	Display and tone	H E S	High	—	—
Battery low warning	Display and tone	H E S	High	—	—

Table 11.2   Partial Chart of Task Analysis from an Antecedent Product (Basic Cellular Telephone)

Task Analysis Function	Associated Element	Location of Use*	User Priority /Freq.	1 cs. 2 Hands	Video Ref. No.
Incoming call/message					
Initiating a call					
Dial a call (active dial or predial)	Dialpad ↔ Talk, flap, DIAL softkey	H S	High	1	—
Dial from Directory	Directory → scroll keys or dialpad → Talk, flap, DIAL softkey	H S	High	1	1
Dial back a Caller from the Messages List	Messages → scroll keys → REPLY softkey	H S	High	1	5
Redial a number	Redial Æ Talk, flap, DIAL softkey	H S	High	1	—

Location of Use: H = hand E = ear S = surface.

Video Reference: 1 = Make a call, 2 = Receive 2 calls, 3 = Receive a note, 4 = Change mode, 5 = Retrieving messages, 6 = adding to Directory. Users were videotaped conducting typical tasks. These numbers refer to location markers on the videotape.

* **Note:** User may be interacting with the device with or without a headset.

simply the surface procedures associated with the current work model. Functional analysis gives the team the information to redesign tasks, perhaps eliminating the requirement for a task to exist at all. Task analysis of antecedent products can further be used as a checkpoint to evaluate the feature list of new product concepts, i.e., it can be used to uncover the requirement for a basic feature that might have been ignored in the high-level user value analysis of the new product concepts.

3.3. NEW GENERATION PRODUCTS — USER VALUES

Whereas the Exploratory Stage can be characterized by ideation and far-reaching exploration without any effort to get the design "right", design in the Refinement and Analysis Stage is more directed. In the Refinement and Analysis Stage the concepts become more highly detailed and defined. The goal of the Refinement and Analysis Stage is to clearly define what mix of attributes the final product must have to deliver the highest customer value and thereby make a successful product.

Based on the opportunities identified in the Exploratory Stage, a second series of concepts are designed and developed. Using the new concepts, a thorough assessment of user requirements and values is conducted through the use of one- to two-person interviews or focus groups. With this process, analysis is not done by observing users doing a current task with a current product rather they are shown new concepts and asked to react to how this concept aligns with their future needs. As in the Exploratory Stage, new product concepts can be communicated to users with *scenarios*. However, in the Refinement and Analysis Stage, scenarios are more explicit and better detailed to facilitate the presentation of new concepts to end users, such that they will better understand the implication of the product for their work.

Scenarios are presented to groups of customers for their reaction. The scenarios are easy for the customers to understand because they are short, to the point, and they outline a specific task with specific goals. Based upon customer feedback, the key customer values and the required product attributes become known to the design team.

Storyboards scenarios can be developed into video-based scenarios. Video is useful to seamlessly and realistically convey new product concepts to end users, possibly resulting in better user feedback.

Video can be a particularly effective technique because:

- The designer is not constrained by prototyping software.
- The designer does not have to resolve the all of the user interface details.
- Futuristic technology can be easily conveyed (Tognazzini, 1994) (e.g., natural voice recognition).
- Concepts are more immersive and thus more readily understood by most users.

Table 11.3 Example of Detailed Attributes from the Orbitor Project

Attributes Contributing to the user value of *Call Closure through Multitasking*
Note: Detailed attributes are also extracted for each of the other key user values

1. User has access and is accessible at all times:
   - Use the device everywhere
   - Receive both notes and voice simultaneously
   - Receive notifications of all types of messages in one device
   - Leave someone a electronic note if they are on a call
   - Leave personalized voice messages

2. User has efficient communication management tools:
   - Dispose of calls as they arrive
   - Call someone directly from a message center
   - Handle all messages through a graphical display
   - Select options by touching on the display
   - Add new information with single action

3. User can screen for critical sources of information:
   - Preset who gets through to me
   - Identification of caller

A video is the equivalent of an architect's scale building model. It is understood at some level by all the clients, and captures the overall look and feel of the building without necessitating any premature detailed design work.

In the Orbitor project, storyboards and a video were created using scenarios to illustrate key capabilities. The scenarios depicted the product in context and permitted a comparison with the use of existing products (to give users a baseline for evaluation). Concepts were also communicated to users with physical models. With consumer electronic products it is important to assess both the display-based interface and the physical interface together in the users' environment. As Alan Kay noted over 28 years ago in his visionary design of the Dynabook laptop computer, "even the computer's weight is very much part of the user interface" (Davidson, 1993).

3.4. OUTPUT OF CONCEPT REFINEMENT AND ANALYSIS STAGE

The major output of the Refinement and Analysis Stage is the verification of the customer value hypothesis. This is expressed in terms of a list of detailed product attributes which have been verified through testing with users (see Table 11.3). Table 11.3 shows a list of attributes in a simple tabular form. The next step in the design process is to reformulate this list into a high-level flow chart to represent the sequence of tasks and the interactions between various tasks (see Figure 11.4). The user feedback should also provide the information required by the design team to make design trade-off decisions (i.e., attribute mix and weighting required to optimize a design concept for a specific target group of users).

From the user feedback to scenario-based concepts, the team can also extract some of the following:

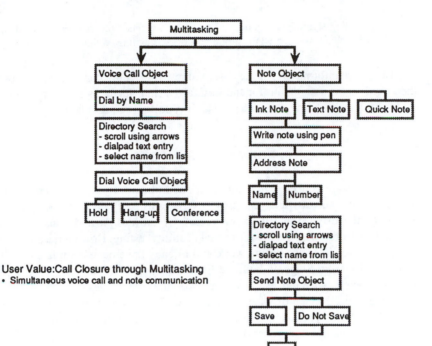

Figure 11.4 Example of high-level task flow chart.

- Users' conceptual model.
- Priority of the tasks based on perceived level of importance to the user.
- List and sequence of the major subtasks within each task.
- List of objects used in a task.
- List of related information required by the user to accomplish a task.

In addition to this information, other factors are equally if not more important in understanding how users do "real work". The design team might also consider the following:

- Understanding any additional constraints in the environment in which the work is done (e.g., office, home, car).
- Noting if this task is done while doing another related or unrelated task; e.g., driving a car, working on computer, writing, participating in a business meeting.
- Identifying other people who may be involved in completing the task.
- Identifying who initiates which task.
- Understanding what defines closure of the task for the user.

- Understanding significant ergonomic issues; e.g., is this a one handed or two handed task?; or is this task done while sitting at a desk, standing, walking?

The above information, the key user values, and detailed product attributes are then used as the foundation for the Formal Design Stage, as metrics for design trade-off decisions, and as input for usability testing requirements.

4. FORMAL DESIGN STAGE

The set of design concepts, in conjunction with the information gathered in user values analysis and task analysis, provides the basis for the Formal Design Stage. The Formal Design Stage is characterized by the design and construction of detailed UI prototypes suitable for formal usability testing. However, a substantial amount of user interface design work will already have been completed prior to the Formal Design Stage, in both the Exploratory and Refinement and Analysis Stages. As well, when the design team reaches the Formal Design Stage, they will have internalized much of what is required to deliver a successful final product (this advocates having a single design team participating in and completing all of the stages of the design process).

4.1. ROLE OF SCENARIOS IN THE FORMAL DESIGN STAGE

In the Formal Design Stage, scenarios are used to move between the user information gathered in the Exploratory and Refinement and Analysis Stages and the first detailed version of an interface. Scenarios are built around the early product concepts (created in the Exploratory and Refinement and Analysis Stages), the task analysis from antecedent products, the list of key user values, and the detailed list of required product attributes. In the Formal Design Stage scenarios are used to choose, design, and verify the conceptual model and metaphors to be used in the final product.

Using a "storyboarding" technique, the high-level user interface for key features of the product to be rapidly mocked up. After these storyboards have been refined, they can be developed into a *paper prototype* (discussed below), detailing the key interface dialogues. The interface *dialogue* refers to the structure of the interaction between the user and the system.

Using a combined narrative scenario and paper prototype is a good technique to design and verify the high-level flow (dialogue) for the most important user tasks. The scenario and paper prototype is tested in usability sessions in which users are asked to follow a narrative scenario and interact with a paper prototype. The paper prototype is interactive; it changes with the story-line and reacts to the users input (the usability session moderator acts as a "computer" and constantly flips paper to update the paper prototype).

To give an example of a fragment of a Formal Design Stage narrative scenario:

Imagine you are walking down the hall on your way to a critical presentation when you receive notification that your boss is calling. While carrying on a voice call with your boss about modifying a few key details of the presentation, you receive a note from your son's school principal...

This Orbitor scenario/paper prototype was used to test the multitasking capability of one of the designs. It allowed the design team to develop an understanding of the cognitive load imposed on the end user by such features as multitasking. The discovery of the human limitations of multitasking early in the Formal Design Stage was highly beneficial.

4.2. ROLE OF PROTOTYPES IN THE FORMAL DESIGN STAGE

Prototypes are the first concrete embodiment of the user interface design. They allow users to experience something resembling a real product and thus provide more useful critical feedback. For the design team, building a prototype immediately highlights some of the erroneous design assumptions that may have been carried over from the Exploratory and Refinement and Analysis Stages.

A series of low-fidelity, paper-based prototypes are used primarily in the early stages of the user interface design process to map out both the *dialogue design* and the *detail design*. High-fidelity, computer-based techniques are the principal tools used in refining the exact interaction and graphic details. Both types of prototype can be subjected to usability testing.

Although prototyping is a very powerful design tool, as with iterative design it should not be an excuse for not doing a thorough-enough user analysis. The limitations of the prototyping tools can begin to negatively influence both the design team and the users (e.g., some tools make it difficult to create anything other than a standard Windows interface). Finally, prototypes, particularly high-fidelity simulations, can give the design team as well as managers and clients the impression that a project is much closer to completion than it actually is.

4.2.1. Low-Fidelity Paper Prototypes

Paper prototypes are very useful to try out a variety of dialogue concepts inexpensively in a short period of time. Paper prototyping allows for early user feedback and rapid iteration of the concrete user interface design.

In building paper prototypes only key states of the user interface are initially depicted and tested. This ensures that the high-level work flow and navigation issues are addressed and that basic usability requirements are met before the designer is caught up in design details. As the design is further refined, virtually all states can be drawn. This makes it easy to get the "big picture" of how a

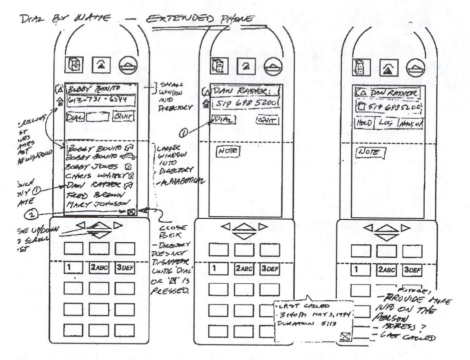

Figure 11.5 Paper prototype.

particular task would be supported, simply by laying out the entire sequence of drawings on a large table.

In the Orbitor project, paper prototyping resulted in a detailed depiction of most of the important states of the user interface (see Figure 11.5). These were hand-drawn sketches of what the user interface would look like at full 1:1 scale. This *full-scale* paper prototyping was useful to keep the design team conscious of critical ergonomic issues (text legibility, size of icons and touch targets) associated with a small display interface.

Informal usability testing was conducted with local users (often fellow employees) on an ongoing basis. This was a way of receiving fast and inexpensive feedback to support the ongoing iterative design process. Overall scenario-storyboarding and paper prototyping were the most useful and widely used techniques for rapid design of new generation products such as Orbitor.

4.2.2. High-Fidelity Interactive Simulations

As the design team begins to focus on the optimized and preferred user interface, the paper prototypes are transferred to an interactive computer simulation. Some of these simulation applications include MacroMedia Director, Super Card, and Visual Basic. A high-fidelity interactive simulation is used to integrate all of the disparate elements of the paper prototype. During the transition stage between

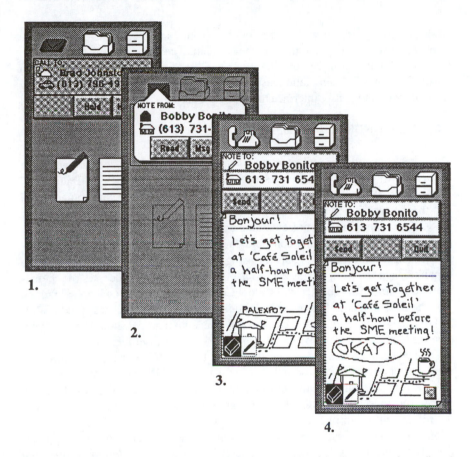

Figure 11.6 High-fidelity interactive simulation of multitasking (simultaneous voice call and note).

paper and a computer simulation, it is fastest to revisit problem areas of the user interface simulation and first refine them using paper prototyping. This takes advantage of the speed of paper, while capturing only the output in a more finished interactive computer simulation. Interactive simulations are used to develop and refine the interaction sequences, interaction timing, graphics design details, and animation sequences. The interactive simulation gives the design team a feel for the real-time flow of the interaction dialogue (see Figure 11.6).

An interactive simulation is further used for formal usability testing with end users. The information received from usability test sessions is a key element in the design decision process, and ongoing usability feedback is required for efficient iterative design. The subject of detailed usability testing is outside the focus of this chapter (see Neilsen, 1993; Wiklund, 1994; Bauersfeld, 1994; Hix et al, 1993).

In the Orbitor project, seven formal usability test sessions were conducted with over 50 subjects in total, to refine the various elements of the interface. The interactive and realistic nature of the simulation served to convincingly demonstrate the strengths and weaknesses of the Orbitor interface as it evolved. The implications of new developments in the simulation could be quickly grasped both by users who had seen previous iterations and those encountering the simulation for the first time. The simulation also proved an effective tool for communicating the intricacies of the user interface to managers, partners, and potential customers.

4.3. THE CONCEPTUAL MODEL

The terms *conceptual model, mental model,* and *metaphor* have been defined quite differently by various designers (see Norman, 1988; Laurel, 1990; Bauersfeld, 1994; Zetie, 1995). While many of these designers use users' conceptual model and users' mental model interchangeably, Collins (1995) states that, "conceptual models are externalized representations of mental models, in words or pictures, that can be shared. The users' conceptual model represents the users' understanding of their task. It includes goals for using the system and knowledge of how the capabilities of the computer system relate to the objects and processes of the real-world domain." This chapter will follow Collins' definition of conceptual model.

The development of a conceptual model is central to the success (and usability) of a new-generation interface. A users' conceptual model should be explicitly designed into the interface by the design team. From the user feedback to concepts developed in the two earlier stages, the design team should have insight into what attributes contribute to a workable conceptual model. However, this model will often evolve through usability testing and iterative design in the Formal Design Stage. The conceptual model provides a guiding framework for a design team in the refinement of an interface, and it also guides users through the interface by allowing the user to systematically discover the various functions of an application. The conceptual model is communicated both through the *flow of the dialogue* in an interface as well as the use of *metaphors*.

4.3.1. Task Model — Dialogue Design and Detail Design

The primary means of communicating the users' conceptual model and supporting the tasks identified in the Refinement and Analysis Stage is through *dialogue* design. Dialogue design includes the contents and ordering of windows and dialogue boxes in an application that allows a user to complete a given task. The flow of the dialogue in the interface should be designed to follow the flow of the tasks identified in the Refinement and Analysis Stage. The dialogue should be structured to maintain consistency in the behavior of objects: they should not arbitrarily appear, disappear, or be changed.

Although ideally dialogue design for each task should precede detail design (window layout and type of controls), in reality these are often done concurrently. This is particularly true for small screen devices, such as Orbitor, where the limited screen real estate will often impact the ideal dialogue flow.

Dialogue and detail design for relatively simple graphical user interfaces can be largely completed through the use of the prototyping techniques described earlier. Larger and more complex interfaces (e.g., a multimodal user interface) would require the use of more sophisticated tools, such as flow charts, state transition diagrams, or an on-line dialogue design and management tool.

With user interfaces for standard operating systems (Macintosh, Windows, etc.) the designer can refer to style guides to help with the detailed design. With new-generation products such as Orbitor, the detail design comprises a significant proportion of the new "look and feel" of the product. It also constitutes a major amount of the design effort. For this type of project, graphic and visual interaction designers should be part of the design team from the Exploratory Stage onward.

4.3.2. Metaphors

A *metaphor* is used to map an object or action in an interface to something else the user might already understand. Metaphors should communicate the users' conceptual model of the new interface by expressing it in terms of other objects or actions with which the user is already be familiar.

Metaphors should be selected for their appropriateness to the target market and they should also be matched to the experiences and capabilities of typical users. All of the metaphors used in an interface should also be unified with respect to each other (i.e., they should follow a common theme). For new generation products, the goal is to build upon and extend users' experience with existing products.

Metaphors, particularly visual metaphors (e.g., graphical icons) are useful for improving the initial discoverability of an interface for new users. While the user interface concept being conveyed may be either an object or an action, it is easier to communicate a metaphor that is related to real-world physical objects. The real value of graphical metaphors is not that the user intuitively understands it from prior experience with the mechanical real-world equivalent, but that it is both simple to discover and memorable. Well-designed graphical icons can make use of recognition memory.

One of the problems with overly-explicit metaphors is that they become constrained by the properties of the physical real world object. Thus, a major functional gap evolves between the capabilities of the application and the more limited capabilities of real world objects. Some designers have shown that users do not perceive explicit graphic metaphors and that they will perform the same with or without them. (Spool, 1996).

A well-designed metaphor should strongly encourage exploration, discovery, and learning without penalty (e.g., including the ability to undo mistakes and try again). For products which will be used on an ongoing basis, the interface should be designed to facilitate the transformation of new users into expert users (who do not require explicit graphical metaphors).

Using a brainstorming technique (see Michalko, 1991) with a team of designers is a fast way of developing a range of metaphors. For new generation products,

Call Environment
- voice communication
- not communication

Communication Object
- Caller' s Name
- Caller's Number
- Location Icon
- Call status icon

Integrated Message Center
- voice, text and ink messages
Filing Cabinet Environment
- business cards
- personalization preferences

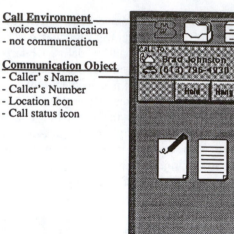

Figure 11.7 Hierarchy of controls and metaphors.

antecedent products (studied in the Refinement and Analysis Stage) can be a good source of metaphors. As computers become ubiquitous, established ideas in the desktop computing environment can also be a source of metaphors.

4.3.3. Hierarchy of Control and Metaphors

The interface design should be based upon an understanding of which are the highest priority features and of the order in which a user would want to move through the steps of any given task. The interface should be organized so as to maximize the discoverability and perceived ease of use of high priority features. Perceived ease of use is defined to include a minimum number of key presses, a minimum number of dialogue screens, and a minimum amount of time and effort required to complete a task and achieve a goal (this is verified in usability testing).

The location of a feature is determined by its importance to the user and the frequency of access, as verified in the Refinement and Analysis Stage. Frequently used features are allocated to the top level of the interface. In the case of the Orbitor interface, priority is given to the most important time-critical task: real-time voice communication. Highly used features are either located on the first screen or on hard keys that can be accessed directly at any time (e.g., navigation arrow keys). Less-used features are located on-screen, one layer down (e.g., telephone configuration controls were located in a folder within the filing cabinet environment; see Figure 11.7).

The first screen should support the most important frequent task. With the Orbitor, a system of spatial, object-based metaphors was used to create an understandable hierarchy of primary and secondary foci of attention. The size of an object, the location, and the level of detail were all used to communicate the hierarchy. The most important objects were large, highly detailed, and located in the foreground. Smaller, less-detailed objects in the background were still easily accessible, despite the visual cue indicating their reduced importance. Also, within any screen there was generally a top-to-bottom, left-to-right hierarchy (building upon the users' experience with the typical layout of newspapers, books, and other paper-based graphical information).

At the highest level, an environment metaphor was used to logically organize the various features into three groups (Call Environment, Message Center Environment, and Filing Cabinet Environment). This metaphor was chosen to make it explicit to the user that there were three distinct modes in the interface. For example, the Call Environment was used only for real-time voice or note communication. The Message Center Environment was used only to view stored voice messages, ink messages, or text messages. We wanted the user to view these not as abstract or arbitrary modes, but as spatially distinct places (environments). "I know I am in the Message Center because I see messages and they look graphically distinct from objects in the Call Environment or the Filing Cabinet environment." Within each of the environments, the interface was modeless, i.e., any input from the user had the same consistent response anywhere within that environment. The user could also navigate at any time between any of the three environments without any destructive effects.

At the next level down within each environment an object metaphor was used; all communications links were represented by graphical objects. For example, a voice call between two people was represented by a single "call object" in the foreground. This "call object" had text to identify the caller's name and telephone number, an icon to identify the location (home, office, cellular, other), and an icon to represent the type of link (e.g., a voice call on Hold, an active voice call, message, etc.).

4.3.4. Animation — Extending the Range of a Metaphor

Animation is a technique that can be used to extend the useful range of a small and simple set of icons. For example, a static telephone icon could indicate a free line, while an animated version of the same icon could signal an incoming call. Animation can also be used to provide visual cues to the internal structure of the interface, as well as providing feedback to the user as to what is happening. In this way, users can discover the function and location of various objects from the interface itself. With the Orbitor, for example, if a user did not answer an incoming call because she was busy writing a note, the incoming "call object" would be automatically shrunk and moved to the Message Center. At a later time the user would know exactly where to go to look for a message left by the caller.

4.4. STRUCTURED VS. UNSTRUCTURED INTERFACE

An overall interface, or specific tasks within an interface, can be implemented in either a structured (task-oriented) or unstructured (subject-oriented) manner. A *structured interface* is one in which the user is clearly guided through a particular task in a lock-step fashion. The Wizards used in Microsoft products are a clear example of a structured interface. Structured interfaces are ideal for novice users or where there are strict business or legal rules that regulate the sequence in which tasks must be completed. The converse is an *unstructured interface*, in which the user is presented with objects which can be manipulated in many different ways to complete a task. Unstructured interfaces are generally appropriate for experienced users.

It can be advantageous to design an *unstructured* interface for new generation products, particularly in the early part of their product life cycle. The reason is that new generation products are often put to completely different uses from what was originally envisioned by the design team. For example, MacroMedia Director was originally designed to facilitate simple scripted business presentations. It is now the premier package for the development of multimedia games, interactive WWW services, as well as user interface prototypes. With a new generation product, a detailed track record of field use is obviously unavailable, and an excessively structured interface will limit the unanticipated uses.

Similarly, the general user interface for the Orbitor product was designed to be unstructured or subject-oriented for a number of reasons:

- The product would be used frequently (i.e., all users would quickly become experienced).
- The initial interface would serve as a base platform for an evolving set of future service modules.
- One of the key user values was *multitasking*: users did not want to be guided through a single task from start to finish, they wanted to be able to do multiple combinations of tasks in many different orders.

It is likely that future Orbitor applications which are specifically targeted for infrequent use by a particular group of users would be designed with a structured interface.

4.5. HETEROGENEOUS USER GROUP

Consumer products such as cellular telephones have many users with different backgrounds and expectations. A diverse group of users will want to accomplish similar tasks in many different ways. The Orbitor user research indicated that the

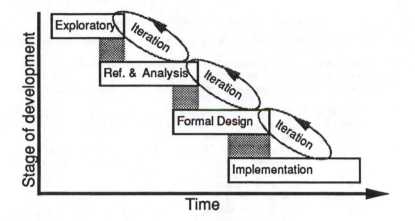

Figure 11.8 Concurrent iterative development model.

product would have to support two levels of users — novice and expert. It had to provide a simple and discoverable interface to novice users, but not at the expense of a fast and powerful interface for experienced cellular phone users. The team therefore designed the Orbitor with context-sensitive help prompts for the new user. Experienced users would be able to personalize the user interface to speed up common tasks by reducing the number of prompts. Short cuts would also be available to the power user. As expressed by Collins (1995, p.66), "A successful user interface will not lose its appeal as the user becomes expert, and will take advantage of any expertise the user brings to the application from prior experience."

5. MANAGING AND DOCUMENTING THE ITERATIVE DESIGN PROCESS

The term *iterative design* has been used to describe the design process throughout this chapter (see Figure 11.8). A concurrent iterative process for the Refinement and Analysis and Formal Design Stages is critical for any new generation projects. However, the Exploratory Design Stage discussed first is not iterative or convergent; in fact it is divergent, and the initial exploratory concepts are deliberately designed to be far removed from what users would expect to see in a current "real" product. The various exploratory concepts represent a breadth of ideas.

One of the key project management challenges is to keep the iterative process on track and moving toward a more usable design. For an iterative design process to work within the constraints of the product development cycle, two conditions must be met. First, the initial design must be reasonably close to the final product design. Second, successive iterations must converge on the final improved product at acceptable speed to meet project delivery deadlines.

Table 11.4   Example of Hierarchical Decision-Making Process

Level 1. Does the new design meet the list of user values and detailed product attributes?

Level 2. Is the users' conceptual model clearly communicated in the design?
  • Are the metaphors appropriate to the user and to the task
  • Does the flow of the dialogue in the user interface match the users' task flow?

Level 3. Does the interface follow basic principles and guidelines for the good UI design?
Some of these guidelines as suggested by Norman (1988) and Neilsen (1993) include:
  • Provide meaningful feedback to the users' actions
  • Provide visual clues (affordances) to the user about the function of an object
  • Show an understandable relationship between a control and its function (mapping)
  • Use a simple and natural style of dialogue and interaction
  • Provide a consistent method of interaction for the user
  • Provide meaningful feedback for recovery from errors
  • Provide shortcuts to experienced users

Level 4. Detail Design:
  • Is this the optimal layout for each screen given certain constraints? (e.g., small display size, anthropometric data regarding minimum touch target size)?
  • Is this the best GUI widget or control to use to accomplish a defined task given certain constraints (e.g., usable in the mobile environment)?

Level 5. When the design is tested with end users, does it meet usability requirements?
  • Note: This is by far the most important decision-making criteria

5.1. POTENTIAL PROBLEM WITH ITERATIVE PROCESS

There are two common problems with iterative design. One is that the initial design is so far from an acceptable final design that it is impossible to evolve toward it. Another is that the initial design might immediately cut-off development in the right direction and successive iterations may show no improvement over the initial design.

Iterative design cannot replace up-front analysis. It is extremely frustrating and inefficient to do iterative design if the design team has no common understanding of the users' requirements. The team must have a systematic decision-making process (see Table 11.4) and clearly defined metrics with which to evaluate each successive design iteration. Optimally, the team should record design decisions and design rationale to avoid repetition.

5.2. DECISION CRITERIA FOR TRANSLATING USER INFORMATION INTO A USER INTERFACE

Having brought together multiple design concepts and user information in the Exploratory and Refinement and Analysis Stages, the Orbitor design team then had to translate this into a working user interface. In the Formal Design Stage, a hierarchical decision-making process was used to guide the design of the user interface. This hierarchy can be expressed as a series of questions with associated decisions to be made before progressing to the next level (Table 11.4).

Asking Level 1- and Level 2-type questions was the method by which high level design decisions were made. More specific questions regarding the high-level model were addressed at Level 3. Detail design issues were addressed at Level 4 and further refined by input from usability testing of UI simulations (Level 5). A hierarchical process such as this can speed up and simplify the constant design trade-off decisions that are associated with any development project.

5.3. DESIGN RATIONALE AND DESIGN INTENT DOCUMENTATION

The transfer of the user interface design intent to a larger software development team can be largely accomplished through the use of high-fidelity interactive simulations. A simulation can capture the design intent more accurately than a paper text document (it readily expresses the "look and feel" of a product). A simulation unambiguously communicates the intended user interaction, graphics, fonts, animation, auditory prompts, and expected system response time. The simulation should also include a text window to annotate the design and record the high-level design principles, general design guidelines, and design rationale.

The key advantage to this method is that the user interface can be rapidly iterated without having to update a separate design specification document. Also, it is relatively easy to ensure consistency between the user interface design intent and the interface of the final product as it is being coded (these may progress concurrently). This will considerably shorten the development time for the product.

6. SUMMARY

The methods described in this chapter apply to the design of new-generation products. They are illustrated by a case study of a new wireless personal communication product called Orbitor. The Orbitor team had to determine the set of key user values and relevant product attributes and integrate these into a superior small, mobile communicator (see Figure 11.9). The list of potential features and services was long, but there were many constraints. The small display size, the need to use the product while mobile, and the limitations of multitasking identified in scenario-creation sessions meant the Orbitor could not be all things to all people.

With new-generation design projects a multidisciplinary team determines the problem space and the customer values, while continuously evolving multiple design solutions. An Exploratory Stage precedes an Refinement and Analysis Stage so that the design team's initial creative output is not overly constrained. Design is done in all stages (Exploratory, Refinement and Analysis, and Formal Design). The Danish scientist, Piet Hein, expressed it as follows: "Art is solving problems that cannot be formulated before they have been solved. The shaping of the question is part of the answer" (Ching, 1979).

Figure 11.9 Early model of Orbitor personal communicator.

User interaction scenarios are used in all three of these stages. Early-on, scenarios are used to facilitate communication and brainstorming in a multidisciplinary design team. They are later used to give users a view of the new product concepts in a particular task-based context. Finally, in the Formal Design Stage, scenarios are used in conjunction with paper prototypes to test detailed implementations of a user interface.

In the Formal Design Stage, the design effort is focused on articulating the users' conceptual model; this is explicitly designed and tested through the use of scenarios in combination with prototypes. The conceptual model in the interface is primarily communicated to the user through interaction dialogue and the use of metaphors. Paper prototypes are later used to create a scripted high-fidelity simulation, and then a fully interactive highfidelity simulation is built. The interactive simulation is used for formal usability testing and also to communicate the user interface design intent to other project partners (e.g., software developers, hardware developers, marketers).

Interviews, focus group sessions, and usability testing are conducted throughout new-generation projects to support the iterative design process and validate the user interface as it evolves. Since user interface guidelines and style guides do not yet exist for advanced non-WIMP interfaces, these design projects tend to require more conceptual design time and more user input.

7. ACKNOWLEDGMENTS

The development of the Orbitor user interface was the joint effort of numerous individuals within the Corporate Design Group at Nortel Technology. In particular, the author wishes to acknowledge the effort of the other members of the UI design team: Brian Beaton for visual interaction design and Bruce Stalkie for simulation development. The author also wishes to thank Jeff Fairless, Des Ryan, Mike Atyeo, Gord Hopkins, Arnold Campbell, Peter Trussler, and John Tyson for the contributions they made to this paper.

8. REFERENCES

Bauersfeld, P., *Software By Design,* M&T Books, New York, 1994.

Carroll, J.M., Ed., *Scenario Based Design,* John Wiley & Sons, Toronto, 1995.

Ching, F.D.K., *Architecture: Form, Space and Order,* Van Nostrand Reinhold, New York, 1979.

Collins, D., *Designing Object-Oriented User Interfaces,* Benjamin/Cummings, Redwood City, CA, 1995.

Cooper, A., *About Face: The Essentials of User Interface Design,* IDG Books, Foster City, CA, 1995.

Davidson, C., The man who made computers personal, *New Scientist,* 138, 30-36, 1993.

Erickson, T., Notes on design practices: stories and prototypes as catalysts for communication, in *Scenario Based Design,* Carroll, J., Ed., John Wiley & Sons, Toronto, 1995, 37-58.

Hanks, K. and Belliston, L., *Draw: A Visual Approach to Thinking Learning and Communicating,* William Kaufmann, Los Altos, CA, 1977.

Hix, D. and Hartson, R. H., *Developing User Interfaces: Ensuring Usability Through Product and Process,* John Wiley & Sons, Toronto, 1993.

Laurel, B., Ed., *The Art of Human-Computer Interface Design,* Addison-Wesley, Menlo Park, CA, 1990.

Michalko, M., *Thinkertoys: A Handbook of Business Creativity for the '90s,* Ten Speed Press, Berkley, CA, 1991.

Neilsen, J., *Usability Engineering,* Academic Press, Boston, MA, 1993.

Norman, D. A., *Design of Everyday Things,* Basic Books, New York, 1988.

Porter, T., *How Architects Visualize*, Van Nostrand Reinhold, New York, 1979.

Potts, C., Using schematic scenarios to understand user needs, *Proceedings of Designing Interactive Systems (DIS'95)*, Ann Arbor, Michigan, August 23-25, p. 247-256, 1995.

Spool, J. M., Users do not see metaphors, discussion in *Comp.Human-Factors Usenet Group*, March, 1996.

Tognazzini, B., The starfire video prototype project: a case history, *Proceedings of CHI'94*, Addison-Wesley, Reading, MA, 1994, 99-105.

Wicklund, M. E., *Usability in Practice*, Academic Press, New York, 1994.

Winograd, T., Ed, *Bringing Software to Design,* Addison-Wesley, Menlo Park CA, 1996.

Zetie, C., *Practical User Interface Design*, McGraw-Hill, London, 1995.

Index